"*All of Me* celebrates rage as a way to reject a culture that isolates women from one another. Such a necessary read!"
—Soraya Chemaly, author of *Rage Becomes Her: The Power of Women's Anger*

"*All of Me: Stories of Love, Anger, and the Female Body* is not your typical feminist anthology, mostly because it busts open binaries, gender and otherwise, in brave and fierce ways. I have been thinking about the importance of feminism with regards to intimacy—in relation to ourselves, to our stories, to our work, to each other, and to the planet. This wide-ranging collection of stories and interviews is deeply intimate in all of these ways. *All of Me* brings you on a journey through people's lives, connecting you to each story. Whether the writers and storytellers are sharing personal narratives or ideas, they are told in intimate, courageous, and beautiful ways. Bravo to Dani Burlison for creating the space for all these diverse and inclusive stories to be shared. By the way, reading this book will crack you open toward feeling more compassion and love. Read it. Read it out loud. Buy it for everyone you know. And then read it again."
—carla bergman, coauthor, *Joyful Militancy: Thriving Resistance in Toxic Times*

"Visceral, raw, and personal, *All of Me* is the barbaric yawp of womanhood unrestrained. Ranging from the confessional to the call to action, this collection of deeply personal writings tears back the veil of womanhood to show the glorious and gritty guts of it all. Unfiltered, unadulterated, open; witness the wounds and the wisdom of what it means to be a woman today."
—Lasara Firefox Allen, author of *Jailbreaking the Goddess: A Radical Revisioning of Feminist Spirituality*

"These stories of resilience center the voices and experiences often overlooked and unheard. *All of Me: Stories of Love, Anger, and the Female Body* is just what is needed in this time to balance the torrents of racism, xenophobia, misogyny, and violence filling our everyday newsfeeds."
—Victoria Law, author of *Resistance Behind Bars: The Struggles of Incarcerated Women*

"An incredible array of voices gather together in this tightly packed, raucous anthology. If ever you felt the need to focus feelings of deep anger, *All of Me* serves as an almost step-by-step manual of rage."
—Inga Muscio, author of *Cunt: A Declaration of Independence* and *Rose: Love in Violent Times*.

All of Me

Stories of Love, Anger, and the Female Body

Edited by Dani Burlison

BTL

All of Me: Stories of Love, Anger, and the Female Body
Edited by Dani Burlison
© 2019 the respective authors
This edition © 2019 PM Press.
All rights reserved. No part of this book may be transmitted by any means without
permission in writing from the publisher.

ISBN: 978–1–62963–705–1
Library of Congress Control Number: 2019933011

Cover by Mikayla Butchart
Interior design by briandesign

10 9 8 7 6 5 4 3 2 1

PM Press
PO Box 23912
Oakland, CA 94623
www.pmpress.org

This edition first published in Canada in 2019 by Between the Lines
401 Richmond Street West, Studio 281, Toronto, Ontario, M5V 3A8, Canada
1–800–718–7201
www.btlbooks.com

Canadian cataloguing information is available from Library and Archives Canada.

ISBN 978–1–77113–466–8 All of Me paperback
ISBN 978–1–77113–467–5 All of Me epub
ISBN 978–1–77113–468–2 All of Me pdf

Printed in the USA.

Contents

Introduction

Dani Burlison

Dear Reader,

Thank you for opening this book. In it, I hope you will find stories that resonate with you and inform your work in the world. Inspired by my two-volume zine *Lady Parts*, my intention with this collection of essays and interviews is to provide a space for the gritty and honest reality of living as a woman in these times; a time when binary gender lines are gorgeously blurred and embraced, where the voices of queer women, poor women, and women of color are being amplified and where women—the whole warrior lot of us—can share our pain and joy and revel in the strength that comes with being survivors.

When the *Lady Parts* zine was first created in 2015, I was preparing for and recovering from a hysterectomy. Having my uterus removed led me to reflect on all of the things women's bodies go through, like complicated relationships with menstruation, reproductive issues like abortion and infertility, body dysmorphia, childbirth, gender confirmation surgeries, and more. I also thought about the various traumas women experience from the outside world, the physical and emotional violence and violation we carry in our bodies, and how voicing our feelings of anger about these traumas is often unwelcome in the world and frequently met with dismissal; we are seen as nothing more than "Angry Feminists." We need to calm down. We need to tone police ourselves and each other. We need to remember our place.

As if we have nothing to be angry about.

Naturally, this pisses me off. So I put together a second zine, focusing entirely on anger.

Working on that issue was eye-opening. At the time, the only resources I could find about women and anger were workbooks for women about how to banish anger from our lives. There were few similar resources for men, though I did find a handful of books marketed toward men about how to tame the lady rage (funny to note that as I write this, times are changing: I know of at least two books about women and anger recently published by amazing feminist writers).

Upon completion of a year of writing and collecting tales of women's anger for that project, I immediately felt a knee-jerk response to wash over the rage in those stories with a follow-up zine all about love; there remains some uncomfortable knot in the depths of my nervous system about the stigma that comes with being a woman expressing anger and the societally ingrained need to suture that "bad" emotion and to soothe it with a sweet healing salve. We read account after account of women being raked across the proverbial coals for calling out abuse and injustice, yet very few accounts of that same criticism for the abuser or the act of injustice itself. Dylan Farrow was often called out as simply wanting to ruin the career of her abusive father Woody Allen. "Why wouldn't I want to take him down?" she asked in a televised interview. "Why shouldn't I be angry?" On another point in the spectrum, international media spent weeks critiquing tennis goddess Serena Williams after she confronted an umpire during the 2018 U.S. Open (and much of it was fueled by racism), yet her male counterparts have historically lost their shit on the court with not so much as the bat of an eye from the media. And the world watched as Trump dismissed the rage of anti-Kavanaugh activists as they confronted Senator Jeff Flake in an elevator; Trump claimed they were paid actors. And the most frustrating part of this is that much of the critique comes from other women, even self-proclaimed feminists. It feels unsafe to be a woman with anger, yet I feel it is a necessary emotion that can create amazing things if channeled effectively. As I wrote in the introduction to *Lady Parts* no. 2:

> We need more outlets. We need each other. We need the more privi-
> leged in our communities to step up and help unload some of the
> burden of the folks who are struggling or targeted or living in fear
> because of the anger of dominant culture. And most of all, in my
> opinion, we need our righteous anger to change the systems that
> brought us here in the first place—through direct action and magic
> spells and community building and through listening to each other.

You'll find stories of anger in these pages. I hope you can hear them, hold them, and use them to inspire your own storytelling.

And, of course, we need stories of love in our lives too. You'll also find those here, whole stories of love and intimacy and what it means to work on loving our bodies, our communities, and our families—both of origin and of choice.

This project also occupies a specific location in the feminist spectrum.

Growing up poor, I always felt a little twinge of awkwardness calling myself a feminist. From where I sat—either in a working poor agricultural corner of the hot Sacramento Valley during my childhood, and later as a twenty-something single mother in line at a food bank or fumbling my way through an education as a first-generation college student in my thirties (while cleaning houses and working low-wage jobs)—the feminism I saw portrayed in the media often felt like a foreign land that I couldn't afford to enter. I felt out of place, like something bigger and deeper was missing.

So I sought out and found my people in the margins.

The version of feminism where I currently reside has always felt deliciously magical and scrappy, maybe too far left for the masses, with its imperfect utopia and inclusion of women of color, poor women, sex workers, trans women, witches, anarchists, queer moms, women with disabilities, recovering addicts, abuse survivors, "spinsters," and women whose bodies don't fit the mold of what society deems valuable. Ultimately, women who have fought to find a space in this world and who have often experienced unbearable trauma yet have found courage and support in sharing their stories of love and anger and the history of their bodies.

These are the people who make this book what it is.

Admittedly, I put together this collection for selfish reasons too. Every voice in this anthology comes from someone I deeply admire, and I wanted to gather them together in one place so I can visit in the dark and trying moments of these times and be reminded of the power in vulnerability and the beauty in resilience.

Someone once said that love and anger are two sides of the same coin, and for women, there are worlds to be explored with every flip of that coin and countless ways in which our bodies experience, process, and express that love and anger. My hope is that readers find a sliver of that truth in these stories and interviews.

Thank you for reading. Now go smash the patriarchy.

Dani Burlison
Santa Rosa, California 2018

For my mom, the ultimate survivor.

Chama

Christine No

There is a word in my language: *Chama*. It is an imperative and an imploration. It means "be patient" in the utmost sense: hold it in, push it down, repress it. It means *take it, bear it.* Do not react. A good woman is obedient. *Chama, chama*—my grandmother's two hands press down on her solar plexus. *Tsk! Chama*, when I tell her, the first time, that my stepfather touches me down there.

Chama—because you are a woman.

Chama—because women bear the whole wet world.

Chama—why are you surprised?

This is why we exist: as vessel, as repository—

I grew up in a violent, abusive household—*like classic, like textbook.*

My stepfather was (is) an alcoholic narcissist (calls himself *Zen Buddhist, Poet, Philosopher*).

He once held a knife to—

He came into my room many nights and—

This went on for over a decade. I grew up in *constant fear of*—

And I tried to break the rule. I did not stay silent. I did not *chama.*

I was not prepared for the repercussions:

My mother told me, *Watch your mouth!* Sent me away for three months.

My aunt said she'd pray for me.

My grandmother murmured *chama, chama, chama* when I appeared at her door—scraped, bruised, hysterical with disbelief.

What else did they know to do?

It has taken me a long time to come to this answer: *nothing.*

They were raised to abide by the same rules.

I've spent years on concrete floors, in motel bathrooms, trying to smash, snort, slice through my body and cut out my heart—to purge myself of *chama*. This singular phrase kept my mother in bed for days, practically comatose—eyes wide, unblinking fish, belly-up. Or she would disappear for weeks away at a time; pulling lever after slot machine lever—*hoping for a miracle.*

Chama landed me in psychiatric care: no shoes and a flimsy gown. Shattered glass girl; weakling, so ashamed. I named my broken vessel *Chama.* I named my stuffed animal, my ugly feelings, *Chama.* What facilities are we given to cope with so much abuse, such violence, other than a mouth trained to keep shut? A heart disciplined to *take it, because*—

This is why I write.

This is why I mine old wounds and leave fresh scars. This is why I speak up about abuse, why I participate. This is why I tell my story over and over again, even though it leaves me emptied, each time. *I tell my story in order to live.*

When kept quiet, unaddressed, domestic abuse perpetuates like brushfire; manifests in new faces, new generations. We entangle ourselves in partners who will do what our stepfathers did.

After all, *this is how we learned to touch and be touched*—

I know too many survivors who have had to *chama*, still do. After all, the further embedded a stake, a coping mechanism, a broken mantra, the more excruciating it is to find and remove, unlearn.

But here you are, elbow deep in your own wounds; careful not to break further your tender self.

And here you are—fighting to heal. *How brave you are.*

Keep Going. You are not alone. You are not invisible.

I see ya—

As far as I am concerned, there is no *chama*. There is no need to hide a chasm behind a smile, no need to turn rage inward, anymore. What happened to me is not my fault. That it kept happening is not my fault. That I loved men who repeated these patterns is not my fault. It has taken me nearly two decades of *chama* to learn these lessons, to break away from toxic unions, to unbreak my heart. But I did it.

I broke the cycle.

Should I have a little girl, she will never have to *chama* in the face of violence. She will never sleep in a closet. She will never remember her mother as a fish, belly-up, look in her eyes far away gone.

And if anyone tries to hurt her, silence her, they will have *her* mother—*I am a Destroyer of Worlds*—to get through, first.

And believe me, I *will* have questions—
And whoever messes with *my* Baby Girl
                    —*they'd better have answers.*

Explicit Violence

Lidia Yuknavitch

In a bar, with friends, listening to a man I've admired for years saying this: "Enough with the sob stories, ladies. We get it. If I hear one more story about some fucked up sad violent shit that happened to you, I'm going to walk. You win! You win the sad shit happened to me award! On behalf of my gender, I decree: we suck!" Laughter. The clinking of glasses. Again, the secret crack in my heart. Stop telling.

The first time I saw my father's specific sadistic brutality manifest in physical terms, I was four. My sister was flopped across his lap, bare bottom. He hit her thirteen times with his leather belt. I counted. That's all I was old enough to do. It took a very long time. She was twelve and had the beginning of boobs. I was in the bedroom down the hall, peeking out from a faithlessly thin line through my barely open bedroom door. The first two great thwacks left red welts across her ass. I couldn't keep watching, but I couldn't move or breathe either. I closed my eyes. I drew on the wall by my door with an oversized purple crayon—large aimless circles and scribbles. Not the sound of the belt—but her soundlessness is what shattered me. Still.

The second time I saw my father's naked brutality he came at my mother—I mean the second time I physically witnessed my father looking more animal than man, his embodied rage—he threw a coffee mug at her head. Hard. He once tried out for the Cleveland Indians as a pitcher. That hard. He missed, and the mug punched a hole through the wall in the kitchen. My sister was long gone—the escape of college. Afterward, there was dead silence in the kitchen. I know because I held my breath. Even air molecules seemed to still. I'd recently written a fifth-grade school report on hurricanes. It felt like we were in the eye.

My father never struck my mother. She told me it was because she was a cripple. My mother was born with one of her legs six inches shorter than the other. She said, "He wouldn't dare hit me," the lilt of a southern drawl and vodka in her never-went-to-college voice, some kind of messed up trust in her too blue eyes. Instead, he molested his daughters.

Our legs were perfect.

Baseball.
Purple crayon.

When I was sixteen a boy older than me asked me out on a date. I was as sixteen as a girl could be. Barely able to breathe with the incomprehensibility of my own body. The heat and pulse and lurch. When he drove me home and parked outside my house, we kissed. Because I was stupid and sixteen I thought we were alone. I got out of the car and leaned back in through his open driver's side window to kiss him some more, my mouth, his mouth, wet heat and tongue of youth sliding into youth, and my father, who was standing behind me there in the dark, grabbed me by the ear and dragged me all the way back to the house. My ear became more than red and hot. Then ringing. Then pain. I thought he would pull my ear off. Briefly, I saw the boy step out of his car—did he mean to save me? I shook my head wordlessly, no. Or maybe it was just in my eyes through the dark. No. He got back in his car.

That night my father hit me with language. Slut. Over and over again.

Purple crayon.
Belt.

The second time I was molested I was twelve. I was on an out-of-state swimming trip with my swim team. Nebraska. Even now, I understand, the hormonal chaos of all of us half-naked in the pool every day of our lives, 6:00 to 8:00 a.m., 4:00 to 6:00 p.m., pushing our corporeal truths up and out—I understand how hard it was for our bodies to find forms for things. A seventeen-year-old boy named Robert asked me to come sit by him on the plane and share his Walkman earphones—to hear a song he liked. He had one in his ear and he put the other in my ear. The song was "Baker Street" by Gerry Rafferty. As I leaned in closely, he reached up underneath my tank top and fondled my barely there tits. I kept stealing glances at the airplane barf bag. But I didn't move. I remember being terrified to move. Not the terror of violence. I didn't think he'd hurt me. It was the terror of my own body. My nipples responding to this thing that made me want to throw up. Or just die there in the seat of the airplane. Crashing, crashing. Wishing for it. "When you wake up it's a new morning/The sun is shining, it's a new morning/You're going, you're going home."

To this day if I hear "Baker Street," which is mercifully almost never, I can vomit.

To this day, I would rather have taken ten plane trips sitting next to Robert than live with my father growing up.

Baseball.
Coffee mug.
Walkman.
Barf bag.

The first time a man came at me with a fist I was eighteen. I passed out. Not from his fist though. I'd passed out drunk. When I woke up all my clothes were on the floor, my legs were spread-eagle on his bed, and I was wet and sticky and sore between them. There was a bruise between my shoulder and my breast. He was snoring, asleep back in bed. I stood up and watched him sleep. I remember thinking he is beautiful. He had long blonde feathered hair and an astonishingly fit body. He did karate. Competitively. In fact, his power and beauty were what made me go home with him from the bar. I mean I went out of my way to catch his eye, wag my ass, throw my huge mane of blonde lioness hair around. I pretended I didn't know how to play pool—which my father had taught me when I was ten—so he could "teach" me. He had blue eyes. Standing there watching him sleep, my legs shaking some, I thought, he is beautiful, and I am not, I am stupid and drunk, and I deserve this and more.

Then I called my roommate from college at 3:00 a.m., and she and her boyfriend came to get me. I couldn't find my underwear. I waited for them in the dark and cold morning on the front lawn. He came out before they got to me and punched me in the jaw—not hard enough to call the cops, not soft enough to keep my ear from aching, saying, "You tell anyone, you crazy little bitch, I'll find you." He smiled. He handed me my underwear.

I waited for my roommate to pick me up. I heard a dog bark. I smelled cow shit from Lubbock stockyards. I picked at a scab on my arm like a kid. You're no victim if you are a drunk-ass slut. I didn't cry. I swallowed it whole.

I didn't tell anyone. In fact, later that year I went home with him again. On purpose.

Purple crayon.
Coffee mug.
Vodka.
Underwear.

The second time a man hit me I was in college. The man was a poet. A pacifist. A hippie. Somehow, I believed things like that could matter. But he had a hair-trigger rage in him. His father had been career military and hit him all through boyhood. The rage in him sat like the crouch of dead dreams in his fingers. Poems came out. And that shot to the bridge of my nose. Probably that's what drew me to him. It was familiar.

Twice in my life I've been homeless, both times the result of emotional trauma. Both times I woke up under overpasses with no pants or underwear, vomit everywhere, a throbbing pain between my legs extending to my asshole. I'm assuming I was raped. But where do you put the story of rape when there's no man to blame? I put it the only place I knew how to. I put it back into my body.

Belt.
Barf bag.
Baseball.
Purple crayon.

I'm trying to tell you something here, but it's starting to sound like what I'm saying is that I deserved these violences. Let me be clear. I did not. No one does. Ever. But when women tell how it is for them, when they self-narrate their ordinary lives, it's instantly sucked up by the culture—there's already a place waiting for the story. A place where the story gets annulled. It's 2012, and I'm still reading about what the girl or woman was wearing that night. Or how she should hold aspirin between her legs. Or how she shouldn't say the word "vagina" on the floor of congress. Or how a friend at a bar wants the sob stories to end. What I'm trying to tell you is that violence against girls and women is in every move we make, whether it is big violence or small, explicit or hidden behind the word father. Priest. Lover. Teacher. Coach. Friend. I'm trying to explain how you can be a girl and a woman and travel through male violence like it's part of what living a life means. Getting into or out of a car. A plane. Going through a door to your own home. A church. School. Pool. It can seem normal. It can seem like just the way things are.

To be honest, the first reason I understand the complexities of male violence against girls and women is that I went to college and read a shit ton of books—and even that wasn't enough education—I went to graduate school, where finally, finally, the books that I read and the films that I watched and the art that I experienced and the teachers that I had showed me just how not normal male violence against girls and women— or boys and men—is. Ever. And yet at the same time, the more conscious I became, the more I also understood that the pervasiveness of that violence has saturated the entire culture. It's both omnipresent and unbelievably invisible in its dispersed and sanctioned forms. So many times the cult of good citizenship covering over the atrocities of girls and boys. Mothers who go numb. Counselors who ask the wrong questions. Coaches and priests and teachers whose desires are costumed and sanctified by their authority. Neighbors who go blind and deaf. Paying bills. Drinking lattes.

The second reason I understand is that I am alive. Still. Differently.

It wasn't that I did not understand the violences against me were wrong. I did. Even at three years of age. It was that I thought I deserved it, and possibly worse: that deserving it, I could withstand it. Mightily. Heroically. You see? As a righteously indignant defense. I could take it. As good as if I was somebody's son. It was a choice.

When my father raised his hand to me in our garage at eighteen, I said, "Do it."

When the poet punched me in the nose in my pickup truck at a stop light, I said, "Get the fuck out of my car, or I will kill you." And I meant it.

I'm telling you this because I know I'm not the only one who came of age like this. Up and through male violence. I'm telling you because there are all the things that need to be done "out there" to stop it. But then there are also all the things that needed to be done in me. To stop it.

Listen, these are not the sad stories. Worse things happened to me. Those aren't the sad stories either. These stories don't carry the pathos to signify culturally in my culture. These stories I'm telling you are commonplace. That's the point. They just happen, and you live them, and as you go you have to decide who you want to be.

Victim.
Slut.
Bitch.
Crayon.
Baseball.
Belt.

When I was thirteen, in junior high, my best friend Emory was beaten and sodomized in the boy's locker room at school by some sadistic members of the football team. Because he was gay. Or at least that's what they were aiming at. In truth, Emory had not yet finished discovering his own sexual self. Like my sister, Emory suffered rectal damage the rest of his life. They used a baseball bat. Emory says, I'll never be in any kind of relationship. Emory says, my chance at being with anyone, a family, feeling okay, died that day. Emory was also a swimmer, and so after swim practice, sometimes we'd sit in the parking lot waiting for our moms to pick us up and drink vodka from a flask an older girl swimmer had bequeathed to me. I never knew what to say about what happened. I didn't even understand it until we were adults. I'm only glad we are still in contact—writing. The tether of words when the world isn't safe like it was supposed to be.

The boys who committed this brutality were never charged. Emory couldn't bring himself to tell anyone, and anyhow, at that time, there were no laws on the books to protect us. Also, he was instructed by his father's lawyer that the term "rape" was not available to him in this situation.

Baseball.
Purple crayon.
Barf bag.

I'm a writer. It's all I really know how to do, besides being a wife and mother. I consider myself a success story. Because I am alive, I mean, and because I think writing and books and art are the reason. As a writer, I'm not so sure I see much difference in the storylines for women and girls who enter the field. I see that some art is rewarded for being "universal," and it is written by men. Other art is deemed confessional. Or sentimental. Or too subjective. And it is written by women. I see that straight white men are published in prestigious venues more often than women. I see that women are told by editors and agents and publishers to take explicitly sexual or violent or subjective language out of their work unless they can bend the language toward the culture in a way that will sell. These are gendered terms, laden with a force as real as my father's. I write my heart out. I do. For better or worse. I write my heart out, because my heart, well, she was almost taken from me. Every year of my life until now. It's something I can "do." A verb. Something that has at least a chance of interrupting another girl or boy's story with other options. Write. Make art. Find others. It's a choice.

Listen, I know this is a bit of a dreary story. But whenever I get told that, by friends or agents or editors or publishers, I think, if this dreary story is hard for you to live with, how are we supposed to live with you?

When my father was thirty, he had all of his teeth pulled. Just bad genes with regard to teeth, I guess. Early dentures. When he came home from the surgery he turned all the living room lights off, became part of the couch, and turned the television on. It was a horrible week waiting for his mouth to heal. I don't know how to say it—things went too dark and horribly submerged. If my mother or I spoke, he yelled, but we could barely understand him. Laughter and crying kept getting caught and confused in my throat. My mother made soup. Mashed potatoes. Ice cream. I drew on the walls in my room. It was like his rage had gone underground, under the beds, the house, the dirt. But we could feel it, pulsing. Pervading everything.

They sent his teeth home with him. I never understood that. I just know I stole one. A molar. Off-white as a baseball and like a wrong pearl. I have it still.

Sometimes I think about the children that didn't come out of me. Four. Three of them were zygotes. The zygotes were sucked out of me in what can best be described as a process involving a hoover upright old-school vacuum. That's what it always looked like to me. Though medical technology has advanced since I was in my teens and twenties. And yet it's 2012 and I keep reading about ideas like forced sonograms where the newly or barely pregnant woman is made to watch. I saw a congressman interviewed who actually said, "Well, no one can really be made to 'watch,' the woman could just close her eyes." While a camera wand is shoved up her. It makes me think of the film *A Clockwork Orange*. It makes me think how, yes, we are forced to watch, every day of our lives, we are forced to watch how our culture still doesn't get what it means to live every moment of a life in the body of a woman.

Baseball.
Purple crayon.
Underwear.
Belt.

The zygotes that did not become children—I think about them. Who would they be? Would they have lived? It's a question I feel I've earned the right to, since one of the children who came through my body died—nothing wrong with my body or hers, sometimes babies just die. Though for more than a decade I believed it was my body that killed her. My body I'd made into a war zone to mirror the culture as I saw it. When Christians in particular talk to me about "killing babies" and abortions, in my head I think, trust me, I know the difference between a dead baby and a zygote. Once a white Christian woman with shellacked blonde hair and the smallest green eyes I'd ever seen told me I was going to hell on my way in to Planned Parenthood. I thought to myself, lady, I've been there and back. Only it was called "family."

Those zygotes, would they be boys? Girls? Would I have survived? I had no money during that part of my life. I stole food and did things I'm not proud of so that I could eat and have shelter and go to school. I also worked three jobs. And still I needed food stamps, just to stay alive. What would they have eaten, the three zygotes, where would they have lived? Would there have been a man under the beds, house, down in the dirt, his rage and violence waiting? Would I have let him in the door, his face so familiar I couldn't recognize it?

I carry deep shame in my body for the zygotes. I don't know a single woman alive who is "happy" to have had an abortion. Or two. Or four. And it's not just me. Other women. Republicans. Democrats. Unaffiliated women. Atheists. Christians. Muslims. Buddhists. Armies of us walking around carrying our body secrets. Our shame over the zygotes. Or maybe there's something deeper than shame—maybe there's a second self I had to kill in order to live. The Lidia who believed she deserved it. Could take it. Should. It was a choice.

My father's tooth is in a pink plastic box that was my mother's. Inside it too, a lock of my hair and two of my baby teeth and that little bracelet they used to give babies that spells out L-I-D-I-A. I'm the one who put my father's tooth in there after my mother died. I don't know why. Sometimes I get it out and look at it—hold it in the palm of my hand. So small. The man who terrorized us. His DNA. So large the culture that let him.

I am a survivor of sexual abuse and male violence. I've had three abortions. I also had one baby girl that died the day she was born. I have a husband and a son now. My husband plays cello and makes films and writes, and in the evening he hits the heavy bag; he's proficient at Muay Thai and Jiu Jitsu. My son can't throw a baseball properly to save his life. His favorite color is purple. He draws and draws. Me, between them, I am alive, unflinchingly.

Grab My Pussy, I Dare You

Michelle Cruz Gonzales

When you are caught on tape saying women let you do what you want, that *you* could even grab them by the pussy, because *you're* famous, *and* then you say you've *never* done such a thing, that it's all *talk*—women who you've *groped, kissed* without consent, *bullied*, made to stand on tables so you could see up their skirts, or *raped* will speak up.

Women who felt they had no power, no voice, women who you only did it to once, women who thought no one would listen, women who maybe spoke out before and no one did, *will* speak out.

These women won't stomach you any longer. They will speak out, and they won't stop.

When you shoot your mouth off and bully and insult and demean—women will start to speak out, and they won't stop. *And* women who have pushed it all down, harassment at work, on the streets, leers, whistles, catcalls, "smile, why don't you smile," "okay, fuck you, bitch," "suck my dick," will listen, and we will tell our stories, and we won't stop because there is no end to the litany of examples, because this is what it's like being a woman in America.

Men show their dicks to us on public transportation, rub up against us, and leer, and suck their teeth, and sometimes they get off the same bus stop and chase us across the street, forcing us to run into traffic. This is what it's like to be a woman in America, you should know that, of all people you should know.

But you shrug it off, give it a cute name, say it's normal.

Then you say, "They're liars. It's all lies," you say. Fiction. Anyone could make up a story like that.

But here's the thing. We don't have to make up stories. There's no shortage of adult men leering at girls, fingering them, "sit on my lap," "it feels good, don't you want to feel good?" There's no shortage of *nonfiction* tales that I or any number of my friends could tell—the men who tried to lure us into their cars, yes, more than one, the men who turned vicious when rebuffed or rejected or exposed.

"Look at her and look at her words." *You* said. "You tell me what you think. I don't think so."

"These vicious claims about me of inappropriate conduct with women are totally and absolutely false," you said. You have proof, you say, evidence.

Then you say we are the ones lying. That there are no witnesses. That you have evidence but we don't. You say that no one was around. And *we* know; it's how you operate, in the dark, under the covers, safe in first-class, money, power, influence. You say you have proof, but we can't prove you groped, bullied, leered, demeaned, raped. You're right, we don't have proof, no DNA evidence, no fingerprints to lift from our skin, no audio, no video, just stories and stories and stories that we will tell, that we will keep telling, because we are full, and you have lifted the lid.

Pandora is out of the box. Medusa's head full of snakes is yanking apples off trees and biting into them, letting their juices run and run and run.

On Anger and the Black Female Body

an interview with Artist Kandis Williams

Dani: I want to talk about misogynoir. Can you explain what this term means?

Kandis: That term was coined by Moya Bailey, who practices intersectional, institutional critique. Misogynoir refers to the intersection between racism and sexism. It kind of makes this totem where black female bodies, or black female-identifying bodies, are at the bottom of the totem. That "We Are Not Well" article just kind of speaks to the complex complaints against systemic racism and sexism that black women face and the lack of credibility and validity that their lives and lived experience is given will often just create these pathologies around their behaviors and that make them either untreatable, like either symptoms of depression and psychosis and stuff become untreatable because there's just a general sense of unwellness. And having a black female body in this culture, it feels like you carry this burden back and forth and back and forth and back and forth from your individual self to the systemic representations of your body and your agency and your potential, you know. Like this kind of credibility of black women around whether or not they've been raped or sexually assaulted—we live in a culture that doesn't believe black women's bodies can be assailed. It's just a constant barrage of hypersexualized images, like constant assertion of black female hypersexuality to sexual deviancy to hyperaggression. Like Mammy, Jezebel, and Sapphire. People who don't live around black women will pretty much never see a caricature of a black woman that doesn't do that. That doesn't do "sex kitten diva" or Condoleeza Rice. You know, scary political, Michelle Obama as a gorilla.

Dani: How does this affect you personally in terms of, first, relationships, and, second, your creativity?

Kandis: I'll answer backwards. In terms of creativity, I think I share this with a lot of black artists. Especially black scholars, where creatively it's always made me search for systems of representation that resist the normal patterns of representation. I'm really interested in all the signs and symbols and systems of representation that don't get disseminated, or they get disseminated poorly, or that survive these colonizing tactics. In that way it's always been a weird sort of inspiration knowing that I'm not going to look at mainstream or normalized issues of communication. That's been a journey creatively that I think is nice. Especially with the readers and with being a visual artist, I just feel really thematic similarities and resonances, I think, in the task of being a creative body, that's "this body that's marked by these codes." I think a lot of people are struggling with how to represent that and how to represent that lived experience and where to put that lived experience in the creative process. So this just recently happened. I met a guy. I was at a café, at a café in the middle of the day, and I met this dude. He was a self-identified Chicano dude in his forties in a band.

Dani: This is in Los Angeles?

Kandis: L.A. Yeah. We start talking. We hang out. He drives me back home. We meet up the next afternoon to hang out. We meet up the next afternoon, and we sit and talk and have a coffee. Then the next day, I'm like, "So, what. . . Are we going out at night? What's going on? You want to meet up and hang out? Are we friends? What's going on?" He was just like, "Oh, I finally googled your art." Changes the subject. He's like, "I finally googled your art," and he sends me a picture of an oiled up, tall black woman who's naked, from behind, photographed from behind.

Dani: Oh, my God. What?

Kandis: Yeah. I was just like, hmm. . . Of all the things that you could do. . . I can't sleep with you now. I was just like, did you really? Wow. What did you google: "Tall, black nude woman?" He's like, "No. I googled your name, and then tall black ebony." I was just like, "What the fuck?" I've never slept with someone and then gone home and googled their features. Have you ever done that?

Dani: Like, "asshole white guy."

Kandis: Literally. Asshole white guy. Green eyes, 5'8" green-eyed white dude. I'm going to jerk off to this right now. Have you ever done that?

Dani: Uh, no. That's so fucked up.

Kandis: That's insane. All women face this, but I feel like black women face a kind of weird marginalization, even in that, where other women also fail to see the way other women appropriate black femininity for their own sexualization is insane. How many times I've gotten dressed with white girlfriends, and they're like, "I'm going to put my hoops on tonight, girl." It's just like, I know you're not. . . What are you. . . No. Also, no.

There's a kind of weird power or sexual mystique in that, but then it comes from this same degradation, this animalistic treatment. I'm blown away by how easy it is for people to objectify me based on three words about how I look: tall, black, woman. I literally don't even know what people are looking at when they look at me. I feel like they must be like blurry-eyed, goggle visions of Beyoncé to King Kong. It might set someone in any direction, so I really don't know until I've been around a person for a while at this point why the fuck they'd want to be around me.

My last relationship was really hard. [He] was someone who I thought was really smart, who I was talking to a lot about past encounters with these fetishistic things and how they had hurt me, or how I had to process them fully, and we were in therapy together. I thought that he was hearing me about these specific things, and then he's on Tinder, like sixty-mile radius, so he can have a drink with another [black woman]. This is someone who can't sit at a table and talk to his mother about how she fetishizes black culture and blackness in a really weird racist way. He still wants to casually have a drink with a black woman. It's thrown me now, because this is the fourth relationship with a white person where something like this has happened. I feel like I somehow mistake a passionate or intense physical connection with people just wanting to experiment, wanting me to be a gatekeeper or a door opener. People who want to be adventurous or shake off a norm. People want to prove some political thing to themselves.

Dani: That objectification and maybe that assumed image that they will obtain by dating somebody that's different than them?

Kandis: Yeah. It's uncomfortable. The last two partners I had, the one before the last person was a girl, who I was seeing for about a year and a half also, and then our sex life just sort of fell off. I realized that she had been seeing this other girl for probably about the last two months, three months. This girl is a tall, black woman. I was with this woman in Berlin. When we finally broke up, the first two parties I went to alone, some friends approached me and were like, "It's crazy, we thought you shaved your head." I was like, "No, I didn't shave my head. Why would you think I shaved my head?" Oh, because they've seen my girlfriend with a girl who looks just like me but is bald, for the past two weeks.

Dani: Oh, Jesus.

Kandis: It has gone around our small Northern European fucking art community that this woman was fucking another tall black woman. That's a community where I know all the other black women in that setting. There's not that many of us. The German boy I was with before that girl told me, when we broke up, that I wasn't allowed to break up with him because he had developed a fetish. This is a man who was in his mid-thirties at that point. He had developed a fetish, and there weren't enough black women in Berlin to satisfy that, naturally, so I couldn't break up with him. Dude before him: Irish guy. I'm thinking all these people are individual people. Having the same fucking things happen though. This Irish dude, we break up, and we were off and on for almost three years. We break up, and he literally took a fucking job in Africa, Dani.

Dani: No!

Kandis: Moved to Africa for about a year. Came back from Africa, only had sex with black women. I saw him when he got back, we had a random one-night stand. I go to write an email from his computer in the morning, and his screen saver is all black porn. I was like, "You're a writer, and this is your screen saver, black porn?" He freaks out at me about how he's not going to be ashamed of his love for black women anymore. He's not going to be ashamed of that desire. He loves black women, and he wants the world to know it. I'm like, "Your screen saver is porn. That's how you're showing your love of black women?"

Dani: Wow.

Kandis: People don't see "I like black girls" as dehumanizing or objectifying. So many people see that as empowering actually, that's the added layer of insult that I feel in relationships. I'll have partners who understand the racism I face in my life, understand the sexism I face in my life, understand the classism I face in my life, and still be like, "But you're so pretty. Everything's fine." [They] don't want to be with the political part of me, don't want to be with the emotional part of me, can't handle the intellectual part of me, and still want to fuck. The scenes I've been in, the cities I've lived in, I have an entire sexual history that's these relationships. I've been raped twice. Once by a best friend, once by a boss. I don't know what my sexuality does to people, and I don't know what my physical presence does to people, and I don't feel comfortable anymore.

Dani: I listen to you talk about all these different experiences in these different communities. It sounds like that racism and objectification is almost worse in these more progressive, artistic communities that are supposed to fucking know better.

Kandis: Totally.

Dani: Is that your experience?

Kandis: Yeah. I think, in a way, artists and the way artists make money, the infantilization that comes with not having a stable income. Again, it's this system of signage and representation, like being interested in a visual world. I burned a bunch of really weird late fifties nostalgic flash-cards that my ex was collecting, he was always collecting these sort of nostalgic fifties white images. My world was getting cluttered with them. He called them "normal," and just having that around freaked me the fuck out. I knew he was interested in them for his own work, but because I didn't like his work, and because I didn't trust his character, and I didn't trust his analysis of his own racism, it just became this weird feeling of being trapped by people's inability to perceive themselves as culturally racist. Or like my partner's inability to understand the discomfort, that physical discomfort, that I had in our home or in our studio practice or in our work. I burned them. That is the lashing out. The lashing out, feeling so unheard, and then needing to scream to be heard.

Dani: Right.

Kandis: Another weird example with this last dude: every time he filled out a job application that asked him about how he would encounter diversity as a teacher, he mentioned dating me. I'm like, "I'm your first black girlfriend. You can't do this, and we're failing in our relationship. Don't mention this in a job application. It makes me feel like you're racist." He'd be like, "What?"

The most stable women I know who are black women in the art world have black partners, and there are very, very few of those women. They're some of the few women who resist being sexed up and dolled up. Or resist being in positions where they might be sexually assaulted. It's hard. I don't know personally where to place my own sexuality anymore, because it feels like I want to fuck someone who's passionately into me but who knows what the fuck they're into.

Dani: Got to check their screen savers on their computers.

Kandis: Literally. I need like three references. The two people I've hooked up with since my last relationship, one was a taller black woman, and we talked and hit it off and went home together three times, and we went out to a party, and we were dancing together, and she sort of pushed me away and was like, "Hey, come on. People are going to look at us and start thinking things." I was just like, here we go. Here we go. This is going to have to be weird and hyper-discreet. I feel like there's ways where even as black women relating to each other physically, we both developed such shells about when to let people in, how to let people in, how to get to know people, when to get to know people, when to start trusting people, when that trust should be public. You know what I mean? It's like we're judged for any kind of partnership that we might have. Anyone who's having sex with us. We're judged for all that in a way. Like when black women are raped, it's because they want it. Obviously. If a black woman calls someone out for hurting her feelings, she's nine times out of ten bitter or petty. Any black woman who speaks up for herself, speaks up for herself for being marginalized or being treated differently, is a bitch.

Dani: Right. I know we've talked about it before, that whole stereotype of the angry black woman and how it's affected your relationships and the way that you communicate things that aren't working for you or that you're legitimately upset about. Can you speak to that again?

Kandis: It's weird. It's like a dissonance. I turned to a bunch of texts by Carolyn West, who is an analyst and a black woman and an author. She wrote a text called "Mammy, Jezebel, Sapphire and Their Homegirls: Developing an 'Oppositional Gaze' toward the Images of Black Women." She also wrote a text on Mammy, Jezebel, Sapphire and their applications for the psychoanalysis of black women. The first therapist I saw, I was talking to her about how I was developing what I felt like was serious PTSD symptoms around even the discussion of interraciality, because the resonances of several relationships back to back and that treatment, that I was feeling not okay and not addressing it was kind of catching up with me, emotionally. Also, Trump's America. Fucking white nationalist government, and coming back to the States for a year, and making three really intense shows about this stuff. It was like the sky was falling. What protocol can I do to help deal with these tensions? She was like, "Well, the first thing you can do is admit that you have converter complex." I was just like, okay. I have a converter complex? What the fuck would that mean?

Dani: The couple's therapist?

Kandis: No. This was just my private [therapist]. She was an older white woman. I was just like, yeah. So I want to convert people is what is happening? It's the silencing thing that actually is the killer. It's feeling like you're screaming at a wall that just will never open up. You won't make a dent in it. There's an answer that negates anything you say. You're being hysterical. You're being childish. You don't know enough. You've been abused. Your people have grown up like this. [And in relationships] it's that kind of shit that you constantly hear. You tell people you're in pain. Something that they've done has hurt you. Yet their response is "Has it really? No, it didn't." Then there's a discourse around this. Let's talk about it. Let's compare your body to other black women. I've seen this other black woman. I've met this other black woman. This black woman on television, Beyoncé, Oprah. It's like they compare you to this entire cosmology of the world of black women.

I can't make someone understand my humanity who's not equipped to understand my humanity. Who doesn't understand the sounds and the shapes and the feelings or who understands the complete opposite, who understands me to be like a part of an image, a network of images that means I don't have feelings, or I don't have certain rights to being vulnerable or being upset or being anything but sexy and in control. Singing and fucking, wearing tight clothes.

Dani: Right. Just being there for someone's entertainment.

Kandis: For someone's entertainment or general political stock value. Literally. I feel like this last relationship and the one before that really made me feel like a handbag in a lot of ways. It made me feel like I was an accessory to someone's white guilt.

Dani: That makes sense, based on what you've told me before.

Kandis: Like an accessory to white guilt that I feel like has no actual place in white society or in white intimate space. I lost weight. I lost hair. I was crying every day. I really just didn't feel heard or seen or protected. To have my intimate partner really feel the need to protect himself from hearing me was really troubling. I didn't get to feel validated, because I slept next to this constant source of invalidation.

Dani: I think I'd be in a rage.

Kandis: I've been crying about the same stuff for almost two years now. I'm exhausted with it actually.

My breakup reader is this reader on the movie "Get Out." It's kind of loosely based on that. I found some articles on dissociative phenomenon, like what they call "the sunken place." I feel like there's this thing called mental stigmata. It's like a marker of hysteria that when hysteria persists it's a permanent symptom. It's like a kind of PTSD. It's basically "the sunken place." It's like the sort of dissociative phenomenon where you have a temporary amnesia. You can't really respond to stresses in the same way. You have audition anxiety. You have hyper-suggestibility. There's all these weird complex dissociative states that are products of PTSD, and I really feel like, especially ending this interracial relationship, it is my problem in a way. I feel like I have created a system of repetition, reengaging; there's another symptom of PTSD is just reexperiencing. You're constantly reexperiencing the trauma. I think I've trained myself to be attracted to triggers, actually.

Dani: It's what you're used to. I totally get that.

Kandis: I think it is this reexperiencing of a lot of it. Because it isn't just something that one person has said to me. Almost every white partner has lashed out at me in devastating ways. I feel like it's that same passion of like, "You're different, and I want to devour you," also is like, "You're different, I want to spit you out." It's like that same intensity. If they don't like the taste, it's just like, get out of the fucking box of chocolate. It fucking sucks. Relationships with white men are violent and dangerous to the ego and self and body. It just feels so unsafe.

Dani: Jesus Christ. I'm so sorry.

Kandis: Especially being an artist, I feel really aware of the lack of language that we have, especially around how we process guilt, how we process sexual repression, and how we process how colonialization and capitalism have worked their way into our intimate lives. We do have a really sick sexualized culture, actually, that doesn't protect our bodies or our reproductive rights but puts us in meat markets. It's still the fucking slave economy. We just have that. Of course, I guess white men are at the top of that fucking beastly totem, looking down like gargoyles on the rest of us.

Tales of a Culture-Straddling Resident Alien

Vatan Doost

She was a cherry-red Dodge Raider, a boxy, top-heavy predecessor to today's compact SUVs. She featured one of the first styles of mobile phone (though broken), a giant contraption the size of a house phone attached to the center console. To boot, she even had an inclinometer on the dash that looked like a snow globe with a golf ball inside, letting me know when the car was going to tip over.

She was my first car, and I couldn't wait to slap a sticker on her. Isn't that one of the greatest joys of owning a car? I had a prized one I'd saved for years, and I rocked it proudly the minute I could. It had a cartoon-style drawing of a guy with Uncle Sam's hand covering his mouth. It read, "Censorship Is Un-American" and was promoted by MTV and Rock the Vote in 1990. Heck, yeah—thought my twenty-year-old, just finished undergrad self—censorship is totally un-American.

One day not long after, while visiting my parents, I came outside to find my father sitting in the driveway behind my Raider, razor blade in hand, calmly scraping off my sticker. What the—? I was never going to score another one of those! Why? My dad, a first-generation immigrant from Iran, spelled out his obvious truth for me: this is America, and in America you shouldn't be driving around with the word "un-American" on your car. We were lucky to be here, and we shouldn't do anything to jeopardize that. Naturally, I thought that was ridiculous. I was pissed and heatedly explained the semantics and context, arguing that the sentiment was actually super-duper American, like foundational to what this country was built upon. But in the end, my sticker was gone, lost in translation, and, to my dad, my car was now free from misunderstanding.

The Demonization Begins

Born in Iran and raised in the Chicago from age five, I grew up joking that I was from the Middle East but raised in the Midwest. My parents left Iran in 1976, three years before the infamous Iranian Revolution of 1979, which rocked the country and changed it forever. The people rose up and overthrew the shah of the Pahlavi dynasty, which was backed by the U.S. and largely thought to be a puppet regime for Western interests. Unfortunately, though the uprising was populist and nationalist, including many women and intellectuals, it was the Islamicists who grabbed the reigns after the coup, replacing a pro-Western monarchy with an anti-Western authoritarian theocracy.

My childhood consisted of hearing Ted Koppel reporting on the Iran hostage crisis on *Nightline* every single night. The show, at the time a staple of the American media diet, was in fact launched exclusively to cover the crisis. The original title was *The Iran Crisis—America Held Hostage: Day "xxx,"* where xxx represented each day that Iranians held the occupants of the U.S. Embassy in Tehran hostage. CBS Evening News anchor Walter Cronkite was also famous for covering the crisis. In the States, hatred for Iran became a unifying factor for Americans. Iranians living in the U.S. spent years pretending they were Italian, Spanish, or pretty much anything other than Iranian, for fear of hate crimes and discrimination.

Little did I know that things wouldn't be changing anytime soon. From that day forth, the Iranian people were to be demonized without fail or apology in American mainstream media ad infinitum. As a kid, I would watch news reports repeatedly show clips of angry Iranians burning U.S. flags, yelling "Death to America," day in and day out. Iranian women were shown in black chadors, shrouded, angry, ugly, and violent.

During that time, my entire extended family still lived (as they do now) in Iran, and travel between the two countries was restricted for many years. I missed childhood with my relatives and never got to say goodbye to my grandmother in the years of the heated conflict between Iran and the United States. Phone calls became our only lifeline. We regularly dealt with scratchy phone connections, strange echoes, and unexplained clicking noises just to hear their voices from eight thousand miles away.

Worried by the myopic reports broadcast daily, I remember asking my aunt about the angry Iranian mobs that I saw on American television. In my eight-year-old mind, I envisioned they were outside her apartment, even more foreboding and threatening than they were on the screen in our living room. But I was dumbfounded when she told me she hadn't seen them at all.

A sweet and patient woman, she reminded me that Tehran is a huge city, and that what happens in one corner isn't necessarily happening everywhere. For the first time, I learned how the broadcasts were nothing more than a construct, a thread drawn from the whole. If they filmed one impactful incident and then broadcast it on repeat, it would seem like the whole country was up in flames, full of dark, angry people.

Didn't they know that people like my aunts and uncles, cousins, and grandparents lived there? Didn't they know these were good people who were also victims of the harsh new reality in Iran? The dehumanization of the Iranian people was well under way, both by the dark new establishment in their country and by the Western media.

And the news reports certainly had their intended effect on the American psyche. I'll never forget getting into an argument with some kids in fourth grade, when one of them got up in my face and yelled, "What are you going to do? Take us hostage?" If this dark cloud had reached the kids, I could only imagine what it was doing to the adults.

I somehow hoped that in all the images, reports, and videos, someone would show the human aspect, that the Iranian people were also victim. But there was never another, kinder perspective shown, never the human story of suffering happening in Iran after the regime change, never a nod to three thousand years of history that included the first human rights doctrine by Cyrus the Great, numerous advances in mathematics and architecture, and insanely beautiful traditional crafts. Only enraged people in black who all hated America. And no one ever bothered to ask why they were so irate.

United States of Amnesia

America has a serious amnesia problem. I wish I could say I came up with "the United States of Amnesia," but the U.S. has had amnesia for so long, countless people have noted it long before me. Why would people be burning your country's flag and yelling death to its establishment? You really have to have beef with someone to do that, right. And yet, I never heard the media ask that question.

For the record, I have to say, burning a country's flag is a far cry from dropping bombs on its people, as the U.S. has done since in Iran's neighboring countries Iraq and Afghanistan.

To make a long, complex story shamefully short, between 1951 and 1953, Iran had a progressive, democratically elected prime minister named Mohammad Mosaddegh. He was a man of the people, but he pissed off the Brits when he decided to give the natural treasure of oil back to the Iranian people by nationalizing the oil industry. Since 1913, it had been under British control through the Anglo-Persian Oil Company. In 1953, Britain and the U.S. staged a coup to overthrow Mosaddegh and chose his successor—naturally, a puppet. And that was just the beginning.

The history between my two countries—the one I was born in and the one I was raised in—is long and complex, but the U.S. has repeatedly screwed Iran over. I'm in no way making any apology for the Iranian government and the atrocities it inflicts upon its own people, but when's the last time you heard of an Iranian terrorist in the news? 1979? Definitely not 9/11 or any of the atrocious terrorists acts in the States since. Those were mostly Saudis, and the U.S. has great relations with them.

I've watched Iranians get marginalized and demonized for the past thirty-eight years, and I'm just so fucking sick of it. Did you know that Iranians can't get visas to most countries in the world? It's like an unfounded global prejudice. Wake up, America, a people and its government are not always synonymous. Maybe we can see that more clearly now that we have an asshole fascist dictator running the show here.

The difference between Iranians and Americans is that because Iranians by and large don't relate to their government, they also don't equate a people and their government. Your government can suck, but you can still be cool. But in the Western eye, rather than having empathy, the patina of oppressive governments somehow casts a shadow on its innocent people. The Iranian people have been getting dragged through the mud along with the politics they have little to do with.

Through Their Own Eyes

Over the years, I kept hoping to see or hear a kind word about my people in the media, but it never came.

Then something amazing happened in June of 2009. The West got to see the beauty and passion of the people of Iran, because we got to see them through their own lens. Iran has a very young population, with about 70 percent of Iranians under thirty-five. In the 2009 election, they came out in hordes in support of progressive candidate Mir Hossein Mousavi, who was projected to win.

In what was heavily disputed as a fraudulent election, Mousavi lost, and the streets of Iran became a battleground of protests and violence. The young, tech-savvy Iranian population, using proxy servers to bypass government control, took to Twitter and YouTube to broadcast what was happening to them in real time. For the first time, we saw the real Iran, not what the Western media has wanted us to think all along. We saw people who wanted nothing more than to be free, and we saw their government brutally oppressing them. A beautiful girl named Neda got shot during the protests, and for a week, everyone was Neda. People across the internet turned their profile pictures green in solidarity with what was dubbed the Green Revolution.

Suddenly everyone gave a shit, because they were seeing the human aspect. Pictures of passionate Iranian faces hit the media like a big, beautiful, fierce wave. I'll never forget when one acquaintance came up to me with wonder and delight, proclaiming, "Wow, the people of Iran are really beautiful." No shit, Sherlock. No one would've ever seen any of that if not for the Iranian youth taking the media reins into their own hands.

And here we are now, all these years later, and amnesia has struck again. Another Republican in office, and the battle drums beat once again. Iranians got clumped into W's asinine Axis of Evil. (What the fuck does that even mean? Are we living in a graphic novel?) And now they're the target of Trump's hateful rhetoric and travel bans, while he gallivants around making friends with multiple human rights abusers. And once again, no one stops to ask what Iranians have done to deserve this. I guess I'll just have to wait for the Iranian people to painstakingly remind the world that they're just humans hoping to be free again one day.

Fear, Safety, and the Realities of an Undocumented Student in a Border State

an interview with Deya

Dani: Can you tell me about how you came to the United States? And where you and your family came from?

Deya: I'm an undocumented student, from Mexico, specifically, so I feel like part of the process, for us, it's complicated, but I always think back that it's never as complex as people coming from Central America. It's weird to think about it, but I always think that somehow being from Mexico is kind of "easier." I came to the United States when I was seven years old.

Dani: And did you have siblings that came with you, or was it just you and your parents? What was the family structure?

Deya: My dad left two years before, so actually probably within a year of my brother being born he came to the United States. I had some memories of my dad, but my little brother didn't until he came to the United States. Then after my mom made the decision that her, my brother, and I would travel up with an uncle, my mom and my uncle got separated from us, so we kind of made it to the United States probably two months earlier. We were staying with my aunt for that period of time in L.A. I was seven and my little brother, he was three. He actually turned three years old when we came.

Dani: And what was that process like for you?

Deya: It was a little more complicated there. It's still hard to talk about it, because my mom gradually told me her process. From what I understand, they crossed the mountains, whereas my brother and I, we did a different process. The thing is, I'm not too sure if I'm allowed to share the information.

Dani: I understand. So then when you got here you were in Southern California? You said you were with your aunt. Is that where you grew up after you got here?

Deya: Actually, for me, I stayed with my aunt in Compton, specifically. I stayed there for probably eight months. And then we moved to Providence, Rhode Island, in the East Coast. That's where I grew up most of my life.

Dani: Oh, wow. That's so far away. How did you end up in Rhode Island? Did you have family there?

Deya: My mom's sister, she lives in that state, and my dad was staying there, a few of my uncles too. So we went, and we had just saved up enough money to travel to the East Coast.

Dani: There's just so much terrible misinformation in the media, specifically, and in the White House about undocumented immigrants and that experience. From your own experience what do you feel like people should know about what it's like to be an immigrant, especially a woman, in the U.S. today with everything that's going on? I know that's a really big question. . .

Deya: Oh, yeah. I feel like it's complicated, because, one thing is [for people to] do individual research, if possible. Don't believe everything the media tells you. We fall into that I guess sometimes, when we believe what we see in the media, and that's not always the case. Hey, I came here when I was seven. Was I thinking about being a criminal? No, I honestly just thought we were moving to a better place. Me not knowing that it was the United States was kind of a shock, because I was like, "Whoa, what is this?" You know. "Why aren't they speaking Spanish?" I wasn't aware. And you know, with the president . . . we have to say "the president."

Dani: It's so hard to say!

Deya: I know, right. I know. But I mean, we can also look at Bush, we can look at Clinton, and we can look at Obama. Obama did have high deportation rates, if not the highest reported. And my issue is, yes, there's false information always going around but also the fact that so little amount of people own so many media outlets. It's still very biased. Even trying to explain to people my experience, because I say, "I'm from Mexico, grew up on the East Coast, but before I started high school I came back to California, and here I am at UC Santa Cruz." It's complicated for me, because it's personal, but at the same time you do want to give a perspective. Honestly, I'm just tired of being tired, and I'm tired of waiting. I just wish people were more open to ideas.

Dani: In addition to the political stuff and the administration, with the misinformation that's happening in the media too, I feel like most people are pretty misinformed or have their own ideas about what it's like to be an immigrant in this country, and it seems like, just from where I'm sitting and the conversations I've had with different friends, that it seems like a pretty scary political environment and social environment to be in. Has that been your experience too? Just interacting with people or being out in the world?

Deya: Yeah, it's a little scary. But honestly, where I'm at right now, and where I'm standing and how I'm doing right now, it's because of people who did what they had to do, I guess, speak out, I'm here. I have the privilege to have DACA; I'm here because of also the AB 540 law in California. Yes, there's fear, there's always gonna be fear, but I don't let that dominate me anymore, rather I wanna voice the opinions of others who have similar opinions as me, or don't. But it's finding that middle ground too.

Dani: It sounds like there's a pretty good community there at UC Santa Cruz? Are you involved with student activism around immigration issues?

Deya: I'm part of the Undocumented Citizen Services as a student, I'm one of those who use that resources, through ELP. I'm also part of something on campus, an organization called Hermanos Unidos. And it's based in multiple campuses throughout California; UCs and Cal States.

Dani: I'm wondering how you manage to stay focused on your school and take care of yourself with all of the news, especially around the detention centers at the border. I'm wondering how you manage to be a full-time student and really focus when there's all this intense news happening.

Deya: It's in my face, I'm not gonna lie.

Dani: Right, I can only imagine.

Deya: I can't ignore it. Personally, I can't. I don't even know how to go about it, because I think for me it's just that it's always gonna be there. I try to literally be as aware as possible. I do read multiple media outlets, I do put myself in uncomfortable situations and have been in uncomfortable spaces on campus too, because I think that helps sort of, though; for example, I've gone to Republican student meetings here on campus.

Dani: Oh, wow.

Deya: I know, right. I don't support it most of the time. I don't really support it, period, but there's conversations that happen in those spaces, and I want to understand why. Like why to get so concerned. So putting myself in a space that I usually am not welcome in does help me understand certain things. It's complicated. I also think about family. My parents are in Compton, and I'm up here. As much as I'd love for them to visit a lot, I'm just scared that one day there's gonna be ICE or a random stop. The times they've been here they love the campus, they just don't like the distance. But my fear is just them traveling up here. I wish they could enjoy it. I'm here because of them, you know.

Dani: Yeah. It happens up here too. ICE was in our neighborhood about two weeks ago. They just randomly show up in certain neighborhoods, and it's really unsettling.

Deya: Yeah. It's like, what can we do? I don't know. I focus my attention somewhere else, that's my thing. I can't just sit back, but when I do need a break, I leave my phone in my dorm. I'm really lucky I'm at UCSC, and when I can I take a walk with a friend or just take a lap around the campus and pray. It's hard.

Dani: I feel like Republican gatherings seem to be pretty male dominated too, so you add that gender stuff on to it. I'm really curious about what kind of dialogues you've had in that space.

Deya: It's intense.

Dani: I'm sure! You're really brave.

Deya: I feel like in both environments, it kind of taught me to be aware and know my things. Like, yes, you're gonna go in there sometimes, you're gonna go in there debating. I don't even know how to explain it, because it's like, yes, most of them are guys, most of them. There are women in there too, but they happen to be predominantly white women. When you look at the spectrum, there are some people who identify as Latinos who are Republican, there are some African Americans who do identify with that party, and it's just understanding that this is their ideology. I respect it, I have to respect it. But at the same time, if I respect it, they have to respect my opinion as well. And that's the kind of treatment that is given in that org, surprisingly, you know. Most of the students in there happen to be in a very limbo state, where they're not for the Republicans nor are they for the Democratic Party, because right now the government is . . . excuse me, but it's super shitty.

Dani: Yeah, Democrats are not always my favorite people either.

Deya: I'm not for either of them, honestly. It's hard, they helped me, but right now they're helping no one, I feel, but themselves.

Dani: It sounds intimidating going into those spaces. Do you feel heard? They give you space to talk and they actually listen? Or is it confrontational?

Deya: Sometimes it can get confrontational, because there's those die-hard Trump supporters in there as well. They're everywhere, but, you know. . . Why do they believe in this? And then also learning how to talk to them, because some people are aggressive. We have to be very informed in order to have these discussions with people like that.

To me, those spaces, they made me want to read more about the policy and understanding the Constitution more, understanding the California law, and Santa Cruz County, my hometown. It's hard to say hometown, but one of the places I grew up and I call home is Compton, then there's Providence, Rhode Island. Mexico, it's just like when people say, "What's your home?" I'm like, "Complicated."

Do all Trump supporters, are they all racists and bigots? We all feel like we know someone who voted for that president, but it's just like, are they racist? I don't know.

Dani: There are so many people that want to be supportive and be good allies, and I know a lot of times there's kind of a blind spot, especially with the do-gooder, upper-middle-class, middle-age white women, for example. I'm wondering if you have any advice or suggestions about how people can be better allies to people like you, people that are immigrants in this country right now.

Deya: It starts with your own community. You know, I feel like people can help undocumented folks or any kind of person that's marginalized by starting in your own back yard. Go change policies in your neighborhood if possible, you know.

For me, like in Compton, it's a complicated city with a beautiful culture to me. A lot of it has to do, again, media representation after that movie came out, *Straight Outta Compton*. I mean, cool, you know, it's cool that they made it out the fastest. They did, you know. But I wasn't raised in the nineties, I was born in the nineties. If you want to make a change, a difference, start with your own community. It's hard to be politically active sometimes, you know. And that's what matters at the end of the day, because, A, that is why the Republicans won. And if you have the privilege to vote, exercise your right. If you have the privilege to help out your community, go for it. We can go and save children in Africa, they're striving up there too, but here at Flint, here in Compton, Santa Rosa, Richmond, Oakland, where's the help at when you need it?

Dani: Yeah, we have a pretty great community here, and there's one organization a lot of people I know work with, and they've been offering free trainings through the Rapid Response Network that trains community members on how to document ICE activity, how to alert people that there's

ICE activity in certain neighborhoods. Do you know if there's anything like that happening in Santa Cruz or Compton, where your family is?

Deya: From my understanding right now, in Santa Cruz, yes. In Compton, I don't think there is.

I try to convince my friends, "Hey, try voting!" I can't tell them go vote for this policy, because I'm like, "It's your opinion. You have to vote your opinion." But most of my friends choose not to vote, because they disagree with the government. I get it, you have the right to be mad. When they tell me, "I'm protesting the government by not voting." I'm like, "No, that makes it worse, because you're letting other people choose for you now." It's a simple thing, in voting sometimes. And perhaps even introducing a policy where people are allowed to vote.

Dani: Right. That's something that's been so frustrating for me in my activist community too. Just seeing people like, "Oh, it doesn't matter." Or, "Fuck the government, I don't believe in this or that." There are so many people that these policies could affect that can't vote! You know, if they have a felony on their record, or if they're on parole, or they're not a U.S. citizen, but they're living here. These things impact people other than just the people that are actually voting. It's so frustrating for me. It's really important, I'm glad that you brought that up.

Deya: Another thing is that I have never encountered the level of hate. . . I don't know how to say it. I have encountered it. It's just that I will always receive hate from Trump supporters or conservatives because of my documentation. But at the same time, I've also encountered really more aggression, more anger from my own people, from Latinos. We have to call that out, I feel. I'm sorry, but just because someone's Latino, that doesn't excuse us from our behavior either. I don't think it's fair. When Mexico was in the World Cup, and they won a game, New York City, a city near me, they burned a Central American flag. I'm like, "No, don't do that." Why are you disrespecting our brothers and sisters? This is why a lot of Latinos, we are so divided. The one thing that I feel like that unites us is the immigration issue because a lot of us deal with it. And to me that's frustrating, because there are Latinos who are racist too, who hold prejudice, and that needs to be addressed. It's just like, what can we do from here, you know. How can we help out those children that are in detention centers? They happen to be majority from Central America. And understanding what Mexico is doing as well. They just recently started kind of helping, a little bit, the Central American folks.

If I fight for my issues, I have to fight for other issues too. It's not just about DACA, because as much as DACA's given me opportunities, I'm not happy with it. The goal is the Dream Act, and even then it's like pushing a new kind of Dream Act that favors, I think its 1.4 million undocumented youth. Our dreams are here. I'm here because of my mom and my dad. I'm here studying this [Sociology and Legal Studies]. I'm here talking to you because of my parents. And many undocumented folks, so even then, the term undocumented can be complex. But people forget about our parents. They're the reasons we're allowed to dream. It's hard to say. My mom, my dad, they're giving their best years to a country that doesn't want them. Yes, we pay taxes. Do we get any money back? My parents, I don't think so. They have to pay. They play by the rules. The one thing that they did wrong: they crossed. I did too. I was seven. My brother was three. When a country markets: here is the land of the free, the opportunity, you're selling this to the people. The United States destabilized many countries, and now they're coming to this country, because, it sucks, but there's just way more opportunities here.

I'm a Hysterical Woman

Phoenix LeFae

There's been a lot of talk in the news media recently about women and our emotions, how unstable we are, how nasty we are. The last big election cycle stirred up everything from pride, to disgust, to double standards, to outright clear and present misogyny. On more than one occasion, I cried tears of anger, joy, frustration, you name it.

Growing up I hated crying, especially when anyone else was around. If I fell down, scraped my knees, and bled all over myself my reaction was to try and suck it up, put on a brave face, and walk it off. I was inundated with messages from the world around me that taught me being emotional was bad; especially crying. How many times in my life have I heard the phrase "hysterical woman?"

I fought against the desire to cry time and time again. I would push emotions down; swallow them whole, eat them over and over again. Because it was more important to look strong, calm, and together; rather than be seen as a "hysterical woman."

I worked in the corporate world for over a decade, where a woman showing emotions is never allowed to happen. A woman being angry, a woman crying, a woman doing anything but holding her shit together was never acceptable. To cry when upset or frustrated was considered a weakness. To show anger was to be a bitch and then have to endure jokes about it being "that time of the month."

Crying is weakness. Crying is for sissies. Crying is for girls who want attention. You don't want people to think you are a "hysterical woman" do you?

But there were times when the grief got too big. There were lots of times the sadness overtook me, and I needed to let the tears flow. And I found myself in a dark room, lit by the soft glow of the television, playing a sad movie, sobbing. Only then was it okay, only then was it safe. And only when I was alone. My go-to movie was *Beaches*, and it still makes me cry, but no one knows that, because I only watch it when I'm all alone.

And there have been times when the tears came unwanted and impossible to hide. There have been arguments and hurt feelings. There have been times when I was so frustrated or mad that the only thing I could do was cry. Unbidden and unwanted these tears are the worst, because they are the ones witnessed by the people who may have helped to cause them in the first place. They betray my strong and solid exterior by showing there may be crack in my armor. I hate these tears.

There have been people who have accused me of using emotions as a weapon. There have been people who have sat staring blankly when the tears flowed, unsure of what to do with me in such an unusual state. There have been people who attempted to comfort me, only to make me more uncomfortable; aware of my hysteria.

For the most part I hold my shit together. For the most part no one sees me cry. For the most part I keep my "hysterical woman" locked behind bars in a dungeon in a pit, only rarely being let out for a little reprieve. However, as I near ever closer to the age of forty, I'm starting to notice a change in my emotional landscape; tears flow often for things sweet, for things beautiful, for things utterly broken. I find myself crying often, so much more often than I want to; as if the years of swallowing my tears has finally caught up with me and there is no more room inside, no more places to hide the feelings, and so they spill out.

I feel so ashamed and guilty. I feel so unlike me. And yet, it feels like this is who I am becoming, and this is who I've always been, just too afraid to see it. Those stories, those "tapes" that play in my head and tell me that strong women don't cry can go fuck themselves. It's time to write a new story, it's time to be my full emotional self; sadness, anger, and all of it. The "hysterical woman" that I've kept trapped has broken her bars and is clawing her way out of that pit. She is coming for me, and I'm waiting for her with open arms.

How the European Witch Hunts Continue to Influence Violence against Women around the World

an interview with Silvia Federici

Dani: The first thing I want to ask you is what led to you focusing your research and writing on the witch hunts?

Silvia: It was a combination of factors. Partially was that I was encountering references to the witch hunt as I was regressing in history, going back and back to the beginning of capitalism, the sixteenth and seventeenth century. I was very interested in understanding how capitalism developed to begin with, what social forces, what event, what crisis led to this amazing change, the change from the feudal to the capitalist organization of work. At the same time, I also encountered that pamphlet that Barbara Ehrenreich and Deirdre English wrote [*Witches, Midwives, and Nurses: A History of Women Healers*]. For me the most important aspect of the pamphlet was really the chronology, was seeing that the witch hunt was placed in the sixteenth, seventeenth century. Immediately I realized this is really the beginning of capitalism. Why a witch hunt? Why such incredible persecution—which is really unheard of historically—exactly in this period? So that's what motivated me to try to understand all the background.

Dani: You mentioned this a little bit in your collection of essays too, but I'm wondering if you could talk a little bit about why you feel it's important to continue educating people about this time in history?

Silvia: I think it's very, very important, because, first of all, I think that this is the time, in a way, in which some of the most structural elements of the capitalist system of work were established. So there's something that shows there's a continuity. There's a continuity between the developments in this period and the forces that are operating in our time as well. And it's very telling that, for instance, in very recent times, even today, we have a return of witch-hunting in several parts of the world.

It's in a different context but still using much of the ideology. It's using much of the teaching of the Church and the kind of accusations that were [brought] against women in the sixteenth and seventeenth century. So I think that this is the period of formation of this new social system. For example, today we're speaking of a return of primitive accumulation. A return of processes that, in some ways, evoke the kind of displacement, separation of people from the land, that really were at the beginning of capitalism. So, those structural elements have not changed. I think what I've been trying to show through the book is that there are conditions of existence of a capitalist society, of a capitalist organization of production and work, that were set historically from the beginning. Of course, then we restructured in different ways in the course of capitalist history, but nevertheless the period that goes from the sixteenth to the end of the eighteenth century, it's a period in which some of the most important elements and foundations of the developing capitalist society were set. That's why that period is so important to me.

Dani: One of the things that you write about in this book [*Witches, Witch-Hunting, and Women*] is the fear of women's power, especially during the period of the sixteenth and seventeenth centuries, and I'm wondering if you can talk about how the fear of women's power is playing out in similar ways today.

Silvia: I think, for example, there is a major, major campaign that's been unfolding at the political level, social-political level, and also through the media, that it's systematically distorting women's power, as I wrote in *Caliban and the Witch* and later, and presenting this power as something dangerous, as something perverse, as something obnoxious. So, in fact, the witch is the personification of women's power, but presented in this most destructive way. I think it's not an accident that even in the movies and even in the collective imagination, the figure of the witch is now being used again.

Now, for instance, her sexuality. Women's sexuality is always, always represented, particularly in movies and in the media, as something aggressive, as something that is ultimately anti-male, and even anti-life. The woman now, you have the classical image of the woman who has destructive power, Superwoman, always half naked, upper bodies presenting in the most provocative way, and at the same time it's a body that now is armed, it's now destructive, it's now all these very, very destructive powers. And also, in some of the persecutions that have been taking place, often the woman is targeted. If the woman is known to be a *curandera*, to be a healer, to have a particular relationship with the land. So again, women's concern for the question of reproduction is presented as something mysterious and perverse. In other words, she has powers that are not legitimate, that are presented as ultimately destructive, asocial. So I think that is continuing. It's a way of appropriating. It's also seen as connected to the powers of giving death. Or it is presented often as women who have this particular relation to life and death. I think it's part of a whole regime of disciplining women, of expropriation of women, appropriation of their labor, appropriation of their capacity to reproduce.

Dani: Something that comes up for me as we talk about this too, that's been really frightening for me, and you mention this in your writing, is this backlash against feminism and against women's power. Targeted violence against women with things like shootings. Do you feel like things might continue to get worse? Do you think that consciousness around women's rights are shifting? How are you feeling about this moment in time with all of this backlash happening?

Silvia: I think it's a very scary moment, but at the same time I feel that it's a moment in which more and more women are really rising up. I've been incredibly amazed and encouraged by what is taking place in Latin America. Just now, in just the last few days, in Argentina. There's been a crescendo in the last couple of years that is not subsiding. On the contrary. A few things have happened in the last weeks. One has been the big referendum about abortion where people have voted, and now it has to be recorded by the Senate. It has to be really made into law. And the other is the new powers that have been given to the military by the government, by the Macri government. The response of women has been amazing. They have gone out in huge, huge numbers, and the latest they have done, just the last few days, they have launched the Operation Spider, where they have basically gone everywhere in the city, including the metropolitan and the subway, telling people to come out to support the law for abortion and basically to oppose this whole attack that is coming down from this new right-wing government.

And I think that the case of Argentina is not isolated, is not unique. I've been traveling quite a bit in Brazil, in Mexico, Uruguay, and I've been impressed by this surge. And also the ability, the capacity, the clarity the women have. They're very, very clear that what you need to change in order to do away with patriarchal power is to change the whole economic system, and that you cannot separate struggling against male supremacy from struggling against capitalist exploitation, the politics of extractivism, and that the destruction of the nature, of the environment, that all of these are part of a whole social system and social culture. They have to be part of the same struggle. I think that's a very high level of consciousness that, certainly, as important as the women's movement of the seventies was, that I think in a way was revolutionary, did not have this very, very broad understanding. There's been a maturing of the understanding of what we're up against. It is very well articulated.

The violence against women is on a continuum with the violence against children, against the earth, the water, the contamination of the earth and the water, the cutting of forests, that this is all part, on a very perverse, exploitative conception of human beings, the relation of human beings with the natural world. That gives me strength, gives me hope.

This is not to ignore that right now there is a huge backlash, and I think it's in response precisely to the fact that, really, women are present in the struggle and leading struggle in a way that has not been true perhaps before. And demanding autonomy. And refusing to be infantilized. And refusing to be forced to work without remuneration or without a compensation. Forced to a subservient position.

Dani: Along those lines of this violence against women, there's another essay where you draw parallels between the torture inflicted on women during the witch hunts and then the systemic violence and rape against African slaves. And you say that violence against women didn't disappear with abolition, but it was normalized. Can you explain what that means here?

Silvia: Oh, yes. When you see, particularly when you look at the black community and just focusing on women, for instance, the sterilization has continued into our days. In the sixties and seventies, for example, scores of black women, immigrant women, Latina [women] were sterilized, particularly when they were on welfare. We have learned recently that even into the seventies particularly black women in jails were being sterilized. So the whole chapter of sterilization. And lobotomy. Dozens of women were lobotomized in the United States and in Europe. In Sweden, for instance, as well as other countries. Dozens and dozens of women. Women were depicted as particularly good candidates for lobotomy, because presumably the task to which they were assigned, housework, didn't require great mental capacities. And these were theorized openly.

I've been very interested on the question, because we have forgotten the story of lobotomy.

Dani: Right. And it wasn't that long ago.

Silvia: Yeah. We have forgotten it. How many women. And now women are not being lobotomized, because now so many have been put on these psycho-pharmaceutical drugs that are equivalent of a sort of lobotomy. So I think when you see the history of the medical profession, and when you see the history of the treatment of women in jails, and particularly low-income women and women of color, but not exclusively, you also see that that violence is not as continual. For instance, I've learned that during the Great Depression, when you began to have the beginning of a social assistance program, of a welfare program, and women were unemployed, were able at times to get some welfare from local governments. They were always in danger of being kidnapped—I don't think we can use another word—and forced to be either sterilized or cut off from the welfare rolls. I didn't know that. I didn't know. Then I read the report of a writer that describes numbers of white women, proletarian, working-class, would become unemployed, and they were all scared, because they felt that a social worker was following them and checking on whether you talk to men or not talk to men. And, in fact, many women were labeled as promiscuous under the guise that they were weak-minded, feebleminded. If they were poor they were locked up and intimidated until they accepted sterilization. In some cases, they were locked up for life, because there was fear that they would have children who then become dependent on the state.

So that's that old sterilization of poor women, and the violence across the former colonial world, in Africa, India, Indonesia. For example, in the nineties under the guise of population control, when they would have these sterilization safaris, accusing women of being those who bring poverty to their society. Saying that poverty exists because women have too many children, when exactly it is the other way around. There is a lot of work that's been done showing that it is because people are poor. People are not poor because they have too many children; they have too many children because they are poor, and they need the children. Those children are their security for the future.

Dani: Right. Absolutely.

Silvia: In situations where there's no pension, no guarantee against a work accident, and etc., and where you need the children in many different capacities to provide a viable income for the family. So then they have these sterilization camps where thousands and thousands of women were sterilized. In many cases they did not realize that it was irreversible. They didn't know that it was irreversible. And the contraceptives that have been pushed in so many parts of the world, like Depo-Provera, that women cannot really control. They implant them, or the IUD, and then you cannot take them out, even if you discover that they're not good for your health. Some have very negative effects. Those are forms of violence. They might not be as terrifying as being burned at the stake, but that whole underlying texture of violence has not really ever ended.

Dani: Something I really appreciated too, that you brought in class issues and issues that women of color are facing, but also the issue of transgender women of color. Could you talk a little bit about that?

Silvia: Yeah. Two things. First of all, the question of procreation. First of all, about women of color, there was a report that came out a couple of years ago where they actually used these words. They said, "Today, if you are a woman of color, and you are low income, and you decide to have a child, you literally place yourself outside the boundaries of the American Constitution," because you become vulnerable, liable, to a whole series of crime that exist only in your case. For example, women who found themselves in a car accident and told the police that they were pregnant were then arrested and charged with negligence toward the fetus. There is a proliferation of many states that are now busy putting bills that give more and more rights to the fetus, describing and defining the fetus as a person, and so the rights of the fetuses are going up, the rights of women are going down. Now it's dangerous because you can be charged with negligence, with having put in jeopardy the life of this presumed person, which actually is not. My theory is that this is a way of forcing, scaring women, poor black women, away from having children. It presents itself as a defense of life, but actually it's a way of saying, "You're going to have a child, we're going to make sure that you're going to really be watched and penalized for doing that." Because there's no other way you can explain such nonsense.

And about trans women, I think that some of the highest number, and growing, of women of color and transgender women are being subjected to the most violence. This is happening now not only in the U.S. It's happening in Mexico. It's happening in Brazil. I just read, actually, an article about the killing of trans women in Brazil, and, really, the number is staggering.

There is definitely a part of America who is ready to reinstitute the witch hunt. I think that people like Sessions are right there, using the Bible to justify the most unjust legislation. I think if it was up to them, we'd be back to corporal punishment for children and for women, and we'd be back to really witch-hunting. I was scared to see there was a suit basically asking the Supreme Court to prohibit right-to-life groups from following women to the doors of the clinic, because now they go there screaming "baby killer." So they were asking to forbid them from chasing them through the door, and the Supreme Court turned it down, which was quite amazing. Basically, they have the right to intimidate you, that it's been now legislated by the highest organ in the country. That, I think, speaks volumes as to this moment. We're going back to really older models of discipline.

Dani: One of the things that you mention also in the book and that I've been reading a little bit more about over the last couple of years, but I don't think a lot of people are aware of, are the witch-hunts in parts of Africa and the camps in Ghana. Can you talk about those a little bit and the similarities that you draw between those witch-hunts and the European witch-hunts?

Silvia: There actually are a few documentaries. One of the latest is *The Witches of Gambaga*.

Dani: Oh, that's a really good one.

Silvia: Yeah. I've been trying, as in the case of the witch-hunts of the sixteenth, seventeenth, eighteenth century, I've been trying to show that you may have multiple factors, but there is a common background, and that common background is really the kind of an attack to the basic conditions of living that has been moved with the globalization process. The fact that there are now forces and programs that are out to displace large numbers of people from their land, expropriate them from their land, so their land is shrinking, so there is a whole rearrangement also in communities, particularly with regard to land, land ownership, who has access, who does not. So I was showing that this is one of the grounds of the terrain on which these witch hunts are developing, both in Africa and in India, that in many, many cases they are really connected with processes of land displacement.

Another factor that particularly for Africa has to do, again, connected with globalization, with the new forms of marketing. The new forms of trading. So, for example, in part of Africa local traders, women traders, everyone was trading, selling at the local market have been accused of being witches by big guys who are involved with export/import. It's very interesting how they see these women as a danger. These are women who, in fact, are working locally, and they believe that the resources of the community should be invested locally. So there is all this tension.

And then there are other factors, but an important one is also the arrival, since the early eighties, in all these areas where people are destined to be expropriated, where land is being privatized, community things have been broken down, the arrival of all these fundamentalist sects, originally, and probably even today, financed by very right-wing groups in United States, who basically are turning communities against each other. They are turning people against each other by saying that if you are not rich, there is all this panic, conspiracy going on in the community, that Satan is out there, and you have to watch over your shoulder that people are not conspiring against you. So now, for instance, in Africa you have people who look at a car accident maybe as something that is being caused by evil forces.

So you have communities where the new economic programs are really tearing social relations apart, are sending a lot of people out to migrations, are causing forms of mass impoverishment, and causing changes that people locally do not understand, because the price of cotton, the price of coca, is not decided. Why is it that this year they can sell the crop and next year they cannot sell it? All those changes are determined far away from their locality. What is happening in their community is actually the effect of decisions that are being made in London, in Chicago, in New York. So that this globalization and the forces that are impacting people's lives are more and more difficult to understand. They are creating a kind of terrain of suspicion. Why is so-and-so getting rich? Why we are getting poor? Why can't we sell our crop? So there is an environment of disruption, breakdown of solidarity, shrinking resources, struggle for survival, and women are at the center of it. Women are those who have been most penalized from it.

Dani: And it's disproportionately older women that are suffering, is that right?

Silvia: Of course. Particularly older women. In the camps, for instance, the camps in Ghana, it's mostly older women, and so there's an element of it that says older women are burden to the community. They become an easy target. They are also those who know a lot about the community.

Older women are the ones who are seen as having more knowledge, more powers, and the whole question of the older woman is not useful any longer. There's a long history of the older woman being seen as resentful and a negative force. As resentful of the young. It's an image, the one of the older woman, that can be easily manipulated by those who have the interest in creating divisions.

Dani: One of the other things you mention is that a lot of feminists seem to overlook what's happening in these communities.

Silvia: I think some are responding to what happened a few years ago when women in United States, women like Alice Walker, were criticizing genital mutilation and then there was a whole thing, "Well, that you are not supposed to." But I don't share that, because I think that it depends what your analysis is. My analysis is to say, "Yeah, people are being made to kill each other but what are the causal factor and what are the forces?" I think that I've been going out of my way to show, "No, look, this is really very much something that has been constructed, something that has been engineered," as many of the ethnic rivals have been engineered. For instance, I spent time in Nigeria and I have no doubt that some of the way Christians and Muslims have massacred each other was nothing spontaneous. That there was an enormous investment made in having those communities fight each other. Even the question of where the weapons that were used came from. Who could afford to have those type of weapons that were then used? Then you know that it's nothing spontaneous. And now all of a sudden you have all this movement, like Boko Haram. Very, very strange, huh? Who's behind them? Who has the power? Why they have such an impunity after all? So I think it's misguided to pull back and say, "Oh, but they're burning women on the stake. We are not going to say anything, because it can't cast the best image." No. It's important to understand outside of a framework that blames cultures or blames particular groups, etc., and instead [to ask], why now? And what's behind it? What is the context in which it's happening? When you begin to see that, you will find, in fact, that the Africans who have analyzed or the Indians who have analyzed the situation, they themselves identify globalization. For example, in the article that I have written for the book, that actually it was written before the book, I quoted a number of works who are making this connection. I begin the article saying that we have to lay the blame at the doorstep of the World Bank and the IMF, because they are the ones, in fact, who are responsible for destroying the kind of terrain, the kind of changes that have been brought about by the anti-colonialist struggle. That in a way the crisis that was highly engineered, and the process of structural adjustment that was applied, which really was destructive for so many countries, they really are a process of recolonization. They really aim to recolonize, to give again the power to EU, United States, over the resources of these countries. Which is what has happened. That in the name of paying the debt, these countries have been sucked dry of their minerals, of their oil. Their land is being used for green gasoline, to plant elephant leaf and not food crops. These are the kind of devastation which then also sets up for the next stage, which is turning people against each other.

Dani: It's so terrible.

Silvia: And this massacre is continuing. When you look at the Sudan. When you look at the Democratic Republic of Congo. When you look at the land battle in Kenya, and then in South Africa. None of that is innocent when you look at it. When you look at how they developed. Populations that went along next to each other, different ethnic groups that lived in perfect peace for a long time all of a sudden begin to machete each other. What's happening? Who is fueling those divisions?

Dani: My last big question for you, switching gears a little bit, I'm so curious, as someone who is a scholar of witch hunts, I'm wondering what your thoughts are about the Trump administration constantly calling "witch hunt, witch hunt" any time they're questioned or challenged.

Silvia: That's very, very interesting, right. I don't think they're thinking of the old witch hunt. I don't even know what he knows about past history. But what worries me. . . Of course, the man is a liar, but you know. . . I feel tempted to say pathological liar, but I don't think it's a pathology. I am more inclined to see a kind of calculation, yeah? The man is really perverse, but it's calculated. He learns that to defend himself in a condition in which he cannot, or to defend his administration, the best form is to attack people. That's the impulse. It's always to attack and to intimidate and to scare. And now he knows that he has the power to do it. But I think it's important to see how much of that is also intended to distract people from a lot of things that they are actually doing, how they're really systematically dismantling. Right? There is a part also of buffoonery that the American people, we are being entertained. Every day there is a new soap opera. It's an ongoing, perverse soap opera that it's actually hiding important strategic changes in the political economy of the country. Without exaggerating that, because I think that the Republicans are not so far from the Democrats, that there is an important continuity. But there's also a lot of experimentation, I think. How far can we go? How far can we go in denying people's rights? One of my fears, and this applies to social movements, human rights, etc., is that the kind of extreme behavior of a Trump and the people around him, because he's not alone, you really have a collection of characters there, my God.

Dani: I know. It's astounding.

Silvia: Sixteenth-century torture chamber.

Dani: It's terrifying.

Silvia: Oh, my God, you don't want to see them after dark. Bolton and Sessions, oh, my God.

Dani: It's a nightmare.

Silvia: For me, the story of the witch hunt is one of the points of entry. It's been one of the main points of entry to understand the logic motivating capitalism and, in particular, the position of women and the violence against women within it. In that sense, it's something I continue to work on it. And also trying to look at the forms of witch hunts that are not being realized through the fire or through the knife but looking at ideological forms of witch hunt against women. For me, to bring together this new material about gossip, the witch hunt in Africa, it's something that I do because I think it's important, and because I hope that other women will see the importance of these specific developments and will see that even today in the twenty-first century in large parts of the world, several African countries, India, several states in India, Papua New Guinea, you can still have a hundred men take women, cover them with gasoline, and burn them. That this can happen, that something like this can happen. It's so horrendous. It's so barbaric. And yet it's happening. And yet you don't have a massive outcry against it. So I hope to raise some concern and some more desire to make connection with past and present.

Dear Man with the Indigo Cardigan

Anna Silastre

I was wrapped around a toilet at the Courtyard Marriott while we were on the phone. I opened my throat like a goose and tried to fill my body with as much wine as possible. My mom had gone down to the lobby for more bottles and snacks to celebrate, since we were snowed in, and the hotel restaurant was under repair. It was her first time visiting me since I'd moved to New Jersey. We had laughed about the storm's great timing, how she would have missed the moment when I got the news if her plane hadn't been grounded. We hugged each other, you know. Right there in the hotel lobby. And I didn't feel weird. We hadn't hugged like that in a long time. She was proud of me, and I felt like suddenly all this made sense. You believe in fate, alignment, the magic behind a buried cicada. Why didn't this count?

I heard her come back and locked the bathroom door. I palmed the mascara from my cheeks and took another sip. If I blacked out I wouldn't be able to hear you anymore. Maybe you'd stop talking altogether or hang up, or maybe I'd somehow get the courage to hang up instead. Either way, I wouldn't have sense enough to care what you felt or thought. I emptied the bottle into myself and myself into the bottle until neither of us was left.

A year earlier I had stripped on stage at the Whiskey Tip in Santa Rosa for North Bay Cabaret. A mactivist had called my cabaret friends and me "shoddy bimbos" and "womanizers," so at our next show I read a poem as a would-be artist, then stripped off my Christmas onesie to "Overnight Sensation" by Motörhead. Back then no one got to shame me.

Until I met you.

Not the "you" I met at first, though. The "you" I met at first laughed at that story. But now here you were, on the other end of the line, convincing me that I didn't deserve this thing I so desperately wanted.

"It's really disturbing that you want to teach kids how to have sex," you said. "And you made it all up anyways. Maybe I should have made up some liberal agenda and put it in *my* letter to get in."

"I've told you a million times—this is my thing, it's my calling."

"And you won't even be around anyways!"

"It's only once a week, I'm still moving to New Brunswick!"

"You'll always be gone, and then you'll be gone trying to sell your sex thing—is that what you want? To be a salesperson? I thought you were a teacher."

"I am!"

"You'll never have time for a family. You'll be like those horrible moms at your preschool."

At the time, I was teaching at an expensive language immersion preschool in Jersey City, where parents could monitor their toddlers through an app and pick them up after happy hour.

"I'm not even thinking about kids."

"You don't even know what you're talking about with sex ed—you don't know anything!"

"I'll learn!"

"You just used me, you don't even care about me."

"But that's why I'm moving to New Brunswick! For you!"

"I never thought you would value 'getting ahead' over relationships—you're not the person I thought you were."

"I care about you, I care about people."

"No, you don't, you made that whole sex ed thing up—you only got in because you're a minority."

"That is so fucked up."

"I have less opportunity these days as a white guy, and you're not even considering that. You're selfish, and that school is fake, and *you're* fake. You don't care about helping anyone but yourself."

When I was in high school I escorted my friend Kylie to homecoming on behalf of our magazine club, Eyes Open. Every year our school hosted a rally where the homecoming queen candidates walked in a circle and did a little wave to the audience. That whole homecoming tradition to us was disgusting and seemed to prize a specific tailored appearance over anything unique or comfortable. To make our opinion clear Kylie wore a white dress smeared with red paint and a stencil that said "Grade A" and I dressed as a butcher. We did that kind of shit for years.

Copwatch.

Take Back the Night.

Women's group after women's group, feminist meeting after feminist meeting. Herbal teas and tinctures, zines and poetry nights where we'd opened ourselves up and compared the dark entities inside.

In short, I considered myself to be someone who cared.

But you knew this, and that's the point. You knew how to push me. And I'd like to think you wouldn't have twisted me that way, that you did these things unknowingly as some emotional response. But you're too smart, and this wasn't love. But I refused to believe that.

My mom knocked on the door. I came out while we were still on the phone and told her I would be just a minute. When she asked if I was okay you'd heard her. You got angrier, told me I was setting you up to make you look bad. You called me manipulative and delusional, that I had made myself upset, that you were just telling me your feelings. How dare I make this about me? How dare I twist your words to her? All you wanted was to love me.

I hung up. I drank a few more glasses and texted my friends and watched the snow cover everything outside. They called you trash, but I knew: they just didn't *understand*. I didn't understand. Was this my fault?

My mom poured me more wine and told me it would blow over. She said you seemed to care about me, that you wouldn't behave this way if you didn't. But, she said, I should think about myself, about my future.

So there it was. I *was* acting selfishly. I already had so much. Did this mean that everything you said was right?

I used to know myself. I used to know the things I liked and what my soul craved and why, and I used to do what I needed to feed it. But now I couldn't reconcile my conviction to do what makes me feel fulfilled with the notion of hurting someone else. Since meeting you, the compass that once guided my beliefs spun uncontrollably. I was morally lost.

The next month I deferred my acceptance to Columbia and lost the scholarship I'd received to pursue my doctorate in Curriculum & Design.

•

When I was twenty-two my boyfriend and I had moved back home from Santa Barbara. I waitressed, quit, substitute taught preschool, quit, and found myself jobless on the floor of an apartment we could barely afford. I can still remember the way the threads of my carpet wove around each other, plush and purposeful. I filled each day listening to Randi Rhodes on Green 960 and Cloroxing the counters and knobs. Some days I went to the pool after making sure no one was there and pretended to study for the LSATs. I had no direction and no contact with other people. Only a handful of my friends knew I had moved back, but it didn't matter; I had somehow developed a fear of going out that prevented me from seeing them anyway. To make it worse, I had started compulsively picking my face and shoulders so I looked like a half-descaled fish, which justified me hiding myself from people.

No one wanted to see someone like me.

I tell you this as a scale: my depression in New Jersey was many multiples of that, to a point where I wanted to die. I have struggled with episodes of depression all my life, but there in New Jersey, I planned it. I even told you about it, and you mocked me, said I should call a hotline. A couple times I almost did.

I blame you.

Normally this wouldn't be fair. But I have never been so mind-fucked by someone else, and I guess I haven't completely reached the place where I can accept the fact that *I let this happen.*

How did I get there? How did we get here?

You seemed great when we met. You were nice, quiet, smart. You wore this cool indigo Ralph Lauren cardigan and sang "Semi-Charmed Life" on karaoke. Your sense of humor was a little bland, but your heart seemed like it was in the right place. You talked about magic, about fantasy. We pitched our stories to the same people at the writer's conference where we met, and you seemed sweet when you were nervous. You liked my writing and asked to hear my stories. You cared.

But to be clear, you were not the reason I moved here. I moved because of the friends we made at the conference—Alexis, Allie, Eloise. I moved, because one day I sat across from Mark Fitten who told me that at some point a person needs to set fire to their life and follow their dreams, or else they will always regret never trying.

You remember the "squad," don't you? We crashed a Yale reunion with them, drank all night, stayed up talking, skipped lectures to hang out and write. We were fast friends and even talked about vacationing to Italy together.

Later you said that you didn't actually like them. You said you used them to be part of a friend group I seemed to like. You wanted to show me that you were friendly and fun, even though you didn't like karaoke, drinking, or parties. You went into details about why each of them were weak, weird, or sleazy, and you told me you would leave if I talked to Mark again, if I met him for coffee, or if I went to that small reunion they had in the city.

That was the first sign.

You remember that reunion. I sucked down a carton of cigarettes behind my bug-infested basement apartment in Jersey City for hours on the phone with you, arguing over why I should go. You said people that care about each other don't just ditch them to hang out with other people, and since you couldn't make it because you had to spend time with your dog I shouldn't go either.

You know, when I told them I couldn't come, they knew it was you. Fin dropped you a hint through a comment online. Do you remember how you got angry at me for that? How you told me I was imagining you manipulating me? That it was really me manipulating other people to dislike you? "Why would I do something like that?" you said.

My family said your worries would blow over. It was a new relationship, and there would be other times when I could go out with people. I should wait. Building trust takes time. You'd get to know me and be comfortable eventually.

But it never happened. I lost those people as friends. I never saw them again.

There were other signs I should have heeded before I even moved. I would have listened to them, except you brought up the rape thing and fucked with the way I see myself.

I don't know why I told you. I guess I trusted the person you created for me to meet in Connecticut. And then one month after we'd met and I'd gone back to California, I returned to the East Coast for another workshop at Skidmore.

Do you remember Skidmore? Do you remember the instructor who told me he liked my story? He wanted to help me develop it, publish it. It was about two sisters who burn down a butterfly forest out of rage over a guy. I guess it's ironic now. The instructor had invited us to his house in Nantucket. He wanted to talk about writing, about possibilities.

But you told me if I spoke to him again, you would never talk to me. You said my story was trashy and inappropriate, because the protagonist flashes her breasts after sneaking out on a roof. It was a moment of defiance that you didn't understand. You said he liked it because he thought I was like that character, trashy. You said there was no way he could be *that* interested in my writing anyways, because it just wasn't *that* good. Who did I think I was? It had to be something else.

And then there was the kid. Do you remember him? He invited me to go swimming in the Hudson with him and some others in our workshop. He wanted to share work. I missed an entire lecture fighting with you about it. Even though he was extremely out about his homosexuality and very much interested in a working friendship, you banned me from speaking to him too.

I was ready to end things right there on the phone, two days into Skidmore. This was too much for a new relationship. But then you went there: *It's no wonder you were raped with the way you behave around men.*

I hung up on you and screamed into my pillow. The whole dorm probably heard it. My roommates must have thought I was crazy, and I guess they'd be right; it was the beginning of a long and slow mental deterioration.

You called back and apologized, said you loved me so much you just wanted me to be safe from possible predators. You were looking out for me. I needed you to remind me about men, because men are dangerous. Didn't I agree? Isn't that what I'd always been fighting against? Fighting for? You were on my side. I just didn't realize it. And then you changed the subject and told me all the places you would take me when this awful, scary workshop was over. You would take care of me.

Later on, a good friend would warn me about this. He'd tell me it was great you "cared" so much, but wasn't it strange that you made the world seem so dangerous? Wasn't it strange you didn't trust me to handle myself, to be independent?

But back then, I couldn't believe someone would do that, not to me. There had to be other reasons for you being the way you were.

That night at Skidmore, you talked me into exhaustion, telling me I must not care about you, I must only be out for myself. I began to doubt myself, to examine myself as flawed in ways I hadn't considered before. Was I unaware of the way men perceived me? Was the predation I experienced my own fault? I couldn't believe that it was, but coming from someone who apparently cared about me, it was hard to not consider.

And that became a standard equation for our relationship: If I did X, I was a lowly, uncaring piece of shit, and all you did was want to care for me and love me. And if I didn't agree, you would repeat yourself continuously, interlacing your argument with criticisms about who I was and the choices I made, until I was too tired and too sad to argue.

You chipped at me until you found an insecurity, a weakness, then dusted it off and held it to a flame until there was nearly nothing left but the dark ruins of my pain and fear. And a very fast train.

·

When I was eleven years old my mom left me in Paris's Latin Quarter. She was upset at me for forgetting where we were, where our hotel was. I told her that I couldn't remember. It was something I've always had trouble with. I couldn't remember where anything was, what I had done, where I had been. I still struggle to remember people's names, birthdates, places I've gone, or the direction of water. Large parts of my childhood, my teens, my young adult life, are subsumed by blank walls. All that remains are the feelings.

But the Latin Quarter, I remember. We were standing on a sidewalk; black lampposts and the smell of old things wafted from the buildings. She walked away angrily and told me to figure it out for myself. I watched her leave, down the street and walk around a corner. I thought at the time that I would figure it out. I would look at the colorful little map we'd gotten from the hotel and find the street names on the corners. She'd see.

I remember walking to a little cafe and getting a small snack then sitting down to stare at that map. But all I wondered was whether or not she would come back—and feeling like she wouldn't.

She'd done things like this before, usually when my dad came up in conversation. Once she opened the car door and told me to get out. I was seven or eight, and she drove off. During several visits, which were supervised at my grandmother's house, she'd walked out, frustrated that, in her eyes, I seemed to care more about my father each day I was now living with him instead of her. She'd lost custody when I was six years old. I don't know what exactly triggered that, and when I've asked my father he only says that she was unstable, undiagnosed, and had refused any sort of treatment. After I found out a lot made sense: no it wasn't normal to speak in code on the phone; no it wasn't normal to believe my father, a resident at UCSF, was paying off psychologists, attorneys, and judges; no it wasn't normal to try and ruin his wedding because otherwise I'd never see her again.

When I was older I told her this, hoping some sort of self-awareness would make her better, make us better. It only made things worse. I spent a lot of time gathering my things outside her house. I came to understand that objects carry little value, because at some point they will be gone.

Even when I moved to New Jersey, she told me she would throw out my things and never speak to me again: I had flown out hours after I watched my father's mother die. He told me not to change my plans, that I had to go. It was hard for him and hard to leave him, but I went. It had happened sooner than expected. My mother was planning to meet me in Jersey and help me move in, but my grandmother had wanted to be buried in New York with my papa, so I had to cancel our plans to go to her funeral. She saw that as me choosing my father over her.

When she told me she threw out all my things, I mourned. Her sister tried to tell me it was because she loved me so much. My moving had caused her stress. I needed to understand.

Sitting there, at eleven years old, I had tried to understand. I waited for her to come back, and she didn't. I imagined the sort of trouble I'd be in if I didn't go find her, if I didn't show her I figured out how to get home. I understood how she would feel, how she might react. I had to put aside my fear, my worry, my sadness. So I followed where I saw her walk and ended up in some square. There were cafe tables, tourists, impressively old buildings. But I didn't see my mother. I tried to use the French she taught me to ask if anyone had seen her, but no one knew what I was talking about. Besides, if I told anyone what really happened I'd be in a shitstorm of trouble.

Then I heard her.

"There you are!"

She was standing in line across the square for some museum. She was waving at me and smiling. I wasn't sure if I was about to be publicly flayed so I didn't move. She waved me over. I walked over, trying to smile, unsure what to expect.

"Where have you been? I've been waiting in line. Isn't this great?" she said.

"I was at a cafe."

"Oh, okay—look at this!" she said, showing me the museum pamphlet.

We spent the rest of our time in line talking about how weird it is that Europeans make out in public. We never spoke of the way she'd abandoned me.

You knew this story, though. Do you think this is why it worked? The things you did? The way you promised me things, places to visit, then took it away if I did something you didn't like?

When you told me this was how you were because you were ill, because you had a need to control things that you tried to medicate, that you wanted to fix, I tried to understand. I said I would understand the way I understood with her.

So I never went to Brooklyn to visit my cousin, because you didn't like the people there. It was your illness, I understood. I didn't go out drinking with my one and only new friend Gabby, because girls who did that didn't care about their boyfriends. It was your illness, I understood. I didn't go out after dark, I threw away my sexy clothes. I couldn't talk to Laura, because she was once friends with my ex; we never hung out, even though she was the only friend I had who lived out here. And when you continually brought up your ex and how you told her you would never let a girl come between your friendship, I couldn't say a word. You wouldn't even delete the porn you kept of her off of your laptop because, you said, you'd have to watch all of it in order to make sure you knew what you were deleting. Is that what I wanted? you'd ask. It was your illness, I understood.

But it got harder for me to understand you and the things that you did, especially as I found myself more and more isolated.

I missed weddings. I left my Christmas vacation with my family in Hawaii early. I missed a party in the city with my cousin, another party with one of my best friends.

And I didn't go to a single writing event.

Instead, I worked as a preschool teacher, because it was the first job I could find. My hours were long, because I needed to pay for everything, and you couldn't understand that. I worked, watched Netflix, and slept. You slowly stopped willingly spending time with me. You held your time over my head like a carrot. It was the only aspiration I had left in me.

I applied to Columbia with you, because it was the one shot in the dark I had, and it sounded amazing. I didn't think I would get in.

But when I got in and you didn't, I lost that too. By that point I had and was nothing but trying to understand you but failing.

On some days I walked to the path and waited for trains to go by one at a time, building up the courage to jump. And when I couldn't, I felt like I had failed that too. So I got on, rode into the city, and wandered nowhere, then went home and cried on the phone to the few friends I had left who regularly called to check in on me.

But I knew it couldn't last. The pain of being alone was so deep and vast, it took longer and longer conversations to feel okay again. I felt myself burdening them. I needed something else.

So I applied for a new job. It was the best decision I ever made.

•

After Columbia, things fell apart and got worse. You resented me every day and questioned my motivations, my appearance, my intelligence, constantly. At one point you told me that no one likes a know-it-all, and you'd prefer a woman who is simple.

By the time I moved to New Brunswick, as I promised I would, you stopped coming by. You stayed over a handful of times, but it always ended badly. Remember the time we went to the Jersey City Wine Festival? Remember when you thought I went to the men's room, because I had told you some girls did, which mixed up the line? Do you remember leaving the building and throwing your taster glass? Do you remember me chasing you? Do you remember making me beg you to not leave? How about the time after that, when we went to the Whiskey Library for dinner? Do you remember making me cry the whole way home, because I told you not to shit talk me to your friend on the phone while I was sitting right there? You told me I was making a scene and that it was over. Do you remember that?

By the time I started working we were fighting every time we saw each other over more and more ridiculous things, including and especially my work.

Do you remember the time you told me my student's parents think I'm weird, because I call home? Do you remember the time you told me I had no business teaching black kids, because I'm not black? Do you remember the time you told me it was unattractive for me to put so much effort into my lessons? Do you remember how many times you told me I was creepy every time I told you how proud I was of a student? Because you had started a master's in Student Affairs at Rutgers and knew better? Do you remember telling me that I would get fired for having friendships at work? Do you remember how many times you told me to quit?

By November you had broken up with me a few times, then "forgiven me," only to break up with me and refuse to come to dinner with my family.

So when December came and you left me again, because I wanted to go to my holiday work party I was done. By this point you had physically pushed me away from you, refused to touch me, and hadn't stayed over in two months. You had nothing nice to say about me and hadn't complimented me in months. We had nothing positive in our relationship, even after I gave it one more try in January. At one point I even tried to end it, but you wouldn't leave my apartment. You wore me down until I passed out. And, God, was I tired. I was tired of feeling bad about myself and the single thing that had started to turn my life around—teaching.

Then one day, after another fight, my work friend told it to me straight—she saw how I was feeling, figured that I was alone, heard about my stresses, and told me that there was someone out there who would love me for everything I am right now. She kept me at work, stayed with me while I texted you, refused to see you, and never saw you again.

And she was right.

•

I want you to know right now that you're wrong and to stop right there. No number of fucked up events in any person's life allow you to have treated me the way that you did. I hope you get the help and build the confidence that you need, and I hope you find peace. I hope you find someone to love and cherish the way they deserve to be loved and cherished, as I have.

I share a life with someone now who likes me *and* loves me. He thinks I'm funny, loves my cooking and the way I dress, and tells me that I'm beautiful. I think he's hilarious, gorgeous, and has amazing values. We explore each other's taste in music and movies, and we appreciate that we've both performed comedy, one way or another. I still don't have enough courage to be silly the way I used to be or to sing and play guitar in front of him, but I'm working on it. He wants me to get out there and do anything that makes me happy, and I want the same for him. We adore each other's friends and family, and he trusts me and wants me to be free. I have shown him my scars, and told him my failures and insecurities and the fears I'm still working through, and he listens and makes me feel safe. And every morning when I wake him up with coffee he kisses me and tells me he loves me.

For a long time, I did not believe I deserved this. I did not think this could exist for me or that someone could genuinely love me this way. I had allowed you to convince me that unless I changed I would end up undeserving of love forever, which is not to be confused with being alone. I have come to know loneliness and aloneness and understand the difference. I am no longer lonely when I'm alone, because I love myself, and I will love myself and will work on loving myself more as time goes on. Man, I have never been happier or healthier in my entire life, and that is something I will never let anyone take away.

Sincerely,
AS

Fire and Ice

Dani Burlison

My hometown sits a dozen miles off of Interstate 5 in Northern California's agricultural Sacramento Valley. The population of that rural community in Tehama County was roughly 175 inhabitants in 1992, the year I moved away and into a bigger town, ten miles away. "Town," or Red Bluff, was known primarily for its big annual rodeo, its soaring summer heat, and the infamous case of Cameron Hooker, the sociopath who picked up a hitchhiker from Oregon and kept her as a sex slave in a head box under his bed for seven years. About ten thousand people lived there. Clint Eastwood was rumored to have visited during nearby hunting trips for wild boar. The National Guard was called in during winter storms to evacuate the outskirts, including my neighborhood, during floods. As a kid, I play-fished off our front porch as the water rose from the creek on our property, creeping first through the adjacent prune orchards and slowly surrounding our house, working its way into two of our ground level rooms. I remember a pair of my socks, folded together in a ball, floating across the foot of water that filled our laundry and storage room that doubled as my bedroom.

Tehama County's demographics are largely working class and working poor, and Red Bluff sits at the intersection of a maze of highways leading to Mount Lassen or Oregon or Sacramento—depending on which long hot road carried you through. The town was a big red dot on *Time* magazine's 1991 cover story on California's Methamphetamine Highway. The Sacramento River curves its way through the county. Valley Oaks pepper the landscape that stretches out to meet the Sierra Foothills to the east and eventually to the Shasta-Trinity forest in the northwest. In 1992, jocks and tweakers drove low-budget pimped out mini-trucks and primer gray mustangs; the rednecks drove Chevy trucks. No one had minivans.

In 1992, Red Bluff got its very first Walmart, offering employment options to add to the fast-food chains and the local paper mill where everyone seemed to work. The only job I could get after finishing my independent study program was a temporary part-time gig filing paperwork for my probation officer who took a liking to me. I was assigned to him a year before when my boyfriend and I were in a horrible drunk driving accident. I was technically a "runaway" at the time, living in a filthy house full of meth addicts, where I sold various substances to buy ramen and generic charcoal-filtered vodka. After the accident, I had a short stint in a foster home on a chicken farm before settling back on the couch in my mom's trailer. I didn't have a lot going for me.

Then I got pregnant.

My boyfriend of three years wanted to keep the baby and presented some ideas of how our life would be with a child. His grandfather had a pink mobile home near the High Desert State Prison in Susanville that we could rent for cheap. He, my boyfriend, would get a job as a short-order cook in the prison. I'd get my driver's license (finally), and I'd wait tables or work night shifts at one of the local gas stations until we saved enough money to move back to Red Bluff. The plan was for the boyfriend to attend culinary school and for me to open a daycare. We'd buy cute dish sets and curtains, a new stroller, and a train set.

But the boyfriend, who reminded everyone of a younger, hesher-y version of Keanu Reeves, wasn't the best boyfriend in the world. He drank a lot. He slept around. He dabbled in meth. He sometimes had freak-outs and pushed me around. Still, as the weeks moved on, I started checking out books about pregnancy from the local library. The books told me all about when the baby's limbs and heart and fingerprints would form. I bought a couple of pale green onesies at the Salvation Army, washed them, folded them and tucked them away in my box of clothes. I craved strawberry Kool-Aid but vomited so profusely that after a few weeks, I weighed a mere ninety pounds. I learned that most morning sickness passes after the first trimester. The boyfriend picked out a name from a list we read together, convinced the baby was a boy.

I almost believed his plan would work. Then he started disappearing.

He stopped showing up for dinner or movie dates. He stopped calling. For several days at a time. Rumors of him being with another girl burned their way through Town. When I finally saw him out at a friend's house, he was dizzy and manic from speed and cheap whiskey, ranting and banging his head to Metallica. He started getting pushy and mean: *a result of his meth binges*, his friend would say. I started thinking twice about being stuck in a pink trailer at high altitude with him and panic churned in my gut. I'd have no means to escape if I needed to, especially during cold winters when snow would pile up all around us. And I was growing more and more certain that one day I would need to escape.

I thought a lot about having a baby. I didn't know much about raising a child. I knew how to change diapers and warm bottles and how to wrangle creamed corn and mashed peas into a baby's gummy mouth from the times I fed and babysat my youngest sister. I knew nothing about brain development or attachment or when to call a doctor. I didn't have friends with babies. I couldn't find an online community for support, because no one was online yet. There were no computers or cell phones or internet. Just newspaper ads and snail mail and churches to connect people. I didn't know much about raising a baby, and I began to feel a need to cut ties with the boyfriend. I watched my mom and how she was tethered to my youngest sister's dad, even after she filed a final restraining order and walked away. I knew I didn't want that for myself or for a baby. I couldn't do it alone, and I couldn't do it with him or his family. And, frankly, I had nowhere else to turn. No one was going to save me.

My mother, who had raised nine kids mostly on her own was just starting to take care of herself and could not afford to have me and a newborn baby sucking up her limited resources. I hadn't seen or heard from my father in years. My older siblings had all moved on and started their own families. My boyfriend's parents hated me. I barely finished high school. I could barely drive a car. I only knew how to cook a couple of things: cinnamon streusel bread and mashed potatoes from recipes in my mom's ancient *Betty Crocker Cookbook*. There was no nice couple with perfect teeth and a landscaped yard and health insurance willing to take my baby and raise it if I opted for adoption.

And I was still a child myself, in every sense of the word.

My mom discovered I was pregnant when I started vomiting blood and she took me to the hospital, where the doctor did a pregnancy test and announced the results as he pulled back the yellow curtains in the emergency room. He gave me some pills to help with the constant nausea and some brochures about adoption and abortion and prenatal care.

The decision was not easy—it was anything but that—but if my young teenage self knew anything, I knew that it was the right decision. I felt it in my bones the way you feel the days get longer after a long dark winter, and you know that warmth and green grass and the big bright sun will make everything better.

Because I was several weeks pregnant, and because I had never been to a gynecologist, the nice woman at the feminist women's health center in Redding, about thirty miles north, told me I'd need two appointments. The first to give me a full exam and to insert laminaria into my cervix, which would swell and help to soften and dilate that tender and strong little place at the opening of the uterus. The second appointment would be for the following morning and would be for the whole procedure, which would leave me no longer pregnant but cramping and bloody and maybe a little emotional.

I had no idea how the pain would shoot through me from those little bits of seaweed jammed into my cervix. And I had no idea the impact the protestors—that I was not expecting that first day—would have on me for the rest of my life.

Those fucking protestors.

They lined up, with their twisted, screaming red faces and Jesus posters and their pictures of dead babies and unleashed a Christian fury like I had never imagined. Men, mostly, but a few women too, with bad haircuts and polyester pants and wide, gaping mouths condemning me to hell. I remember someone—a man, I think—throwing something like a bloody Kleenex or rotten piece of fruit my way as my mom ushered me out. I remember security guards, emotionless, making space between us and them so we could get to our car and go home. I remember worrying that the girls I went to high school with would be there and tell everyone back in Red Bluff that I was a baby killer.

I wondered if any of them, with their angry screaming and spitting, thought that they'd be good parents. I wondered, selfishly, what kind of life I'd have raising a baby in a pink trailer next to a prison.

I remember cramping so badly that I threw up as I opened the door to my mom's Dodge Dart and again when we pulled into the driveway to her trailer. And I remember the phone call later that night, or early, before the sun came up the next morning. The clinic had been burned down and would be closing indefinitely, and we'd have to drive forty-two miles south to Chico for my final appointment, and that the doctor I was scheduled to see would meet us there.

It was fire and ice, walking out through those protestors. I didn't know then that I'd carry the taste of it—the sensation of being simultaneously burned at the stake and held under cold water—with me throughout my life as a woman.

The boyfriend was supposed to stay with me the night before my abortion. He never showed up or answered his phone. My mom drove me to his house as the sun rose the day of my final appointment and pulled him out of bed, still drunk and reeking of Southern Comfort from the night before. We drove Highway 99E in silence for an hour before arriving to one lonely misguided Christian activist on the steps of the Chico clinic. The procedure was painful. I bled way more than I should have. We spent the entire day there so they could monitor my vitals and make sure I didn't need a transfusion. The day was a blur, but I remember returning home along that long, flat highway, cattle fields and orchards rolling by outside my window as I nodded and woke over and over, the pain medication still winding its way through my veins. My mom gave the boyfriend money to get 7-Up and Tylenol while she went to a friend's. He left and never came back. I lied on the couch, cramping and alone, shaking with regret and relief, watching that damn U2 video with all of the buffalo running and running and running to their deaths off a cliff.

I never regretted my abortion and have always been immensely grateful that I had that choice and that my mother supported my choice, but I carried the hatred those protestors spewed (and some abandonment issues from the boyfriend) with me for years. I look back at that eighteen-year-old girl and wish I could have offered her comfort and helped her to feel empowered and strong at a time when she was completely alone. I wish I could have been there in the weeks that followed, when the boyfriend's mom showed up and screamed at her for "killing her grandchild and putting her son through hell." I wish I could have held her hand at doctor appointments a year later when she was told she couldn't have kids and, again, years after that when she did get pregnant and a family member tried to talk her into having another abortion.

It wasn't until twenty years later, long after scar tissue and infections in my uterus gave way to two healthy babies and the distance between the fear and rage and shame inflicted on me by those protestors grew and grew, that I discovered the story behind the clinic fire that day. A serial, anti-choice arsonist named Richard Thomas Andrews burned the clinic down. He was a sixty-year-old "pro-life" activist with ties to the Operation Rescue organization. He was caught in 1997 and later sentenced to seven years in prison for six abortion clinic fires that caused a cumulative one million dollars in damages to clinics throughout Northern California, Oregon, Idaho, and Montana.

Fear, Anger, and Hexing the Patriarchy

an interview with Ariel Gore

Dani: The last time we talked about this, Trump only had been in office for just a couple months, and one of the questions I asked you is how you saw anger playing out within the queer community—how scary things were—and you responded that you were actually seeing people, particularly within the queer community, being a lot nicer to each other, feeling really vulnerable, kind of putting aside differences. Then you had a really funny comment: "Except for on social media where it seems like everyone is kind of drunk."

Ariel: Right. They're still drunk, I think. I mean, understandably.

Dani: Exactly. Do you feel like that's still relevant? Or are people being testier?

Ariel: It does seem like fatigue and stress are factors. You know, all kinds of people are interested in activism. You can just tell that people are fatigued and stressed out. It's like a domestic violence situation where, after a while, you are just kind of shaking all the time. I think where I live now [New Mexico], there's more immigration issues that the activists that I am around are involved in, and there's just tremendous fear and anger and heartbreak. But I haven't really personally experienced people being testier with me, you know. It's probably because I leave the house less and less. I guess I'd stand by that. I mean, it's hard. It's like the left and . . . "callout culture." That's not really infighting, but that was a way to make progress. You can see people can't really deal with that sometimes. I think people are just trying to adjust and figure out, how do you at least survive and try to help each other see if you're being a dick or if you're being complicit. . . Also keeping in mind that people are so called out every day that they might not feel like they can deal with it.

Dani: Right. I'm so glad you brought that up too. That's something I've been thinking a lot about. Being in activist circles for a long time, and then seeing a lot of people, it's like their first step into maybe doing direct action or even going to a protest or trying to be aware of what's going on. It's really frustrating for me to see those people getting shunned so much. They're doing their best, and they don't have twenty years of direct-action training, like a lot of other people in the Bay Area. I'm seeing this kind of elitism, actually, in the anarchist activist scene, and it's like, come on, people, alienating the newcomers, basically.

Ariel: Right, and well, that's the thing. You don't want to excuse people's willful ignorance, but we need new people.

Dani: No shit.

Ariel: We need people who have not entirely interrogated their own issues, you know. There has to be a way to be with each other and to be kind of helping each other along, like the newcomers. If someone comes to band practice, and they suck, do you help them, or: "You have no talent for music. Off with you"? In every arena, I guess, that comes up. Especially when you have, I think, a lot of really young activists who are becoming politicized in a way that we didn't have for a long time. Why isn't that super exciting? Instead of, "Don't you know how to go limp?" Well, no. That's not something you just learn in high school.

Dani: Right. Not everyone went to New College.

Ariel: Right. That's the thing. I'm less and less willing to put my body on the line, just because I know that if I get kicked in the ribs, it's going to hurt for the rest of my life. It's like, we need people who are not over forty-five.

Dani: . . .that have that resilience to bounce back, and also don't have children that they're responsible for yet, maybe, you know. I definitely feel that. I'm like, "Fucking thank god there's younger people stepping up." I'm just too traumatized by that shit, and physically, I'm not going to bounce back if I get hurt in a protest.

Ariel: We have to use our skills in more appropriate ways as we evolve. There's not really a safe place to express your rage, because you can also understand people are coming in a little more traumatized and a little more fatigued than we were for a while. There was that moment, certainly in feminism, in overall activism, where you felt like people were coming to movements less and less traumatized, in terms of like, "I'm drawing the line. There's a five cent pay cut." You kind of wanted to roll your eyes, but you were like, "Oh, my god, that's so great, that minor thing has radicalized you." I think we're kind of going back to the thing where people are more traumatized because of Trump.

Dani: I just know for myself, when I first got involved with activism, we didn't have the availability of information in such a quick way as we do now. I feel super overwhelmed every day reading the news, and the increased incidents of school shootings, and just all of this shit is so traumatic of people to watch. You know, it's definitely. . .

Ariel: At our fingertips. That's the thing. You're not coming in young and hopeful. You're coming in young with a major anxiety disorder.

Dani: I'm wondering, since we're talking about all this trauma with these younger generations, how do you feel about having a kid that. . . Is your son in middle school yet?

Ariel: No, he's going into the sixth grade, which here is not middle school yet. He goes to middle school in the seventh grade. Yeah, I'm not happy about it. You know, it's just like when he was one or something, or whenever it was, Obama was elected. It's like, you know, Obama wasn't a saint, but I thought like, "Oh, what a great time to be breeding."

Dani: I know! Everybody had kids then. It's like, "The world is better."

Ariel: Right. It's just like this stupid hope boom. Meanwhile, their mom doesn't even know. . . I think she's a naturalized citizen, but they're taking that away from people now too.

Dani: That's right. Jesus. Yeah, how do you feel about safety in school?

Ariel: I'm not into it. Even being a visiting teacher on the high school campuses, which I've done for years. I kind of don't do it that much anymore, because you're constantly on lockdown. I don't think I've visited high school in like two years when, at some point, we were not on lockdown. I mean, obviously, they've got all these policies in place for safety, and the kids sort of laugh it off. Seriously? Max can barely even handle going to see "Black Panther" because it's very violent. Next year, he's going to have to be thinking every period about, "Why are we on lockdown?" I'm not into it. We're homeschooling. I don't know what we're doing. Then, private school's like twenty thousand dollars a year. It's like, "Why don't they have school shootings? It's probably because they get to kick people out if they seem a little iffy."

Dani: Right, which is also problematic in its own way.

Ariel: Exactly. I can't navigate this. Then, you know how lefties are. You start pulling your kids out of public school, and they lose their mind.

They're like, "That's what they want." Yeah, okay, well they can have it, because if you put a gun in my face, I do what you want, I guess.

Dani: One of the things also that I had asked you about too was responding to other people's anger, and things, I feel like, have changed a lot since that last conversation. I know, at least for me, I've never felt 100 percent safe around, let's say, straight white men that are out and about, and I feel like, especially over the last year or so, this really scary violent backlash after #MeToo, and people just being so emboldened to express their bigotry in really fucking violent ways. I wonder how are you feeling about that? How do you feel like you can keep yourself safe and be an effective parent and be in the world with this stuff?

Ariel: In between the last time we talked and this time, the major road trip that we took was very different than it had been previously. If I just travel with Max, I'd pass for straight, and they won't love it if you have tattoos, but you know . . . but if I travel with my partner, we're a very obvious queer family, and the last road trip that we took was noticeably more uncomfortable. For a minute there, if you're a queer family going through a small town, at least a couple people waved at you, and they're thinking that the world was changing in that way. Now, it's not like that at all. I guess the people who used to smile at you just don't leave the house anymore. Yeah, the people who hate you are just super emboldened to just yell things at you, when you're just passing through their fucking town, you know. Here in Santa Fe, we had a weird thing with a Lyft or Uber driver. It was long after the election. He's just railing against Hillary Clinton and what a liar she is. Are you kidding me? My kid's in the car. We don't need to hear that. You know, it's sick to see that.

Every once in a while on social media, I see some of that article about *How to Communicate like a Buddhist*. I think, "I should read that," but I never click it. I just feel so angry all the time, but I don't really say anything, because nothing that's been in my face has been quite bad enough to get injured over, so I just feel kind of fearful. This low-level fearful, I guess, where you're back to that place when you were younger and felt so vulnerable all the time.

Dani: Right. Yeah, it's crazy. I think about that a lot. People get called out like, "Oh, you didn't stick up for this person, or blah, blah, blah." Then we also see the people that are sticking up for people that are being targeted with hate or violence; we saw that a year ago, where those men were murdered in Oregon, because they stood up.

Ariel: I definitely rehearse for that situation, because I don't want to wimp out as a white person if that happens in my presence. But you definitely might die. For my own self, I definitely have been erring on the side of just wimping out, because I don't want conflict, rather.

Dani: Well, especially if you have your kid with you, I imagine.

Ariel: Yeah, I don't like to get into it. Seriously, like someone going off on Hillary Clinton. It's over. How can you still be angry about that? Why are they still angry about that? She went home. She's drinking wine. It's over.

Dani: One of the other things that you had said too is about Trump being this archetype of the abusive father and us living in this culture of abuse, and, god, I feel like every day he will say something, like on record, recorded, and then the next day he denies it. It's so gaslighty and crazy making to me.

Ariel: You notice that the white male journalists are the ones who are the most outraged. You know, the CNN ones, the sort of liberal-ish ones, because they're not used to this. This is their first time around, I think, for most of them. I think for some of us, it's very triggering of a million different things, and it's horrifying, but they don't know what it's like to be female. That's good. Someone needs to be naively outraged, but you do notice it. I'm just like, "No, honey. That's how it works."

Dani: How do you, especially as a creative person, as a writer, you've got to get shit done . . . how do you keep yourself informed and get your work done?

Ariel: I guess that's what I mean by that sort of fatigue. I certainly notice my students have a harder and harder time being productive. You know, I teach a manuscript workshop every summer. It's like a three-month thing. It's a lot of work. Then, a summer like this, or at the end of last summer, you just see that people can't work. It's not possible. If you have any time, you just have to go to the ocean or something.

Dani: Oh, my god. I did that this morning.

Ariel: Oh, really?

Dani: Yeah.

Ariel: See? I think that's legit. I still don't take late assignments, but I think that's completely legit. It's not another thing to beat ourselves up over. Our productivity is going to be diminished. I'm pretty perimeno-pausal too, so it might be that. I have this board of things I'm supposed to do every day. It's quite a lot, but I think in another time, just even a couple years ago, it would've been doable. You could definitely get this shit done by Friday. It doesn't look like it's going to happen this week, because I just can't. Now that I think about it, it's not perimenopause. It is the news cycle. To think creatively takes an absence of immediate stress. We don't really have that right now. We can try to turn it off, but it's hard. I can't figure out how to make my phone not beep when something horrible happens. It's like they've figured out how to get your attention.

Dani: Yeah, you have to go off the grid for a while to get into a good headspace.

Ariel: I know. I need a cabin. I mean, and then you do feel like you're not being socially engaged. Like, is that cool to just hide away? I think it's necessary.

Dani: I want to talk to you about your upcoming book project, which I'm so excited about. The hexing book, what can you tell me about it?

Ariel: Well, that's been a fun place to ask people to be. I've been asking people to contribute spells, and it's just a short writing assignment for them, and a way to kind of focus your anger and focus that energy. I thought that I would come across more pushback in terms of hexes and prayer and spirituality. . . You know, it's like meditating for world peace. You worry that people think, "Well, that's not doing anything." All the people who have been contributing spells do that in conjunction with all the other things that they do. It's not like people are just sitting around waving sage, hoping that's going to be enough all by itself.

It's very much a part of it, and it's a way to kind of focus our energy against all that. Again, if we think about this current president as this very archetypal abusive dad, almost like abusive Christian god figure. Not that he's a god, but that's the kind of angry patriarchal god that a lot of us were trained to think of when we thought of who to pray to. In the nineties, at least in California, we had this huge reclaiming tradition in witchy religions, and then that sort of either kind of went underground or mainstream or just seemed like less of a thing. Then it seemed like right before the election, people were back in action. When *When We Were Witches* came out, I was really surprised that most of the audience that was really excited about it was much younger than me. They were more like Maia's age, and people would come out to readings and want to know all about "What was this reclaiming tradition, and how do I get started?" It's kind of cool, and sweet. In witchy traditions, being older is cool. You know, I think it's a cool way to engage more intergenerationally than a lot of political stuff allows for. People are hexing that guy.

It's so out of control. It seems like people are trying to be careful too, because you don't want to hook into it too much. I think it's really helpful also in focusing: "What do we want? Do we want to topple all of Western civilization?" That might be happening. It's an interesting way, whether you believe that magic alone affects a change, or it's part of a psychological exercise, as an activist, it doesn't really matter. I think it's a really cool way to focus and be like, "Okay, what is my intention?"

Dani: Absolutely. That's so great. Yeah, my week at witch camp, the class that I took this year we talked all about hexing, and talked about all of that stuff. I think a lot of people didn't necessarily go this year, because they were nervous about that piece of it, about the hexing. Then there were also a lot of people, especially newer, younger people that I hadn't seen at camp before, that were there because of that.

Ariel: That's actually been really interesting too, is a lot of people who I think of as quite powerful witches, I ask them to contribute a spell, and they'll be like, "What's the title? Absolutely not. We don't believe in that," or "I was trained not to do that," or "My teachers taught me not to do that." Again, if they're white, you can understand why you might be very reticent to keep doing all this unconscious damage and wanting to step back from that and be like, "Okay, again, what is my intention? Do I know what I want? Is my vision totally clouded by this horrible white supremacist training that I'm just beginning to wrap my mind around?" And, then, some people are just like, "Absolutely, let's hex this shit. Ready to go."

Dani: It's just like, "Fuck it, we've tried everything else. We've got to fucking call in the queen of the witches for this shit." Is this kind of magic something that you've actually have a long relationship with or a long history with?

Ariel: I think that has always or almost always been a part of any political engagement or any activism that I've done. I think, the way I grew up is, my stepdad was a Catholic priest. He came from a liberation theology point of view. He ran the chapter of Amnesty International while he was still a priest, but he was excommunicated. I think I grew up with this worldview that spirituality and politics were friends in a way that a lot of people on the left are uncomfortable with. You know, when god comes into politics, we get very nervous, because usually it's to come and take away our right to choose or something like that. Which, of course, is a good thing to watch out for. Are we pretending that god thinks what we think and then putting that forward as some kind of moral authority over people? It's sort of a cautionary tale to look at the religious right, but I think that the left can tend to disempower itself if it refuses to have a spiritual framework or point of view. You know, when that's appropriate. Plenty of excellent non-spiritual atheists are welcome. It's always been a way for me to kind of get over my shyness about being an activist. It's a kind of focus, "What's my intention?" A way to feel like I'm not alone. I'm not just this random powerless queer freak holding up a sign. I feel like all my ancestors are with me, except for that one guy.

Dani: Is there anything else you want to add about either your book project or how you're feeling about the world or anger or anything like that?

Ariel: I've been editing a couple of books by old-school civil rights activists, and those have been really kind of heartening, even in the parts of the book where the writer thinks that was a down year, you know, to see that that's the way that change works, and that change makers are humans who also have interpersonal problems with other excellent activists, and who also get tired, and who also fuck off to another country for a couple years and regroup and come back. Things happen in really lifelike ways. It's not like we just all wake up one morning, and we're this great army, and we're just going to make this happen. That's been cool to think, "Okay, I can do that. I can be human and just keep redoing my commitment. I'm going to try to do what I can today. I'm going to do what I can today." It doesn't have to be some big amazing thing.

Dani: We're all doing our best. It's hard to remember that we aren't perfect.

Ariel: I mean, unless you're Ruth Bader Ginsburg.

Ink

Michel Wing

People ask me what my tattoos mean. I say, "They're tribal." I say, "I like black work." I don't say they are a road map of my disorientation. I do not tell them that the lines upon my skin are the red thread of Ariadne, that they led me out of labyrinthine despair and into possibilities.

People want answers that fit into boxes. They want to hear that a tattoo is your Zodiac sign, or that you saw it on a piece of flash at a cool shop on the boardwalk in Santa Cruz, or that this symbol means "peace" in Arabic. They do not want Greek tragedy and loss, stigmata, the cutting of the thorns into scalp, the raw truth of pain. The designs on my body, although sometimes visible to others, have never been intended for public dissection. It matters little to me how I am perceived because of them or how they might be interpreted. We are our own tongue.

It starts with identity. At a party, where I know almost no one, I find myself asked that dreaded question: "What do you do?" The answer should be simple, but it is not. I am working as a legal secretary. That word, "secretary," fills me with shame. It does not sync with who I think I am, who I ever want to be. I am the classic underachiever; my family calls me "gifted" and "broken" in the same sentence. I leave college not even knowing if I have graduated, move to a new city with a man who is growing more and more abusive. Who am I to look for a job that requires a diploma, real skills? I happen to find work at a law office and find it pays relatively well. I am appreciated for being bright without having to aim too high. Eventually I escape from the relationship but never recover my sense of equilibrium. I teeter from one bad situation to the next, and even a graduate degree gives me only temporary and timid self-respect. Again, somehow, here I am in another city, underemployed and fragile.

And then that question. "What do you do?" After I mumble my response, I politely reverse it. The woman I am speaking to says, "I'm a puppeteer." Not the answer I expect. How does one become a puppeteer? She says, "I made some life-sized puppets, wrote some scripts about Jewish folklore. Then everywhere I went after that, I simply introduced myself as a puppeteer. Soon after, a woman asked me to perform at her son's school—my first job. It became real. I now do acts all over the city."

The power of that naming stirs something deep and forgotten. I enter my first tattoo parlor that week, in the Castro in San Francisco. The symbol I choose is the Japanese ideograph for "poet." The selection of language is not random, as I read and speak Japanese, having spent three years in Osaka and Kyoto. The word "poet" is composed of two characters, "poem" and "person." The word "poem" can be broken down even further into two parts: "word" and "temple." I like that. A poem as a temple for words. The tattoo, only one and a half inches high, sits neatly on the inside of my right wrist, facing toward me. I intend it as a secret message to myself. Even if I am not there yet, this is who I am in the process of becoming.

Perhaps, though, it is too late. Trapped in an endless eddy of depression, everyone flows past me in a terrifying stream of humanity, far out of reach. The nightmares are constant, relentless. I lose track of days, stop eating, and begin to use a razor to cut lines in my skin to remind myself I am alive.

The second tattoo is also a Japanese ideograph. The Japanese language is filled with homonyms. The word "poem" is pronounced "she" and this new character has the same sound. Its meaning, though, is "death." Yet another "she" word is the number four. Because of this, in Japan, four is considered an unlucky number. Buildings don't have fourth floors; tea sets come with five cups. But each time I cut myself, I draw four lines. I don't know why I started this. It just happened. Now, though, it is a pattern, a rule, and all are connected—poem, death, four. The death tattoo is on the inside of my left wrist, on the arm with the most thin, white scars. I never tell anyone what this character means.

Although I still go to work every day, I am disintegrating. I am an island of pain, and I have no belief that it will ever, ever improve. Thoughts of suicide are with me from the moment I wake up, and they accompany me through every activity. When asleep, the nightmares. It is too much. All the years of sadness, violence, invisibility. I used to think

I had to live, because I was meant to write. I find this no longer matters. It's not a big enough carrot. I can't stay.

I make a couple of feeble attempts at ending my life; laughable, really. Sloppy. Then I put some more effort into the planning and think things out. Give away my belongings, write the note (instructions, not a goodbye), arrange for the care of my cat, the disposition of my car. Still, damn it all anyway, I fail and wake up in intensive care. Someone finds me.

The third tattoo has its origins in a treatment center art therapy class. I had been in and out of psychiatric hospitals for years. But when my latest visit prompts the lead doctor to recommend shock therapy, my parents find an eating disorder/substance abuse clinic near L.A., and I check in for a month-long program. At barely one hundred pounds, my shoulder blades fan out like angel wings, and you can count each of my vertebrae. I still think my thighs are fat, my butt too big. In the class, the counselor has each of us take turns lying down on a piece of butcher block paper, and we outline our bodies with a marker. The idea is to give us a more accurate image of the size of our bodies. We are then instructed to write emotions into the outline. Most of mine are in the head—fear, depression, confusion, anxiety. At the last minute, with a pen, I draw a small spiral in the gut, and in tiny letters, I label it. "Rage."

Back in San Francisco, I am now classified as a dual-diagnosis patient (major depressive disorder/anorexia/PTSD and alcoholic/drug addict) and have been approved for Social Security Disability. I am in day treatment programs and go to twelve-step meetings. I head to a tattoo parlor again. On the back of my right shoulder, I have a black spiral inked in. Small but visible. Not hidden in my gut. Ready to explore.

I am trying to get well, but it is hard. Everything is hard. I see a psychiatrist, and we experiment with medications. I have been down this route before, unsuccessfully. Each new drug takes four weeks before we can tell if it might be working. Over and over, the results are not good. So despite the fact that I have gone through treatment, am going to meetings, have a therapist, I am still dealing with unrelenting, daily, smothering depression. The nightmares continue. I am exhausted.

I cannot live in San Francisco on my paltry disability paychecks, but I also cannot earn much money, because I can't afford to lose those checks either. I am in no condition to do anything requiring mental concentration. I stumble into a job as janitor at a women's tattoo parlor. Three mornings a week, I clean the shop before it opens. I don't have to talk to anyone. I run the tattoo guns through the autoclave to sterilize them, set up the workstations for the day, stock all the supplies, mop the floor. There is a laundromat across the street to wash the towels. I have always loved folding laundry. The repetition, the sameness of it, the fresh smell. And I am paid cash. It is precisely the right job at the right time.

Periodically, I work the reception desk on the weekends and trade that time for new ink. My next tattoo is an expansion of the previous one. On my right arm, on the outer edge of the bicep, a spiral. But the spiral begins to unravel, to come apart. It is controlled, precise, spinning out into four separate lines. It reaches to my inner arm, and down onto my forearm. This tattoo is larger, not hidden. It asks to be noticed.

I am six months sober and decide to go out one last time. It's a head banger. Drinking alone in my apartment, the only purpose seems to be pouring glass after glass. When I stagger awake from my blackout, twisted in my sheets, the tequila bottle lies empty on the carpet, and vomit spatters in piles across my room and bed. Later that day, walking with a friend, I have a grand mal seizure and end up in an ambulance. For a week, my memory short circuits, short-term information unreliable, lost in time. It scares me just enough, knowing there might be something worse than dying—living with half a brain. That's my last drink.

But I'm not done being angry. I'm only now tapping into the wellspring of rage. All the years of abuse and mistreatment, the violence. I unwrap memories. The way I was dulled as a child by a mother hell-bent on shaping me into something I was not. My rapist has a face now, and the days, weeks around that time begin to unjumble. My molester still lurks in shadows but physical sensations surge quick and strong—his hands, so large; me, so small. I am hot with never again. I am filled with internal shouts of *get away from me*. The tattoo that forms in my mind next and soon appears on my left shoulder is a spiral thick and bold, bursting apart and erupting into flames. I walk the streets clad only in black, wearing heavy boots. I pick up empty beer bottles in city alleys, smash them against brick walls. The razor cut on my upper arm slices so deep I end up at Urgent Care, requiring stitches. The triage nurse and the doctor can tell it is self-inflicted. They handle me as if I am a dirty word. Slashes two and three I manage to knit together on my own with butterfly bandages. Now my body art includes ropy white keloid scars.

I find another part-time cash job with a small two women–owned company that sells yoga equipment. More physical labor, as I carry around forty-pound mat rolls, heft them up onto a roller, cut off the right lengths. There is a woodshop, where a master craftsman makes back-bending benches, calf stretchers, other items. I begin to help out with the basics, sanding and oiling the wood. I build the boxes and crates needed for shipping. I grow strong, put on weight, revel in the return of this body of mine that can lift, move, throw, create. I rent a room in a house, shared with five gay men, two of them artists. One paints a portrait of me on a large board, depicts me as an infant reborn, emerging ready to fight. In it I have a Mohawk, my vertebrae external, visible, and I wear big black boots. My favorite tattooist recreates the image on my right upper arm, the first design with color, a green Mohawk and blue backbone.

I'd like to say it's been easy since that turning point, but it hasn't. It took several years to find medication that helped to make the suicidal-ity recede into the background. There were many, many days I thought I wouldn't be strong enough, that I couldn't make it. I fought for every inch of healing, every day of recovery. But I am alive. And today I write the poems that eluded me for so long.

Here's how the numbers play out. I haven't been in a psychiatric hospital for fifteen years. It's been eighteen years since my last drink or drug. The last tattoo, the large tribal pattern on the underside of my left forearm, is different from all the others. Because fourteen years ago, I met the woman who filled me up, who made me know I had finally found a home. She herself has colorful tattoos of fantasy creatures—dragons, imps, elves.

We went to a tattoo parlor together, and she had an image inked on her thigh of a sassy fairy with tribal tattoos on its arms and legs. Instead of having a clichéd heart with my wife's name in it tattooed on my chest, I had the same tribal pattern from the fairy's leg inscribed on my inside of my left arm. It serves a dual purpose. First, it is a daily reminder, strong and firm, of us. Second, the tattoo covers an area where I used to cut. Though you can still see the faint white scars underneath, the love is on top—which is as apt a metaphor for my life as any I could ever put to paper.

Merging Sacred and Mundane

Bethany Ridenour

I wrote this essay out of my love for cleaning. The ritual of cleaning, clearing, washing away, moving out physical and unseen energies, and the frequent sweeping away of old ghosts has brought deep healing into my life.

My goals are to challenge the reader to rethink the way we have begun to separate the sacred vs. mundane and to introduce the idea of cleaning as a potent transformational tool for moving energy.

My name is Bethany. I am a teacher and student of ancestral skills. For as long as I can remember I have turned to the trees and animals in the forest for counsel. I believe strongly in the healing powers of nature, believing that strengthening our connection with the natural world can improve our interpersonal relationships and emotional well-being. In my own path I have found that working with my hands with elements of nature brings some of the deepest healing. I feel like it is my path to do what I can to help bridge the gap between humans and nature and bring to light how that relationship can help heal trauma.

There are certain stories that define who a person becomes and how they carve their path. My path, and the work that I believe I am meant to do, is largely defined by the trauma that I survived as a young person.

When I turned twelve years old, I went down a rabbit hole that I did not come out of until I was in my early twenties. Those lost years of my life are a blurry mess of drugs, frequent bouts of being locked up in juvenile hall, visits to the mental hospital after trying to take my own life, and other painful traumatic experiences.

In my early twenties two relationships developed unconsciously and simultaneously that saved my life.

The first one was that I developed an intimate relationship with the more-than-human world: trees, creatures, plants, water, earth, air, fire, spirit. This relationship happened unconsciously and gradually. I did not trust the humans in my life. Most of the people that were supposed to care for me either betrayed me, were trying to institutionalize me— pathologize or "fix" me with medication—or had earned my distrust in some other way. I spent a lot of time running and hiding from the police, my parents, mental health professionals, group homes, and any other forms of authority that were trying to make me do things I didn't want to do.

The best places I could find to hide were in the darkness of the woods or other "wild" spaces. These places became my refuge and where I felt safe. Here, I felt protected by the forces of nature. These more-than-human relatives are the ones that held me. They asked nothing of me, just took me in and took care of me, accepting me just the way I was.

The second life-changing relationship I developed was with the process of cleaning. I became a total neat freak and started cleaning ferociously. This was also happening unconsciously, but I imagine the world thru my eyes at this time felt like a messy, chaotic, and unsafe place. With this cleaning obsession I began to feel a sense of safeness and empowerment. This is one of the ways I survived all the trauma, while avoiding mental health medication. With this cleaning obsession came an intimate relationship with sweeping and the broom. I often swept many times in a day, whenever I felt bad or disturbed I would pick up my broom and begin sweeping. Sweeping gave me a sense of peace and a break from the pain of all the unhealed wounds I was carrying. I didn't know it at the time, but I was beginning to sweep away my trauma.

My matrilineal roots extend from Mexico. Like many Mexican families, this is a mix of Spanish and Indigenous ancestry. This is the part of my blood that I have always felt the most drawn to. Unfortunately, I grew up very disconnected from the culture, since my grandmother left Mexico and worked hard to integrate into the culture of the United States.

This last fall, I was teaching Broom Craft at the Northern California Women's Herbal Symposium. I was excited to see on the schedule that there was a workshop on the *curanderismo* practice of "*limpia*" (curanderismo is a holistic system of Latin American folk medicine). I had no idea what a limpia entailed, but I had often heard my great-grandmother (whose name was Amparo) referred to as a bruja and felt this might be close to some of the medicine she practiced. So I was excited to take this workshop.

The self-limpia we learned about in the workshop was a technique of sweeping our own bodies with bundles of fresh aromatic herbs. This is a way of spiritually cleansing oneself. I was excited about the idea of sweeping in a different way.

Immediately when I starting this sweeping of my body, I got chills down my spine. I could hear my great-grandmother whispering to me, and in this moment I knew for sure that she was there with me, and that she had led me to this. I knew that this was the missing piece with my sweeping obsession, and that she was leading me to healing all along with sweeping.

We each have an ancestral memory of the medicine that our people used for healing. I think if we dig to try to find it, we might just find that we were already being led there, and that we are already doing things that point to that ancestral memory.

Folks mention cleaning as a "mundane" or "domestic" act—I believe this is a conditioning that has happened in order to keep us from anything that gives us power and brings magic into our lives. For me sweeping and cleaning is far from mundane, it is a wild act of disobedience against the patriarchal system that is trying to hold me back. Every time I sweep I feel the power and reclaiming of my space and a reconnection to my ancestors.

By breaking down the dividing walls in my cleaning rituals, I am reminded to do the same in the rest of my life. As I sweep, I am reminded that sacred and mundane meet everywhere; that no one thing is truly separate from the next. This practice gives me a lens that helps me move past divisions everywhere, to remember that there's no division between me and others; between me what we call "nature," spirit, beings, people, the elements, and so on.

Every human who walks this earth has ancestral ties to land-based people. However far back it might be, we all have ancestors that at some point lived closely to the land and had a harmonious, symbiotic relationship with the more-than-human world.

It's important to know who the indigenous people of the land you are inhabiting are and to educate yourself about the history of the area and current struggles. It's also important to remember to not appropriate or steal something that we have no connection to, just because we see the beauty in it. Cultural appropriation is an extension of colonization, genocide, forced removals, and land theft. We can admire something without taking it for our own.

I encourage you to look into your own ancestry, however far back you need to go (for some of us this can take a lot of work, but I assure you it will be gratifying).

What spiritual or healing practices of cleaning or cleansing did your own land-based ancestors practice?

What cleaning magic was and is vital to their worldview?

Notes on Racism, Trauma, and Self-Care from a Woman of Color

an interview with acupuncturist Lorelle Saxena

Dani: In your practice (and in the world) what do you see are the major underlying issues in regards to mental health and general well-being, specifically for women?

Lorelle: Advertising in general, and advertising within the beauty and fitness industries in particular, is really dangerous. In order to work, it has to create a sense of need in the consumer. Too often, that's done by actively making women feel inadequate. If you wake up feeling good about any part of yourself—your skin, your hair, your butt, your sex life, your career—you can pick up a fashion magazine or turn on the television and feel bad about all of it within an hour. And then there's the entrenched sexism that informs expectations of domesticity. Almost every woman I know feels more responsible for housekeeping chores and childcare than their male cohabitants, and feels this in spite of knowing it's bullshit. Advertising for cleaning supplies reflect this: there's always a shiny floor and happy children and amazingly fit women beaming ruefully at eight-year-olds running screaming through a beautiful house. The message we're unable to avoid getting is: you could be this organized, this slender, this happy . . . but you're not. The primary effect of the ads is to get us to buy stuff, but the insidious side effect is feeling like chronic failures. We don't feel deserving of good health, because we feel like we have to get the house and the abs and the job up to the standard set by commercials first. And that's an impossible standard, so we're set up to resign ourselves to feeling unwell all the time.

Dani: Do you see a connection between societal pressures/standards/expectations of women and happiness, confidence, or general well-being for women?

Lorelle: Yes. Absolutely. We've agreed somewhere along the way and very tacitly that the way to be a fully realized person is to be "busy." We've assigned value to an overfilled scheduled and chronic fatigue. We're all supposed to be neatly concealing exhaustion and overwhelm. We're a little suspicious of anyone well-rested and grounded; we grant an implied badge of honor to women who are tired and stressed. What if we granted that badge of honor, instead, for prioritizing wellness and quality of life? What if we decided we'd fiercely protect time on our calendars for doing nothing at all? What if we spent just a few minutes each day not striving but just being? What if we started with "I am already enough," and then went from there?

Dani: In the last few years there has been a lot of research (including DSM recognition) of racism as a root cause of PTSD for people of color. As a woman and a person of color, what do you think about this? Do you think that sexism also contributes to severe stress and/or mental health issues for women?

Lorelle: First of all, this is a really great question. So there are different etiologies for PTSD: there is a single-incident type of trauma, like a car accident or the sudden death of a loved one; and then there are extended, repetitive types of trauma, like soldiering in battle or being abused throughout your childhood. The kind of PTSD people of color face in the United States can be both: an event like the murder of Trayvon Martin and the detailed news coverage can all by itself be sufficient trauma to create post-traumatic symptomology. And the kinds of things that combine to create the other type of PTSD causation are certainly too numerous and diverse to name them all, but we could start with: the constant barrage of media covering police brutality toward people of color; the lack of news stories about heroes, changemakers, writers, academics of color; the graphic coverage of the terrorist attacks in Middle Eastern countries when networks would never dream of showing photos of, for example, severely wounded white children.

That last example has bothered me since I was very little. I'd open my parents' copy of *Time* magazine and I'd see images of brown people harmed in civil unrest: closeups of the faces of parents freshly mourning their children, long shots of children bloodied and shocked in rows and rows of inadequate beds. I never saw photos like that, that blunt or raw, of white parents or children. Never. The reason not to publish photos of traumatized people is to avoid traumatizing the viewer, who is human and therefore vulnerable to empathy. Where that becomes problematic is that this particular guideline, at least in this country, is not applied to people of color. The loud but unspoken message is: white people are the only ones that matter; white people are the only ones who read. It's far too painful to see a photo of a grievously injured person, but only if that person is white. Hurt brown people who live far away? Yeah, that is fine to show. We don't feel for them. No one is traumatized by seeing hurt brown people. But, of course, we are. If we're not, maybe we need to take a closer look at ourselves and ask why we're not. And there's no way, as a brown person, to take all of this in and bring out of it the belief that I am as valued as a white person. It is not just offensive and politically incorrect. It is personally hurtful, it is frightening, it is, absolutely, the exact form of repetitive trauma that can result in PTSD.

I do think that there is reason to believe sexism impacts all women in a similar way, though it's hard to draw a precise parallel, and though I don't believe I can separate my experience as a woman from my experience as a person of color, having only ever been both of those things. I do think that women are subtly encouraged to contain and curtail our desires in a way men are not. Largely, I believe that's due to expectations around the role of motherhood; even women who aren't mothers are expected to be more oriented toward caring for others than toward meeting their own needs. It hurts us. We don't create the lives we really want if we're only focused on supporting others. It hurts everyone around us when we don't let ourselves be joyful and fulfilled. The truth is, women—and men too—can be fulfilled, happy, realized, *and* nurturing, compassionate, empathic, and of service to their family and community. We don't have to choose.

So it's kind of a Catch-22. We're either heroically, miserably martyred, or we're guiltily following our bliss. I've met so many women who exhibit symptoms of marked depression or anxiety that is either exacerbated or caused by their own perceived failure to either care for their loved ones or to follow through with their own goals. It's hard to do both, and we feel expected to do both, and at the same time we might be criticized for doing either.

Dani: If you could pick *five* lifestyle or health changes (including specific supplements or treatments) that you feel could greatly improve the overall quality of women's emotional well-being, what would they be and why?

Lorelle: *1. Trust yourself.* You already know what to eat to feel your best. You know the kind of exercise that most agrees with you. It's specific to you—and finding it is just a matter of tuning in to your own intuition. For example, I feel best when my diet is based on white rice and cooked vegetables. Brown rice and salad don't agree with me, despite what conventional nutrition might dictate. Running is one of my favorite things to do, and I also recognize that it isn't the right exercise for everyone. Try different things, pay attention to how you feel in the hours and days after you eat or exercise, and base your health approach on your own experience. Taking control of your physical health is powerful medicine for your emotional well-being

2. Find a health care practitioner that you're really comfortable with that leaves time in their appointments for conversation and treats you with respect. This person could be an MD, a therapist, an acupuncturist, a chiropractor, an intuitive and informed massage therapist, or another practitioner with whom you resonate. You need eyes on your health besides your own and having a professional—someone who is trained to identify red flags and can help you interpret medical advice, as well as contributing the weight of research and education to your health decisions. Maintain that relationship; keep regular appointments, and share all the information you can within it; it's a long-term investment that will pay real dividends.

3. Meditate. Even if it's just for two minutes a day.

4. Forgive yourself. Have a whole practice of self-forgiveness. It's hard to meet our own expectations and the expectations of everyone around us. Don't beat yourself up when you fall short. Instead, celebrate all the things you have accomplished. Keep a list if you want of all the things about yourself that are awesome and refer to it whenever you're struggling to be gentle with yourself. Treat yourself with the same kindness you treat your children and friends. You are your most important resource.

5. Keep a checklist on hand (or in your head) for those moments when you feel really bad—you know, when you are so sad or anxious or exhausted that you can't even imagine feeling better. If you can't think of what your next step should be, start by trying these simple, close-at-hand steps:

Step 1. Drink water. Dehydration creates fatigue, which in turn can create a sense of hopelessness.

Step 2. Eat. Low blood sugar is one of the most frequent causes of anxiety.

Step 3. Get outside. Ideally walk around a little bit or run or do something that raises your heart rate a little; even sticking your head out the window can help.

Step 4. Take a shower. Sometimes it's just enough of a reset button.

Step 5. Call a friend, go to a coffee shop, write a letter . . . do whatever is within your comfort zone that emphasizes your indelible connection to the rest of the human race.

Step 6. If all else fails or feels impossible: breathe. Wait it out. Don't make any big decisions. This will pass. Hang in, one breath at a time, until you feel ready to start at step 1 again.

Locking Doors

Airial Clark

Most of my life I've had a hard time remembering to lock front doors, or to even close them. Doors feel superstitious to me. I don't trust their utility. Their solidness feels suspicious to me. Like a trick to let my guard down. What's ever been stopped by a door? Sometimes I see a dead bolted door as lack of preparation. A talisman. A prayer for protection. "I'm locking this door wishing that what I want to stay out will not come in." Like knocking on wood to prevent something unfortunate from happening. Or throwing salt over your shoulder. Maybe more like crossing your fingers in hope. When you are poor, people breaking into your home aren't there for a stereo. The people locked inside the box are the valuables. You need a lot more than a door to protect them. That's what my mother taught me.

As a child, my mother's insanity permeated our home, wrapped about us like a cloak, charged the air. You could feel it when you walked up our steps; someone crazy lives here.

I knew from a very early age that the mysterious men my mother was afraid of would not be stopped by a locked door. She lived waiting for the door to get kicked off the hinges, ready for the windows to be busted out. I had no idea who our attackers were supposed to be, but I had a feeling that they would end up needing my protection. I believed she would kill them. She'd feel . . . accomplished.

Because she wanted to win this time. Finally, the predators from her past arriving to finish off the girl she had been, unequipped now to deal with the madwoman she was. She was waiting for them. Night after night, falling asleep in the lopsided, worn-out green recliner. Facing the front door to ensure they couldn't get past her. Guaranteeing she would be their first encounter and determined to be their last.

She didn't need a weapon; she fantasized about strangling them with her bare hands. She told me during her regular late afternoon fits of rage. Afternoons were the worst. That twilight zone when kids old enough to walk from school alone come home to empty houses. "How many lives had been ruined on a Tuesday at 4:00 p.m.?" she asked me more than once whenever I complained about not being allowed at friends' houses until their parents were home from work.

She never beat me, my mom. Never took her rage out on me. She'd go quiet with anger. Eerily so. The first time I read *Carrie*, I thought for sure that Stephen King had met my mother. Her rage felt telekinetic. Static. I lived in fear of being zapped.

She taught me that while I was smart, I couldn't rely on my brain to protect me. What really mattered was that I knew my strength. From about eight years old on, she admired and complimented my wide hands, meaty like my grandfather's. "Hands that can do things," she would say. She encouraged me lift heavy things, to be loud, to be unafraid. Around ten, when puberty started, play fighting became her favorite way of showing me affection.

Slap boxing especially. Showing how it didn't really hurt to be hit in the face, just stung a little. But it passes and when you're having fun, you don't even feel it. No reason to be afraid of someone slapping you. What's a slap going to do? She smacked me in the face until I stopped needing to flinch. Pinching my face until I kept my eyes open to aim straight and slap her back. I was expected to match her blow for blow. All while howling with joy. Just keep laughing, it's fun to play like this. By eleven, we were the same height. A year later I passed her and felt taller than everybody. And still, she would wrestle me to the ground, laughing; pure joy in the takedown. Sometimes I'd have a fat lip or bruised eyebrow afterwards, but it didn't matter. She called me Amazon and told me I was a Viking. She praised my strong arms and sharp elbows. She shared how sensitive a man's throat is to puncture, "Breaking a windpipe is easy."

She would tell me that while men may whistle and catcall at my long legs, those were also my best weapons. A foot to the jaw, to the groin, to the eye, to the stomach was completely reasonable; and you never needed a reason. Don't wait, follow your gut, look for the twitch in his eye that shows he's made his decision to hurt you, then strike first and run! Yell "fire!" while running down the middle of the street, don't scream "help," that never works, strangers don't care about a girl screaming.

Until one day she couldn't pin me. I'm fourteen, flat on my stomach with her knees in my back, pulling my hair, both of us laughing hysterically. I decide to rear back and realized I was standing with her still hanging on. I threw her over my shoulders and stepped on her neck, her face red and voice cackling. "Enough, enough," she wheezed, "you got me, you got me!" And we sat on the dirty living room carpet panting then laughed some more. We stopped wrestling after that.

Still, she spent more nights than not in front of the unlocked door. On warm nights, she left it wide open. Our upstairs apartment on the corner of two busy avenues. Traffic, the ocean sounds my brother and I fell asleep to. Our neighborhood full of tweakers with the meth crisis of the mid-nineties in full swing. Our door faced the building parking lot. She was relentless in her silent seething. If a stranger came up our steps in the night, her weaponized fear was locked and loaded. An unlocked door was an acknowledgement of the battle, according to my mother, raging all around us. She knew what was really happening.

I imagine I slept the same way kids who had loyal guard dogs slept. My mom slept during the day, I would silently pass her in the morning leaving the apartment for school. In those morning moments, I was more mime than daughter. Like all kids, I inherited my primary caregiver's reality. The world was insane and my mother was wise. Going through the motions of a daily routine without needing an adult was normal, and yet I was aware of how abnormal it felt. My mom spent the entirety of my childhood waiting for my abusers to show up at our door. She waited. And waited. Her tormentors never arrived. Never validated her life lived under siege.

As a young woman, on my own at age seventeen, because I was done waiting and so very tired, living here and there, I failed to close the front doors of my shared houses, and I definitely didn't have a habit of locking them. They always noticed. "You forgot to close the door," they'd say the first couple times, helpfully. Exasperation creeped in with the next reminders. Then anger. Sometimes concern. Rarely curiosity. For those who asked me, I'd answer, "An open door just means I can see who's coming."

I knew nothing of mental illness or chronic PTSD or hypervigilance or how trauma lives in the body, sometimes intergenerationally. Until a friend started going to therapy and sharing with me what she was learning. Her mom and mine were peas in a pod. They hated each other of course, each criticizing the other for the same shit. Neither one living up to basic parenting standards. Both having so much empathy for the other's daughter. Slowly I started to question that maybe the world was sane and my mother was crazy?

I tried to unlearn as much of her wisdom as possible. I started looking for other mothers everywhere. Friends' moms at first, but no, that required vulnerability, and fuck that. Older women at my jobs felt possible, but then that got complicated quickly. I tried learning from the moms in movies and TV, but they were all so vapid and cheesy. So I chose Oprah. She was the mother I found in a magazine. Each month a new way of living. Not just living but living my best life one book club recommendation at a time. It was a new millennia, and there was new wisdom for women to claim. I had hope. And I had questions. Did Oprah lock her doors at night?

I still didn't have much faith in locking a door. I did it because I was supposed to; it would be irresponsible not to. Yes, I thought to myself, Oprah locked all of her doors.

When I brought my first son home from the hospital, I used the door chain for the first time ever. I had never slid the tiny metal ball into place before. I felt the superstition at play. But then I reasoned, the door chain will give me more time when it gets kicked in. Those thoughts felt rational. Even though never, not once in my life, had I experienced the violence and violation of someone breaking my front door down. The rage that coursed through me when I realized how traumatized I was and the intergenerational nature of it made me want to break down somebody's door. I just didn't know whose. So I went to therapy instead.

I saw that there was no binary in the world of people being wise or crazy. I knew I had healed parts of my childhood neglect when I let go of that false dichotomy. The world is insane and sane, my mother is traumatized and wise. There are predators of all kinds and not everyone is preyed upon but any of us can be, one unjust ecosystem holding us all unequally. I don't give a fuck, and I give all the fucks. There were the men who hurt my mother as a child, and then again as a young woman, and there was Oprah.

As a new mom, I worried that I couldn't generate the same force field as my mother. I wasn't crazy enough, and that scared me. I felt as if my children were exposed. I didn't have a cloak of insanity to wrap around them and me, and I needed to sleep. So I tapped into my creative field. I willed my fear and rage and desperation into something bigger than me.

Every night before I fell asleep, I felt a Goddess place her foot on the roof of my home. I willed her into being, fifty feet tall, starlit armed with a sword and shield. Vigilant watching. A giant woman of light and energy standing guard above my babies' bed, unwavering in her nightly defense until I woke up in the morning. I did this for years. I slept well. I got up in the mornings and lived our daily get out the door on time routine.

Today, my teenaged children often lock our front door at night before I remind myself to. And I wonder if I have failed them. Because shouldn't I always be responsible for that? No, I tell myself, they are just being rational; raised by a sane person. Using common sense. They notice the door isn't locked yet and lock it without thinking.

For me though, it's still a form of magic. When I bolt the door, there is still a tinge of superstition. A prayer of protection mixed with gratitude. Thankful for trusting in a first line of defense so I don't have to. Thankful for a solid boundary.

Violence, Generational Trauma, and Women's Empowerment in Indigenous Communities

an interview with Patty Stonefish of Arming Sisters

Dani: What you can tell me about your work with Arming Sisters and how the program started?

Patty: I founded Arming Sisters, originally in 2013. Arming Sisters is a nonprofit and it utilizes women's self-defense as a tool of healing instead of a tool of prevention. I focus on indigenous communities, as I'm Lakota myself, but also I do offer courses to nonnatives as well. It's just that those courses are more of a cultural bridge. They act as a cultural bridge in a cultural capacity course as a self-defense course.

Dani: When you started in 2013 did you already have several years of martial arts or self-defense training? How did you end up deciding that this was something that you wanted to bring to indigenous communities?

Patty: At that point, I had already been in martial arts for over about a decade, but when I started it in 2013, I actually started it because I was living abroad in Egypt, and I had been living in Cairo, Egypt, since 2010, going back and forth since 2008. I was approached to give women's self-defense courses there after the January 25th revolution. It suddenly dawned on me while giving a course that I didn't jive with that idea of women's self-defense as prevention anymore. As a survivor of sexual assault myself, it really started to bother me. Martial arts has been a huge healing aspect for me, and it can be utilized as a tool of healing and should be. And this idea of prevention for women's self-defense, it just perpetuates the whole rape culture cycle, because it puts the responsibility back on us, and it continues this whole victim-blaming cycle, and that's just not how it should be. And it's super powerful when utilized as a tool of healing. That's how it started. I decided to launch it, and I took off and came back to the States, and here I am.

Dani: I'm glad that you brought that up. I have a lot of conversations with people about how "we" need to learn all these tools about how to protect ourselves, and I appreciate how you reframed that instead of putting the responsibility back on the victims, you're actually framing it in a way of, like, "Hey, I'm empowering you and helping you find your strength."

Patty: Thank you. The theory is just working from the outside in, especially in regards to native communities, we don't have a lot of access to things like therapy. And, again, survivors don't always want to go to therapy, and it doesn't always work for everybody. And it can be a lot of money and a lot of resources, and it's just not everyone's cup of tea when it comes to healing. What I learned is this: when you see your physical power in action outside of yourself, it kind of creates that domino effect, you know. Like, "Okay, well if I'm physically stronger than I thought I was, and I can see it, well, maybe I'm also mentally, emotionally, and spiritually stronger than I thought I was." And that's something that survivors of sexual assault deal with a lot is feeling weak or helpless.

Dani: I'm glad that you brought that up too. Not everybody wants to go to therapy, and talk therapy can actually exasperate the trauma situations and having PTSD. You said when you came back to the States were you primarily focusing on native communities with your classes?

Patty: Yes. In Egypt it was just me and my coach, and I just really wasn't okay with what he was saying anymore. I started the crowdfunding for it in Cairo, and I came back to the States after that was done. The goal has always been to focus specifically on native women, which suffer the highest rates of sexual assault out of anyone. In the U.S. and Canada, it's bad. We have a lot of healing to do, and I want to be a part of it as much as I can and help facilitate that.

Dani: I've been reading about and hearing about issues around missing and murdered indigenous women and girls for years, but it's never really been through mainstream media, which is very frustrating. And I'm wondering if you could talk to that a little bit. Why do you think it is that this violence against native women seems to maybe not be taken so seriously or get the attention of the mainstream news sources?

Patty: So there's multiple different aspects to native issues in general, from our culture to anything having to do with the law, but we're largely invisible. And we've been placed in that position; arguably, it's a source of ongoing genocide. The way it's still carried out. And the laws aren't there to protect us either. Since the laws aren't there, there's no real backing for us to remain in the spotlight, for us to remain a hot topic issue, so. . . It comes to prosecution of nonnatives, because of 86 percent of attackers are nonnative. There's no real laws, or there's minimal, it's narrowly tailored to where it's hard for us to actually prosecute, even after the trial provisions that were put in 2013 with the Violence Against Women Act. It's still very hard. So it's also a large loophole.

Dani: Is it still true that because of the tribal laws and then the federal laws that non-tribal members can't be prosecuted for crimes that they commit on the reservation, and is it also true that if they commit a crime against a native person off of a reservation, or is it just if the crime happens there?

Patty: At this point, it's just if the crime happens on reservation land. Still the tribal provisions in 2013 that were, with the reauthorization of the Violence Against Women Act, everyone got really excited, and nobody read the fine print. And it's narrowly tailored to: we can only prosecute nonnative attackers if they live or work on reservation land, have a prior existing relationship with the native woman, or have a restraining order actively in place. So that leaves a wide-open space, especially when it comes to extraction sites. So, for example, there is the Mandan, Hidatsa, and Arikara Nation, MHA Nation, in New Town, North Dakota, and there's the Bakken oil fields up there. This is one example, there's many extraction sites that often border reservation lands, be it mining or oil, etc. But because the camps are directly outside of the reservation and oftentimes the work is done just outside of the reservation as well, this leaves a major opening for anyone in those man camps to quite literally walk onto reservation land, attack a native woman, and there's nothing anybody can do about it.

Dani: That's so crazy to me, and again, there isn't' a lot of information out there about that. I don't hear about any of this stuff. I've had to scour places and purposefully look for that information. It's just not readily available, and I don't think that most people even understand that part of the law.

Patty: Agreed.

Dani: One of the other things you mentioned, the genocide since colonization and these different legal issues, and I think I read something about you where you touched on the issues of generational trauma. Can you speak to that a little bit for maybe people who don't understand what that means?

Patty: Generational trauma is the idea that trauma gets carried and passed down through generations. This has now been proven theoretically through epigenetics, but even outside of epigenetics we have the issues where we have entire generations that are missing due to adoption acts, due to relocation acts, and due to residential school. And a lot of times these things are thought of as way in the past, happening in the 1800s, but residential schools are very new. Many of our grandparents went to residential school and because of it carry an immense amount of trauma, down to being afraid to this day to speak their language. That just continues to carry forward and we are quite literally missing entire generations, and it's very new. To put it in perspective, we weren't allowed to practice any of our spiritual ways openly without prosecution until 1978. That's only forty years ago.

Dani: It really was not that long ago.

Patty: No, not at all.

Dani: Another thing I wanted to talk to you about as far as utilizing the trainings. Do you hope that the trainings you offer can help heal some of that generational trauma?

Patty: For sure. I think with any trauma, it can definitely help with. Regardless of what it might be, I think it gets things moving forward. I've had quite a few beautiful success stories of women reaching back out to me afterwards and just marking those classes as turning points. I'm mobile, the courses are mobile. They last in the community for maybe up to a week but can also be as short as one day. But it's just about getting that initial spark going and pulling people out of their comfort zones to remind them that they are strong and they actually seeing their strength, and it really helps kick that healing off. From there it's really up to them and the resources that we have in our communities, which thankfully are getting more and more. And we are healing as nations. We are definitely on a healing path, but it's tough. It takes time. I completely think that it helps them in all aspects of healing.

Dani: About how many people have come through your trainings over the years?

Patty: I've been coast to coast now, given about seventy courses. I've probably crossed paths with over a 1,000, probably 1,200 women now.

Dani: Do you have any specific stories? Of course, you don't have to use anyone's names, but any stories of really witnessing a big transformation in someone after your training, or have you seen people come in multigenerations, like mothers and daughters or grandmothers and granddaughters coming in to your trainings?

Patty: I've definitely had multigenerations, which is beautiful, and I do have a few stories. The one that stands out most to me though is: this one woman came into my course and she was maybe three days in from sobriety. It was very fresh. She'd just gotten out of an extremely abusive relationship. Her kids were taken away from her. She was really coming out of a very low point in many different ways. And she came in not talking, very slouched over, her body language not very present, not confident. She looked down. By the end of the course she was the loudest one in there. It was amazing. She had a lot to say, and I loved it. We've kept in contact through the years, and now we're three and a half years out from that first course. It was the only course that she took. Since that course, and from that day forward, she wound up saving up money, stayed sober, moved out east, is going to be finishing college this coming fall, she'll be finishing her last semester. She has her children back. And she is a powerhouse.

Dani: And how is it for you? I know that it can sometimes be challenging emotionally to be holding space for people that have been traumatized or experienced any kind of distress. I'm wondering how it affects you?

Patty: Multiple different ways. Overall though it's extremely energizing. There's something insanely therapeutic about being around a ton of native women, and we laugh a lot. When you're dealing with so much trauma, something cultural where we have a pretty messed up sense of humor, because we've been through so much we have to laugh. There's a lot of laughing that goes on in these courses. It's beautiful and it's supporting. There's, of course, the drain moments, there's points where, I mean, it's a lot to take on, like you said, emotionally. It is a lot to hold. And physically too, I'll come out sometimes with red marks up and down my throat and torn knuckles and. . . It can get tiring in that sense too, but I absolutely love it. Overall it keeps me going. It's my healing, as well.

Dani: How do you see Arming Sisters evolving, or what are your next steps with where you're going with this work?

Patty: Currently we are unfunded, so the next step is hopefully getting funded. That's something that's extremely needed at the moment. Grant writing is not my forte, but I am learning. From there though, I want to branch out across not only the U.S., but I want to branch into Canada, and the talks are already in the works at the moment. But I eventually want to branch out worldwide, as well. There are indigenous cultures all over the world. I would love to be in Palestine. I'd love to be in New Zealand. I'd love to be giving these courses all over the place and hopefully have community leaders and be able to pass this training on to other people. Because the self-defense classes, they're very simple, and I would like to be able to pass them on to community leaders, so they can take this curriculum and utilize it in the community as more of a permanent aspect. I don't imagine Arming Sisters having, like, a center in every community nor do I want that. I want the communities to take these tools and create their own organizations, create their own healing from it.

Thoughts on Mother's Day

Nayomi Munaweera

At ten years old, I had two rules about life: I would never get married, and I would never have babies. I have broken my first rule twice. I have never wavered about the second.

I came close to becoming a mother once. Not by choice but in an entirely brutalized way. I was twenty-four and breaking up with a man I had been with for eight years. We had met when I was sixteen and he was twenty. He had been a tremendous part of my formative experience, romantic and otherwise. When I was twenty-four, we were engaged and were planning our wedding when I realized through a series of events that I did not love this man and did not want to marry him. I realized that the life I would create without him would be so much fuller, wilder, freer than the life I would have with him.

My fiancé did not want to break up. He cried. He threatened suicide. He called my parents and my friends at all hours of the night weeping and asking them to convince me to return to him. He told my parents he had lost his job over pining for me. It was a lie, one of many that kept me trapped in a crucible of guilt and shame. Who was I to hurt someone so deeply? Who was I to destroy his life as he said I was doing? As a South Asian woman, how dare I choose a man so easily and then as easily give him up? I knew that breaking up with him would ruin my reputation in my communities both in L.A. and back home in Sri Lanka. He too was Sri Lankan. But as the woman, the breakup would cast a certain taint on my character, not his. I didn't care. I had tasted freedom, and I wanted it more than I had ever wanted anything in my life. It was a desire so sharp and clean I could feel it in my body like an ache.

In that final chaotic month, my fiancé begged me to go on one last trip with him and, stupidly, I gave in. In the neon wastelands of Las

Vegas, he begged me to have sex with him one more time. That crucible I mentioned before had become a vice. There was an added ingredient: pity. I slept with him one last and final time. I had stopped using birth control. He promised he would not come in me, and then immediately he did, and I knew with a gutting fear that he had impregnated me. I rolled over and wept while he showered. It was 1997, I had never heard of the morning-after pill, even if it existed then. I took a pregnancy test two weeks later, and it was positive.

When I told him there was a spark of glee in his eyes. I realized that he believed this meant I would stay with him, that I would bear his children and live in his house for the rest of my life. I felt the bars of a prison closing around me. South Asian women are not supposed to sleep with men. We were not supposed to get pregnant outside marriage. We are not supposed to get abortions. But I "failed" on all counts.

Getting an abortion was the hardest thing I've ever had to do in my life. There was a girl volunteering on that day, and I held her hand so hard I think I could have broken it. I stared into her green eyes, and I think she saved me. I wish I knew her name so that I could thank her. A few weeks after my abortion, my fiancé revealed to a mutual friend that he had planned to get me pregnant. He had thought this was the way to get me to stay. If I had the baby, we would be a happy family. If I decided to get an abortion, he would stand by me and prove how supportive he was and win me back that way. I broke up with him, and I've never seen him again. This feels like a blessing.

I deeply regret the circumstances that led me to get pregnant and have an abortion. I wish I could have talked to that younger version of myself and told her that her body belonged only to herself, that she did not have to please the man or the community. I wish I had the inner resources to walk away at the first sign of danger, but that only came with time and experience.

I do not, however, regret the abortion.

I am deeply grateful that I had the privilege of choice. I am grateful that my younger self had the intuition to follow her own path, to remain childless and claim the life that she had only glimpsed then.

In the almost two decades since, I've never felt those deep maternal urges other women talk about. I've never felt that painful desire for my very own baby. Still, I think about her every now and then. The daughter I might have borne. She's always a girl. Of this much I am convinced. I calculate how old she would be now. It astounds me that in a parallel life I could have been a mother to an eighteen-year-old. I am thankful that I was not forced to be her mother. These days, I am learning compassion, for the naive young girl I was, for the baby girl who was never born, and perhaps even for that tortured man who committed this sin.

On Mother's Day, we are always reminded of our own mothers and entreated to call them, to appreciate them. But I am also always reminded of the mother I never was and never will be.

On Sharing Our Stories

an interview with Melissa Madera
of *The Abortion Diary* Podcast

Dani: Where did you grow up, and what led you to start talking about abortions?

Melissa: I grew up in New York. Part of my years growing up, I was living in Washington Heights, New York. That's where I was born. It is a predominantly Dominican community or has been for a very long time. My parents are Dominican. Both of them were born there. I had an abortion when I was seventeen. I was just finishing high school, but throughout my lessons and my teenage years, no one ever really talked to me about sex. I think there was this idea that you just, you're not supposed to have sex. My parents were just like, you're not even supposed to date. I was actually mostly chaperoned on dates with my boyfriend when I was a teenager . . . by my younger sister. I think my parents just didn't know how to talk about that. I went to a Catholic high school, and that was not part of the curriculum.

Dani: Shocker.

Melissa: We had a health class, health teacher. It was just so awkward, and sex was not really talked about, certainly not contraception. Birth control was not talked about. So I just didn't really have the opportunity to take care of myself in that way or ask for what I needed so that I wouldn't be in that situation. It was a very complicated experience for me to have this abortion, especially because my family was a part of that experience.

Dani: What do you remember about finding out you were pregnant?

Melissa: I was very unconscious of the whole experience. I didn't even really realize that I was pregnant until someone else realized it in my family and took me to a doctor's office, and I had a test and the decision for me to have an abortion was made by other people. It was a very complicated experience. I wish the experience had been different, but I don't believe I would have made a different choice. I'm very glad that I didn't have a child when I was seventeen. Like, very glad. What's also really interesting about that experience is, thinking back on it, as being a teenager, being pregnant at seventeen, and my mother also was pregnant at seventeen and had me. I had a different experience, and had different opportunities, because I didn't have a child at eighteen. I would have been eighteen, and she was eighteen when I was born. I'm also very happy not to be connected to that person that would have been the father of that child. You know?

Dani: Yeah.

Melissa: So it's very complicated for me, especially now. I'm just now processing a lot of it. Last year, when I turned thirty-eight, that summer before was the twentieth anniversary of my abortion. It was a very difficult time for me, especially because I haven't had a child, and I want to, but it's not in the cards for my life in this moment.

Dani: How did you go from having that experience, and then starting the podcast? I know there was a big chunk of time in between. Did you share your story to anyone immediately, or was it something that you took a long time to share?

Melissa: It wasn't something that I talked about after, not even with my family members. It felt like a really big secret. So the people that knew, I had a lot of shame around it. I didn't want to talk about it with them. I felt very shameful. It also was something that was not just shameful around an abortion experience but shameful around talking about it as a person who has actually had sex with another person. It was exactly almost five years ago. Before that, in 2010, I was working at an organization that was doing work on abortion; and it was the first time I ever talked about it with a coworker. It was a surreal, weird experience to be talking about something that I just never talked about before, and it had been like thirteen years. I didn't go out into the world and talk about my abortion to everyone. It just became an experience that had been hidden in the back of my mind, and then came to the forefront of my mind. That's sort of how I can explain it.

Dani: Yeah, that makes sense.

Melissa: So, I talked for a little, and then I got involved in some abortion-related activities. I went back to grad school, and I finished my dissertation. Then I moved back to New York, and I became an abortion doula.

I went to an abortion conference. I bought this bag that says, "I had an abortion," and it took like three months for me to wear the bag. Then that was part of the coming out. Then, a few years later, I was just doing a lot of work around it, and I started with Landmark. My abortion came out very strongly in that experience. I had a big, strong drive to connect with other people who have had abortions: I want to talk about my experience, but I also want to know what other people have gone through to feel like my experience wasn't so different or alone, or that other people have had this experience. You know? So, after I did that, there's a second [Landmark] course that you do. It's called the advanced something or other. And I don't know what happened. I was just like, I need to create [a group]. I looked online in New York for a physical space. I just wanted to meet people; and there wasn't a physical space. Then, I thought, maybe there's a podcast or something I can listen to people's stories, and there wasn't anything with audio. I wanted to just listen to people talk. I didn't necessarily want to read, and I didn't really want to write my experience. That wasn't my drive. Then I thought: maybe I can start a podcast, which I did not know how to do.

Dani: Oh, wow! Really?

Melissa: Because I have never recorded anyone. I had never edited audio. I did not even have the podcast on the internet. I don't know how to do this, but after I finished that third course, I was like, "I don't have money to do a third one," and they do this thing there, where people can sponsor you, so someone sponsored me to do the third one. The third one is actually the most important one, because the third one was the one in which you create some sort of project, a community project, based on whatever you want, whatever you need, whatever has come up for you. People can do anything. Like, "I want to make a birthday party for my grandma, with my whole family," or they can be like, "I want to start a nonprofit that works with children in the inner city." So that's what happened, that's how I ended up starting the podcast. Even setting up a website. I was going to start with one story a month, because I thought, "Not a lot of people will share their stories with me," and then a lot of people *did* want to share their stories with me. There's this idea that you don't want to talk about abortions, but the truth is that we do. We just need the right space for it and the right people.

Dani: I'm curious about how your family, because there was this element of secrecy, and maybe some shame, or just this complicated situation with your family . . . how do they feel now about you being so vocal about your own abortion, and dedicating so much of your life to helping other women share their stories? Or do they not know? I'm just kidding. You're like, "I haven't told them."

Melissa: Well, they do know (laughs). It's interesting, because when I started the project, and people have asked me about that, because it was such a secret, but when I started the project, I didn't necessarily go around telling everyone. I did bring it up with my aunt, who was the big part of this process, and with my father. That conversation did not go very well. The conversation with my aunt went a little bit better, and she was just kind of like, "I just didn't want you to do this and stall your life, and I just thought it was the right thing." And my mom said, "I just feel really guilty about the abortion that you had when you were seventeen." She held that in for like sixteen years, and then finally felt like she [could say that]. She has been really supportive, actually, and helpful with this in the financial sense, because I've been sort of not making any money during this process, and she has been really great about helping. She feels like it's something that I need, and she understands that.

Dani: You kind of spoke to it earlier: you have to test the waters, like who's safe to talk to about this? People are so violently aggressively anti-choice sometimes.

Melissa: What I've learned in doing this work also is none of us know how people will react in our lives, because we don't talk about abortion, so we have actually no idea what most of the people in our lives really actually think about abortion. The first person who ever shared her story with me said that when she was going through deciding to get an abortion, she told her best friend, and that's when she realized her best friend was anti-abortion.

Dani: Oh, no.

Melissa: So, I think for most of us, the people that we think we know the best, we actually don't know, because we don't talk about some of these things that we really should talk about. We should know what people in our lives think about these things. They're really intimate, important things that we might end up having to go through, and then we don't know who even will support us. You know?

Dani: When you got started with the podcast, did you ask people that you already knew to be on it, or how did you find people for them to share their stories?

Melissa: Yeah, that's so interesting, because I didn't know that many people, because I never talked about my abortion experience. I wouldn't have known who to ask if they wanted to share their abortion stories. Through the process of Landmark, I met a bunch of people who were like, "Oh, yeah. I had an abortion too and don't talk about it," and some of those people offered to share their story on the podcast. But the first people to share their story were people that I'd met at a midwifery skills workshop, so I was a birth doula and an abortion doula at the time. I would go to random workshops. In this one room, there were like ten of us in a room, and half of us had had an abortion. Those four people offered to share their story and ended up sharing their story on the podcast. Really, I just met people very randomly in my life, who I would just say, "Oh, I'm just starting this podcast," you know, like when you introduce yourself at groups, "I'm starting this podcast on abortion." I barely had a website. I had a name. That was all.

Dani: How many women have you interviewed so far?

Melissa: I interview both men and women and people who identify as nonbinary. Altogether, I've recorded about 295 stories, I think. And sometimes they're couples, so there's two people involved in the story sharing, which is interesting. And they're all such interesting, different, amazing people. It's so shocking to me that I know all these different kinds of people, because I wouldn't have met them if it wasn't for this project. People who are just not in my world life circle, and I met them because we've had this shared experience. You know?

Dani: That's so amazing. So you have quite a variety of types of stories too. Is that right?

Melissa: Very different, and different countries, and different states in the U.S., and different ages. I think the youngest person was eighteen, and the oldest person was eighty-five. And I never know what I'm gonna hear, which is always fun and interesting for me. I mean, I hate using the word "fun," because abortion is complicated, but it is. I get to meet so many different people and hear all different kinds of stories, and it's really amazing.

Dani: Are there any types of similarities that you hear more often, as far as experience, you know, around access or anything like that?

Melissa: The biggest similarity is that we haven't had spaces to share our stories. A lot of people say, "You're the first person that I've ever told the story to," or that they've told the full story to, because sometimes you might say, "Oh, I had an abortion," but you don't go into the details. So for a lot of people, I would say, almost everyone, this is the first time that they've gone through very serious detail in their story when they're telling it. In terms of, like, accessibility, that's varied, because I've recorded people in so many different places, from people who can get on a subway and get to a clinic very easily to people who have to drive or travel a very long way, like hours, to people who don't have access at all in their country. I've recorded people who, in their country, abortion is completely illegal. And they had to get pills or get on a plane to a different country, like people in Ireland, who have gone to England, people in Poland to go to Germany. They have to take a bus. Or they'd get pills in the mail. It's super varied in terms of how people are able to access or not access, or you know, who have easy access, and people who cannot access abortion legally at all.

In terms of people's feeling, that is so varied. Our experiences are so different from each other, and our relationships with our abortions are very different. I think about it as a relationship, like a relationship that I would have with person. That's the relationship that I have with my own abortion, constantly changing, and one that I'm always navigating; and I think that other people have a very similar experience with that.

Dani: You started doing the podcast, I believe, was that when Obama was in office? It's an understatement to say it was a way more liberal administration. It was a different era. I'm so curious about how you're feeling about it now, when there's this huge, aggressive pushback that has to do with reproductive rights. It's like we've totally flopped over on this end of a weird realm. It's like the sci-fi nightmare kind of, so. . . Has that changed things for you? I'm curious if you get harassed or anything like that, like hate mail.

Melissa: I have never really had a lot of backlash. I think that doing work the way that I do it; it's very personal. I'm not being super political, even though it's political. It's always political, but I'm actually, actively trying to depoliticize this experience of sharing abortion experiences. I don't get a lot of hate mail, I think, mostly because I am not really on social media. I just can't handle that much work. It'd be too much work. I share my story, but I don't do it in very political context. I do it in a more personal way, and the people who share their stories, they're saying it in their personal ways. So, I think people don't see it as threatening. It's like, "Oh, people are sharing their stories. That's kind of interesting."

Sometimes I get emails. I have this listener survey on my website, so anyone who's listening can take the survey and let me know what they think about it. Sometimes people who are pro-life listen to the podcast and they say like, "I'm pro-life," but they're like, "I really wanted to know why women have abortions, so I was just listening. Thank you for having these stories up." They listen, and they're like, "It's good to know why people have abortions." I don't know what they think about my podcast exactly, but I do know that they're not necessarily taking it as a threat, which is why they don't really bother me. Sometimes when I'm interviewed for news articles, I might get a weird email from someone that's like, "You're a baby killer," and I just don't respond. I just don't care enough about what they think. . .

Dani: Right. You can't engage with people like that, because they have their agenda, and just let them pray for you.

Melissa: They want you to engage. They want to be in this fight with you, and I'm like, "I'm not in a fight with you." There was one article that was written about me and the podcast in Spanish, and that was the one where I got the most nasty response. It was on Univision's website, and then they posted it on their Facebook page. Comment after comment after comment. There must have been, I don't want to exaggerate, but more than a hundred. They were just ugly. It was the only time, really, that I got a lot of ugly comments. Nobody really bothers me, and still even this day and age, with this nastiness, people haven't really bothered me very much. It doesn't happen that much. I think there's such a range in anti-abortion people. The image that we have, just like they have an image of who people who have abortions are, we have an image of who they are. In our minds, they're all the people who stand outside of a clinic and burn them down and want to do crazy things. But there's so many other people who are just kind of like, "We're not those people."

Dani: "We're just praying for you over here."

Melissa: Those people, I feel like we can actually talk to, to some degree. But those other people, we cannot talk to them. They're just nuts, and they probably will never change. Although, there was this article the other day about a guy who changed his mind about being anti-abortion. I don't know if he was super violent, but he was outside protesting and things like that. I think it was a priest. It was some sort of religious person, and he was like, "I feel bad that I made women feel bad" or something like that.

Dani: Of the other things you do to get away from some of that isolation and to support people is working as an abortion doula. What is that like?

Melissa: It was the first time where I stepped into doing work around my own abortion, but it's very different than meeting people after they've had an abortion. Meeting people during the process is not as connecting, especially as an abortion doula. When I did first trimester abortions, I met them right before their abortion, like just a few minutes. Like, "Hello. I'm Melissa, an advocate here while you have your abortion," where you hold their hand, give people whatever they need. You're offering them whatever they need in that moment, emotionally and physically. Then the second trimester abortions, I would meet the person maybe a few days before, because the cervix needs to be dilated, so I would be there during that time to support them during that part of the procedure, so they would get laminarias, and sometimes it would be one day, and sometimes it would be two days. Then I'd see them during the procedure.

It felt like I was processing parts of my experience, because that part of my abortion experience, the actual procedure part, is very sort of blurry. It's sort of like something that is not part of my memory. There was something about being with people during their experiences that was really important to me. So, it's very different in the work that I do with the podcast, but it is something that, in the beginning of my journey of processing my abortion experience, that's what I was doing, almost like being a support person during people's abortions; but at the same time, I was being [a doula] at births, which was really interesting.

Dani: Why do you feel it is important for women and nonbinary people to share their stories on the podcast?

Melissa: From the beginning, it was always about creating connections and community for people, because there is no community. I think... I'm gonna say this, and maybe I don't know if I'm ready to say it out loud as much, but I do think that we are purposely isolated from each other in so many ways, even in our experiences of getting the abortions, the clinic itself isolates us in so many ways. The abortion community just isolates us. Even when I think about the experiences that I had and the experience that other people have, about how they move in the clinic. One person told me, this will stick in my mind, there was someone in the room with her in the clinic crying, and she went and hugged her, and the woman at the clinic was like, "Stop touching each other." She just separated them. Why would you do that? Why isn't there more of a sense that we should be more connected than separated from one another? For me, this work has always been about connecting us with each other and having us know that there are millions of us out there that we can be connected to, that we can talk to, that we don't have to be marginalized from a community. We can actually be part of a new community of people. When island people say, "Stigma separates us from the rest of the community," I was like, well we can become part of a different community with each other, that decreases that stigma. You know? I feel very privileged to be part of a community with other people, and I see that, and when people share their stories with me, and they're like, "Oh, I've never met someone else who had an abortion," and that's a big deal for them. I see that as really shifting and changing the way that people feel about themselves and their experience and about abortion generally. I feel different knowing that they're all . . . knowing that there are hundreds of people out there that I'm connected to personally through this work. I feel really fortunate to know them.

There's two aspects to this work. There's two reasons why I do it. One is the invitation for people to share this experience if they want to and feel like if it's important for them. Really, no one should share this story unless for them it makes sense, and for them it feels good, and it feels right. Then the second part of that, which is equal to the first part, is that we can listen to each other. We can listen to each other's stories and feel connected to one another, even if it's just through the internet. We might not meet in person all the time, you know. I get to meet them in person, but if you're listening to the podcast, you may not meet that other person, or those hundreds of people, in person, but you feel like you know them. They're people like you, and you can feel like part of that community, and that to me is like I've won if that's what happens. I've done what I set out to do.

In the Belly of Fuckability

Margaret Elysia Garcia

For the last three years, I've been following and writing about the plus size alternative modeling scene. It's a scene where women—large women, tattooed and/or pierced women, women well over thirty—participate in photo shoots, model for alternative clothing lines with "extended sizes," and post an endless amount of selfies on Instagram in an attempt to stake out some public space for themselves. It's an attempt to regain self-esteem lost to them in a culture that dictates that one's value is only relevant and worthy of love if one is young and thin. A culture that dictates women's worth by how "fuckable" they are. The camera—the public eye—it is long understood, does not belong to large women. Nor does sexual expression. Photos of plus size women are an attempt to take it all back.

If you want to be banned from social media, don't show a penis or a vagina or even a nipple. Show a belly. The belly in all its indulgent rolls and crevices and secret folds frightens the internet like nothing else can. The unrestrained, un-Spanxed, unabashed belly of a plus size woman is out there in defiance. No other body part has that kind of defiance. No other body part faces quite the same ridicule either. Large women are seen as mothers, the best friend and confidante. We are the nurse to young Juliet. We are not supposed to take center stage. Our bodies are supposed to be for comic relief and ridicule. But fat women, older women, are beginning to show our bellies.

So what are we afraid of? Why does the big belly get the censors? There's a photo of a big woman on the Fourth of July that was banned on Facebook. She had a red bikini top and tiny blue panties and a big white cowboy hat. But front and center and very well focused was her enormous belly. Banned for obscenity. No one comments on social media on the obsceneness of a thin woman's belly. Or even gives it much thought, except perhaps to congratulate thin women on their bellies' almost nonexistence.

The body-positive movement seeks to change that perception.

We are taught from a young age that the belly is our most unattractive feature (with the thighs a close second). When you grow up fat in our culture it is the part of the body that is never to be seen. Until very recently, bathing suits did not come in larger sizes—even now it's only niche clothing markets that already cater to larger women who do so.

The belly is the part of us that has the potential to make us unfuckable in the eyes of the mainstream. We are tampering with the male gaze by showing it off, by meeting the camera with it first, not last. We are obscuring and circumventing the display of what is supposed to turn us on.

It's not necessarily true, of course. There are those that find the belly attractive. I know cis men who look at bellies and have carnal caveman reactions to the idea of impregnating their partners. There are those that get off on pregnant partners, etc. There's a porn niche market specifically for belly play. But media-wise, culture-wise, the big belly—with its stretch marks and cellulite and/or bloating is seen as unsexy, and the commentators of social media have let it be known that a big belly renders posters of photos of ourselves "unfuckable." The arbiters of social norms think nothing of writing that in the comment section beneath a woman's photograph.

We spend a lifetime responding to people upholding a social norm that excludes us. They have decided we are worth discarding in social media, because we aren't meeting their standard. What these men (and women) don't realize is that the large women who post photos of themselves are posting for their own self-esteem, their own pride, their own coming out. It's not about attracting men. It's about coming out of hiding in our own large bodies and loving ourselves.

The belly is threatening. I look at my own adversarial belly. Two children have lived there and pushed and pulled it into a new shape that has been with me for the last fifteen years. I have not always been kind to mine—suffocating it in girdles and opaque tights, trying in vain to shape it into things it is not. Suffering through crunches that make me pee. Am I afraid to look larger than life? I have yet to have the courage to post a photo of my own belly. I am working up to it. It frightens me to do so, even while I admire those that have the courage to do it.

I have my suspicions as to why the belly is so threatening. Why it makes some so angry they lash out at strangers and demand they cover up in public or that they delete a photo for community standards or face social media banishment. Sometimes you can find a thin woman and a big woman in the same outfit. The Internet goes silent when asked why the thin woman's photo is not banned.

I think it has something to do with thin fragility. Underneath it all is fear that all we've been sold an unworkable concept, but we're too far invested now to turn back. It's a huge industry, this capitalizing on the fear of fat. We've been indoctrinated to accept that in order to be happy, loveable, fuckable, we have to first be thin. We've settled for this doggie treat reward system.

If I diet and lose weight, then I can have love.

If I flatten my hideous belly, then I can have sex.

If we welcome the fat belly into the fold of sexuality and love then our entire industry of dieting, gyms, personal trainers, surgeries, everything to do with denying what we look like becomes unnecessary. What if we just accepted who we are? What if our sexuality was based on the attraction we actually feel to one another instead of social norms? Freedom. And what's more, it's free.

The woman who has bought into the idea that joy and fulfillment can only be attained once one has dedicated their existence to diet and exercise doesn't want to acknowledge that her whole system is lie—that one can look like one enjoys food and, by extension, enjoys life. Enjoys sex. Enjoys.

What if big, full, indulgent bellies were not apologetic? What if that big belly itself were attractive? A fat woman owning the camera for herself hits too closely to the idea that we only deserve attention when we are thin. I understand this self-hatred. I have lived with the anger of hating my body. I have felt unfuckable because my belly might be in the way. We are bellying our way into thin territory.

I don't exactly love my body. But I have gotten to a point where my sexuality and ability to love is no longer alienated by it.

I am a fat woman. I am a plus size woman. A woman of size. Curvy, if you will. These are the terms used on a woman like me. Big girl. Zaftig. I am a number plus an X. I am algebra and variable.

When I sit in a chair, I envelope the chair. Parts of me ooze over the chair. The chair is gone. It is only me. For my children, when they were young, I was the chair, climbing on me, using my belly to stand with their thin taut young bodies that might one day look like mine. A fat woman has the incredible superpower of being invisible to the world and too visible at the very same time. You can stand at a counter waiting for service for an hour while all the thinner women around you are served. The sexy lingerie doesn't come in your size but the matronly nightgown does. There might be room for a dozen teenagers on an amusement park ride but there's no room for you because you require extra. We are assumed to know little if nothing about nutrition; we are presumed uneducated.

On an airplane, I purposefully forget to breathe. I suck up all the empty space within me to make myself momentarily smaller. I try and take up as little room as possible, knowing like I do, that I perhaps already take up too much. I take exceptional care not to eat anything fattening in public. No matter how tired I am, I take the stairs not the elevator, fearing the eye roll of thinner passengers making mental notes regarding the fat chick who clearly needs exercise getting off at the second floor. These are all the ways fat women are visible. The "bad habits" are visible. The humanity, the need for love and respect? That's the invisible part.

Those outside of my body might see things differently. But none of us have ever stopped and thought about a thin woman eating a bowl of ice cream in public and questioned her dietary habits. No one makes a mental note of the thin man who got off on the second floor.

Like embracing the belly, fat isn't a pejorative term to me; it just is. It exists. It's a way to describe what I would look like in a lineup. I'd be the fat murderer with curly hair. Or, at the very least, the murderer with the humungous ass and sizeable belly.

I'm fine with that. It both defines me and doesn't at the same time. I have my mind. My cultures. My children. My relationships. My obligations. My planet. My love of arts and fashion. So much more can define me than how big my body is. But it always sneaks in there, this feeling good or bad about the way I look, about how something fits me. About how I will be judged.

I am a child of my grandmother, a bigger woman, who I take after. She had six children, a miniscule waist and extra-sized hips. I look at her and see inescapable genetics. She was always dressed well, her belly hidden in wide skirts beneath a cinched waist. She worked in a department store and had to be fashionable, even into her late seventies when she retired. She used to tell me, "If you're going to be fat, be fashionable."

Ah! There's another one. We notice the fat chick in the ill-fitting shorts and the flip-flops as being slovenly in public. The thin woman who does the same gets the pass for looking like she rolled out of bed. It's sexy.

So here I am, a woman in her mid-forties unable to buy things off the rack. I stumble upon body positivity through the internet and motherhood and also my relocation away from my homeland of Los Angeles, where fatness is often part of a zip code (you can only be fat in the suburbs). I know that weird feeling of showing up for a job interview and being the fat person in the room and having no chance at the position, because the job requires one to be hip and young, and fat is never usually hip, and the clothes for fat usually make one not look young.

It's helpful to remember that body positivity activists and models were raised in the same thin only world that they are fighting and that all of their—our—my reactions and feelings about our bodies come from this same place. That is to say, they are all over the map. There's how we know intellectually we should react. There's how we actually verbalize and vocalize empowerment. There is also crying in the bathroom mirror. Maybe we just want photos of ourselves without explanation.

I am in awe of women bigger than I am who are not trying to hide their bodies. I am in awe of women showing off stretch marks, these sacred hashes that etch our bodies' transitions from one life into another. I think it's sexy. I am turned on.

Plus size modeling or alternative modeling is always in essence about selling something. Modeling is supposed to help sell clothing, a look, a style. But plus size modeling—especially via social media—is a way to both participate in and combat culture. It's selling the idea of acceptance and self-esteem and normalizing what is already a majority of American women—those above a size 12. It's selling the idea that the belly is beautiful and sexy not in deference to the male gaze but alone and isolated. The gaze is an inconsequential side dish. Sex appeal doesn't ask for permission anymore.

We as a culture are still uncomfortable with that. We have to not care. Last year I bought my first two-piece bathing suit since I was twelve. I bought three crop tops—the thing large women are never supposed to wear. I wear them anyway, and I like them.

It's easy to hide and comply with thin fragility, and it takes no explanation to do so. But a big bare-bellied woman suggests such decadence, such indulgence, and a fuckability all her own.

Last Drink

Leilani Clark

I had my last drink on February 26, 2017, the night of the Academy Awards. My last sip of wine entered my throat right around the moment when *La La Land* was announced as Best Picture. I remember a man sliding onto the stage, whispering in Warren Beatty's ear after he opened the envelope and announced the winner, how surprised the actor looked, and how a second later he declared *Moonlight* to be the real winner.

I remember—the awards were over; I was in my friend's dark, cramped kitchen, ranting about cancer, marriage, the Trump administration, toxic masculinity, climate change—whatever recent terrors rose up in my muddled, wine-soaked brain. Our daughters, both four, were playing in the living room. They stopped and watched me with concern.

"Why are you crying, Mommy?" my daughter asked.

Then: "Mommy, stop talking, please."

We left a few minutes later. I was drunk. I strapped my daughter into her car seat and drove us to my mother-in-law's house, where we were staying for the week. The line between lanes wavered as the red wine coursed through my body, having its way with my prefrontal cortex.

"I'm fine, I'm fine, nothing to see here," I told myself, pushing away the fear that my luck was about to run out. I'd finally get that DUI I'd somehow avoided for the last twenty years. I'd been driving under the influence off and on since the age of twenty-one, when I'd launched like a cliff diver into a lagoon of binge drinking.

•

Why did I drink? For one, alcohol was a quick fix for my persistent generalized anxiety and hypervigilance. I experienced the first sensation of unclenching immediately after my first sip off alcohol when I was sixteen—a sickly-sweet berry wine cooler at a friend's house in Hacienda Heights, Los Angeles. "How Soon Is Now" by The Smiths played on the stereo. After two wine coolers, I found myself rolling around on the floor cracking up at crushes with my best friend. Grumpy goth boys in black tee shirts and black eyeliner gave us dirty looks, but we didn't care. We'd found liberation thanks to Bartles and James.

Alcohol lent me an easy bravado for the price of grueling hangovers. Drinking—heavily—became my favorite key to the door of the landscape of not giving a *fuuuuuck*. Sucking down whiskey straight from the bottle felt like a feminist act. For a few hours, the self-loathing dissipated, as did the uglies that had plagued me since junior high school when I learned from the other kids that I was too fat and poor for anything but disdain and severe bullying. It allowed me to make passes at people and to explore my formerly repressed sexuality; it became a potent and dependable form of liquid courage.

It also my genetic inheritance. The list of problem drinkers—active, recovering, and dead— down both family lineages is long. When I took that first drink, my neural pathways sighed with familiarity.

·

My daughter and I survived the two-mile drive that night of the Oscars. "It's late," my mother-in-law said, frowning as she opened the front door for us. With her help, I got my daughter to bed, and then went into the guest room, where I slept on a thin mattress under a pile of blankets. I watched an episode of *Grey's Anatomy* but struggled to follow the plot; everything was a blurry, and neither the television nor the wine salved the pain of being. It was always the same. A warm, blissful, euphoria followed by a crash back into the anxiety, self-loathing, and anger—the next morning's shame.

I passed out halfway through the second episode of *Grey's*. A few hours later, I woke to my daughter's screams. All week, she'd had furious nightmares. I stumbled to her, my mouth stinking and sour, my brain like a house of crumbling stone ruins. I wanted only to sleep—fuck, let me sleep—but I had to soothe a hysterical child. My mother-in-law got up from the couch and came into the bathroom, where I was trying to get my daughter to sit on the toilet as she screamed and writhed across on the yellowish linoleum floor. I was shrieking on the inside.

"I can't deal with this," I said, stumbling back to bed. Fading back into a thick, drunken sleep, I heard my mother-in-law soothing my daughter, walking her back into a safety and calm with a soft lullaby. Quiet descended in the darkness. I was nothing but a horrible mother. I'd walked away from my one absolute responsibility. But I wasn't capable of soothing myself, much less another human.

I woke the next day, as to be expected, with a searing hangover and the shame to match. Cottonmouthed and nauseous, I somehow got dressed, ate breakfast, and prepared my daughter for pre-school. I hid how awful I felt with small talk. My head pounded and my gut churned. The wine seemed to have burned a hole in my stomach.

•

My Oscar night binge came on the heels of a fifty-day streak of sobriety. In late December of the previous year, I'd decided to try quitting drinking for ninety days. I'd actually toyed with the idea of quitting alcohol for the past decade. I was forty-three, and the first time I'd attempted to stop had been when I was in my early thirties. Actually, it went even farther back; I'd managed to quit drinking between the ages of seventeen and nineteen, until I got sucked back into a punk rock lifestyle centered on cheap beer, wild parties, and five-dollar shows. So here I was again. Plus, my new therapist was haranguing me at our weekly sessions to eliminate alcohol from my life.

"You're playing Russian Roulette," she'd warned me more than once. Which pissed me off, even as I suspected she was correct. Several of my family members are either in recovery or died of alcohol-related maladies. When I drank, I started fights. I became overcome with emotion. I never stopped at one. When this therapist called me an alcoholic, I cringed. It stunk of failure. I couldn't hold my liquor. I wasn't like other people. Why did I have to give up life's greatest security blanket?

To bolster the daunting goal of not drinking for three months, I signed up for an online program with the cringeworthy name of "Sexy Sobriety." I'd read a book by the facilitator, a vegan health coach from Australia. Inspired by her transformation from heavy drinker to a happy, brunch-loving sober lady with glowing skin, expertly applied red lip-stick, and glossy hair, I paid three hundred dollars for the daily challenge, which involved lots of home spa days, journaling, and green smoothies. I could have attended an Alcoholics Anonymous meeting for free, but

I wasn't nearly ready to admit I was powerless over alcohol, much less embrace anything resembling a higher power. I wasn't ready to admit to anything.

.

After dropping my daughter at preschool, I came back to my mother-in-law's house and retreated to the bedroom. It was a sunny, beautiful afternoon, and I had work deadlines, but headache and relentless nausea made everything feel impossible. I rewatched the episode of *Grey's Anatomy* I'd passed out to the night before, ate snacks, and binge-watched more episodes, letting my mother-in-law pick up my daughter from school.

Later that week, I saw my therapist. When I admitted that I'd gotten drunk again, I expected to be chastised—maybe not overtly, but I knew she'd be disappointed in me. Instead, she responded with a kind, compassionate smile. It was only a slip, she said, it wasn't the end of the world. I could keep going on this path. I wanted to believe her. I didn't want my craving for alcohol to be what defined me. I didn't want to be stuck in this pattern forever. I wanted liberation.

From that session on, I started taking sobriety more seriously. Looking back, I took recovery on like a project, with an edge of spirited investigation. I listened to tons of sobriety podcasts: *Recovery Elevator*, *HOME podcast*, *The Bubble Hour*, *This Naked Mind*, *Tara Brach*. When I craved a beer, I'd pop in earbuds and listen to the stories. I read books on the Twelve Steps and sober living. I still do this.

Eventually, I told a few trusted friends that I was taking a long—possibly forever—break from alcohol. When I told my dad, I broke down crying, despite the fact that he'd quit drinking three decades before. He told me his own story of getting sober through a Veteran's Administration outpatient rehab when he was thirty-three. I'd watched that all through eleven-year-old eyes, but I'd never heard his version—how he had lived the experience.

"Quitting drinking is the best decision I ever made," he told me.

At the same time, I resisted Alcoholics Anonymous. I'd gone to a couple of meetings in the past, when I was flirting with sobriety and thought it was the only option for disentangling from alcohol's grip, but they left me itchy and uncomfortable in my skin. I had close family members and dear friends who swore by A.A. But I couldn't get into the *Big Book*, the stories about business men from the fifties who couldn't hold their liquor and ended up pissing their pants and pissing off their wives. The program's language felt patronizing, patriarchal, and archaic—the program infantilizing and simplistic. Or maybe I just didn't want to face reality.

Whatever it was, about three months into my experiment, I came across a book called *Refuge Recovery*, which laid out a "Buddhist path to recovering from addiction." I went on the Refuge Recovery website and discovered a meeting—or sangha—two blocks from my house. I dragged myself there the following Saturday, feeling like a failure just for walking through the door. I couldn't hold my liquor. There was something wrong with me. Everybody else could drink beer and wine and have a good time and know when to stop. And here I was, an addict, a hungry ghost who couldn't control herself. Never mind that everyone else in the room was there for similar reasons—not necessarily alcohol-related but addiction all the same.

A small group of about six people sat in a circle surrounding a lone candle next to a colorful ceramic laughing Buddha statue. The facilitator, a woman with grayish honey-blonde hair and a flowy boho blouse greeted me with a smile. She began the meeting with the ringing of a bell, followed by a reading of the Four Noble Truths and the Eightfold Path. It was like listening to another language, all this stuff about compassion, generosity, nonattachment, renunciation, and—most challenging—forgiveness. We introduced ourselves by our first names—and that was it: no expectation to identify as an addict or alcoholic. The facilitator guided the group into a twenty-minute silent meditation. I sat, fidgety, nervous, distracted by noise of the street. The meditation was followed by reading from the *Refuge Recovery* book and then a period of open sharing. I noticed that talking honestly about sobriety and its many challenges seemed to release the shame, like air releasing from a helium balloon allowing it to sink into a harmless heap on the floor.

I didn't share that first day. But I did talk at the next meeting. Four months in, I couldn't not share. Telling stories about my week felt like survival. I only needed to be witnessed and heard by others who understood what it felt like to crave something and not submit to the craving. When, to my own surprise, I managed to make it six months without drinking, I shared it with the group. The sangha responded with a few claps and smiles. I didn't get a chip. I didn't get a certificate. I kept going. Fifteen months later—I keep going. I keep choosing not to drink.

•

Sometimes, when I remember to take the time to sit on my pillow and close my eyes, I meditate on forgiveness. I asked my daughter to forgive me for being a human mother with all my flaws and thirsty genetics. For having a craving that I couldn't master. For putting us in danger, because I didn't know anything else. I forgive myself over and over again.

Most days, monkey mind still has its way with me. Calm is elusive, and I wonder how I can make it through a lifetime without having another drink. What the fuck? In the midst of the craving, anger, sadness, self-pity, I tell myself a term you'll hear a lot in Refuge Recovery circles: "I love you. Keep going." I return to the breath. This moment. This moment. This moment. This moment, I am not drinking. This moment, I am free from the myth that plagued me for so many years—that alcohol made me whole. In this moment, I am liberated. In this moment, I breathe.

How to Be A Genderqueer Feminist

Laurie Penny

Feminism's focus on women can be alienating to queer people and anyone question-ing the gender binary. But it doesn't have to be.

I've never felt quite like a woman, but I've never wanted to be a man either. For as long as I can remember, I've wanted to be something in between. To quote Ruby Rose: "I called myself a girl, but only because my options were limited." I always assumed that everyone felt that way.

I discovered my mistake one day in junior school, when a few of the girls in my class were chatting about which boys they fancied. I wasn't often invited to participate in these sorts of secret female chats. Even back then, there was something odd about me, a strangeness that was partly about identity but also about the fact that I wore shapeless black smocks, rarely brushed my hair, and tended to jump when anyone spoke to me.

I couldn't think of anything to say that would be both interesting and true. So I mentioned that I often felt like I was a gay boy in a girl's body. Just like everyone else, right?

I could tell from their faces that this was not right. It was very, very wrong.

This was a time before Tumblr, when very few teenagers were talking about being genderqueer or transmasculine. The women I'd heard of who were allowed to dress and talk and behave like boys were all lesbians. I often wished I was a lesbian. But I almost always fancied boys, and if you fancied boys, you had to behave like a girl. And behaving like a girl was the one subject, apart from sports, that I always failed.

It was around this time that I first read second-wave feminist Germaine Greer. She seemed to explain fundamental truths that every other adult in my small universe of school, home, and the library seemed equally anxious to ignore, and it helped that there were also dirty jokes. I clung to *The Female Eunuch* with the zeal of a convert and the obsession of a prepubescent nerd. I wrote Greer a letter with my very favorite pens and almost imploded with excitement when she wrote back, on a postcard that had koalas on it. I resolved right then and there that one day I would be a feminist and a writer just like her.

According to Greer, liberation meant understanding that whatever you were in life, you were a woman first. Her writing helped me understand how society saw me—and every other female person I'd ever met. We were not human beings first: we were just girls. Looking back, though, that militant insistence on womanhood before everything is part of the reason it's taken me a decade to admit that, in addition to being a feminist, I'm genderqueer. That I'm here to fight for women's rights, that I play for the girls' team, but I have never felt like much of a woman at all.

I grew up on second-wave feminism, but that didn't stop me starving myself.

I was anorexic for large parts of my childhood, for many complex, painful, altogether common reasons, of which gender dysphoria was just one. I felt trapped by the femaleness of my body, by my growing breasts and curves. Not eating made my periods stop. It made my breasts disappear. On the downside, it also turned me into a manic, suicidal mess, forced me to drop out of school, and traumatized my entire family.

At seventeen, I wound up in the hospital, in an acute eating disorders ward, where I stayed for six months.

The window in my hospital room did not open more than a crack. Just wide enough to sniff a ration of fresh air before I got weighed in the morning. I turned up with all my curves starved away, with my hair cropped close to the bones of my skull, androgynous as a skeleton, insisting that people call me not Laura but Laurie—a boy's name in England. I was too unwell to be pleased that I finally looked as genderless as I felt. At that point, I just wanted to die. Mostly of shame.

Long story short: I didn't die. I got better. But not before I let some well-meaning medical professionals bully me back onto the right side of the gender binary.

Psychiatric orthodoxy tends to lag behind social norms, and doctors are very busy people. So it's not their fault that, less than twenty years after homosexuality was removed from the official list of mental disorders, the doctors treating me took one look at my short hair and baggy clothes and feminist posters and decided that I was a repressed homosexual and coming out as gay would magically make me start eating again.

Like I said, they were trying.

There was only one problem. I wasn't gay. I was sure about that. I was bisexual, and I was very much hoping that one day when I wasn't quite so weird and sad I'd be able to test the theory in practice. It took a long time to persuade the doctors of that. I can't remember how, and I'm not sure I want to. I think diagrams may have been involved. It was a very dark time.

I was too unwell to enjoy looking as genderless as I felt.

Anyway. Eventually they gave up trying to make me come out and decided to make me go back in. If you weren't a lesbian, the route to good mental health was to "accept your femininity." You needed to grow your hair and wear dresses and stop being so angry all the time. You needed to accept the gender and sex you had been assigned, along with all the unspoken rules of behavior involved. You needed to get a steady boyfriend and smile nicely and work hard. I repeat: these people didn't mean to do me or anyone else lasting psychological damage. Just like every other institution through the centuries that has tried to force queer and deviant people to be normal for their own good, they truly were trying to help.

For five years, I struggled to recover. I tried hard to be a good girl. I tried to stick to the dresses, the makeup, the not being quite so strange and cross and curious all the time. For five years, I shoved my queerness deep, deep down into a private, frightened place where it only emerged in exceptional circumstances, like a bottle of cheap vodka, or a showing of The Rocky Horror Picture Show, or both. But being a good girl didn't work out very well, so I cut the difference, cut my hair short, and went back to being an angry feminist.

And feminism saved my life. I got better. I wrote, and I had adventures, and I returned to politics, and I made friends. I left the trauma of the hospital far behind me and tried to cover up my past with skirts and makeup.

Today, I'm a feminist and a writer, but I no longer valorize Germaine Greer so blindly. For one thing, Greer is one of many feminists, some of them well-respected, who believe transgender people are dangerous to the movement. Their argument is pretty simple. It boils down to the idea that trans people reinforce binary thinking about gender when they choose to join the other team instead of challenging what it means to be a man or a woman. Greer has called trans women a "ghastly parody" of femaleness.

Greer's comments about trans women exemplify the generational strife between second-wave feminists who sought to expand the definition of "woman" and the younger feminists who are looking for new gender categories altogether. This tension has been cruel to trans women, who have been cast as men trying to infiltrate women's spaces. But it's alienating to all corners of the LGBT community.

By the time I was well enough to consider swapping the skirts for cargo pants, changing my pronouns and the way I walked through the world, I'd become well-known as, among other things, a feminist writer.

At twenty-four, I wrote columns about abortion rights and sexual liberation and books about how to live and love under capitalist patriarchy. In response, young women wrote to me on a regular basis, telling me that my work helped inspire them to live more freely in their femaleness. They admired me because I was a "strong woman." Would I be betraying those girls if I admitted that half the time I didn't feel like a woman at all?

So I hoarded up my excuses for not coming out. I carefully described myself as "a person with cis privilege" rather than "a cis person" when the conversation came up. I decided that the daily emotional overheads of being a feminist writer on the internet were enough for now.

And I waited.

Over the past few years, more and more of my friends and comrades have come out as trans. I've been privileged to be part of a strong and supportive queer community, and it has helped that a great many of my close friends are both trans and feminist. For them, there doesn't seem to be a problem with fighting for gender equality while fighting transphobia—which sometimes, sadly, means that they're also fighting feminists.

Many of the critiques of trans politics from feminists through the decades have been openly bigoted, the sort of self-justifying theories that let people feel okay about driving other, more vulnerable people out of their jobs, outing them to their families and welfare advisers, and putting them in danger.

Buried under the bullshit, though, are some reasonable critiques. One is that people who claim a trans identity are only doing so because gender roles are so restrictive and oppressive in the first place. Sadly, many trans people are forced to play into tired gender stereotypes in order to "prove" their identity to everyone from strangers to medical gatekeepers—not long ago, one friend of mine was queried at a gender clinic because she showed up to her appointment in baggy jeans, which was evidence of her "lack of commitment" to life as a woman. I repeat: even trousers are political.

I regret that there wasn't more language, dialogue, and support for trans and genderqueer kids when I was a teenager and needed it most. I regret that by the time I had found that community and that language, I was too traumatized by hospital, by prejudice, and by the daily pressures of living and working in a frenzied, wearily misogynist media landscape to take advantage of the freedoms on offer. I regret the fear that kept me from coming out for so many years.

Would I betray the girls who looked up to me if I admitted that I didn't feel like a woman at all?

When I say I regret those things, I mean that I try not to think about them too much, because the knowledge of how different things could have been if I'd known as a teenager that I wasn't alone, the thought of how else I might have lived and loved and dated if I'd had the words and the community I have now just a little sooner, opens cold fingers of longing somewhere in my stomach and squeezes tight. But when they let go, I'm also glad.

The journey I took as I came to terms with my own identity—the journey that will continue as long as I live—all of that has led me to where I am now.

More than anything, I'm excited. I'm excited to see how life is going to be different for the queer, trans, and even cis kids, growing up in a world that has more language for gender variance. I'm excited to find out what sort of lives they will lead, from the genderqueer activists in the audience at my last reading to the barista with the orange mohawk who handed me the cup of tea I'm clutching for dear life as I write alone in this café, trying to believe that writing this piece is something other than gross self-indulgence.

The barista is wearing two name badges. One says their name; the other one says, in thick chalk capitals, "I am not a girl. My pronouns are They/Them."

So here it is. I consider "woman" to be a made-up category, an intangible, constantly changing idea with as many different definitions as there are cultures on Earth. You could say the same thing about "justice" or "money" or "democracy"—these are made-up ideas, stories we tell ourselves about the shape of our lives, and yet they are ideas with enormous real-world consequences. Saying that gender is fluid doesn't mean that we have to ignore sexism. In fact, it's the opposite.

Of course, gender norms play into the trans experience. How can they not? But being trans or genderqueer, even for cis-passing people like me, is not about playing into those norms. It's about throwing them out. Some "radical" feminists argue that trans and genderqueer people actually shore up the gender binary by seeking to cross or straddle it rather than setting it on fire. To which I'd say: it is also possible to jump over a burning building.

In fact, watch me.

Only when we recognize that "manhood" and "womanhood" are made-up categories, invented to control human beings and violently imposed, can we truly understand the nature of sexism, of misogyny, of the way we are all worked over by gender in the end.

Coming out is an individual journey, but it is a collective weapon. Questioning gender—whether that means straddling the gender binary, crossing it, or breaking down its assumptions wherever you happen to stand—is an essential part of the feminism that has sustained me through two decades of personal and political struggle. In the end, feminists and the LGBT community have this in common: we're all gender traitors. We have broken the rules of good behavior assigned to us at birth, and we have all suffered for it.

But here's one big way I differ from a lot of my genderqueer friends: I still identify, politically, as a woman. My identity is more complex than simply female or male, but as long as women's reproductive freedom is under assault, sex is also a political category, and, politically, I'm still on the girls' team.

I don't think that everyone who was dumped into the "female" category at birth has a duty to identify as a woman, politically or otherwise. Because identity policing, if you'll indulge me in a moment of high theoretical language, is fucked up and bullshit. This is just how it happens to work for me.

We're all gender traitors.

In a perfect world, perhaps I'd be telling a different story. I'm never going to be able to say for sure whether in that perfect world, that world without sexism and gender oppression, that world without violence or abuse, where kittens dance on rainbows and nobody has ever heard of Donald Trump, I would feel the need to call myself genderqueer. My hunch is that I would; and all I've got for you is that hunch, along with a stack of feminist theory books and a pretty nice collection of flat caps.

I am a woman, politically, because that's how people see me and that's how the state treats me. And sometimes I'm also a boy. Gender is something I perform, when I put on my binder or paint my nails. When I walk down the street. When I talk to my boss. When I kiss my partner in their makeup and high heels.

I don't want to see a world without gender. I want to see a world where gender is not oppressive or enforced, where there are as many ways to express and perform and relate to your own identity as there are people on Earth. I want a world where gender is not painful but joyful.

But until then, we've got this one. And for as long as we all have to navigate a gender binary that's fundamentally broken and a sex class system that seeks to break us, I'm happy to be a gender traitor.

I'm a genderqueer woman—and a feminist. My preferred pronouns are "she" or "they." I believe we're on our way to a better world. And you can call me Laurie.

Coming Out as Trans in a Small Hometown

an interview with artist Ariel Erskine

Dani: How was it transitioning in the same community you grew up in?
Ariel: I think initially it was pretty stressful. When I would run into someone there was that moment when I thought: Do they recognize me, and if they don't, do I bother saying anything? Is it better to accept that I'm passable? I'm really extroverted, so I'm like, "I haven't seen this person in fifteen years and I want to say hi to them anyway and see if they can deal with it." A lot of times it takes like five minutes. I was this person you knew really well! I don't really like referring to myself and explaining who I was in masculine terms or using my old name; just because it's not me and it never really was. I've taken off that costume finally. That's the only frustrating part, saying, "I was so-and-so." Some people, you can see the processing. It's kind of interesting and fun as a people watcher (laughs). I run into people I haven't seen in the last six months, and they don't recognize me. For people that do recognize me, they have a harder time processing it. They are the ones who gender me more or try to overcompensate, and it's terrible! I have one friend who I was friends with through my first coming out period, and that next week he ordered for me at dinner. And he ordered me white wine, and I hate white wine! I'm a bourbon drinker. It's not like I had my first dose of estrogen and started loving white wine.
Dani: That really makes you look at how engrained our gender roles are...
Ariel: I came out June 1 [2016]. I was done playing that role. The first month, I sort of eased into it a bit. But by July 1, I was already presenting, I had settled into the name I wanted and knew exactly who I was. I was very quick to be who I am but what has taken a bit longer is to process how society views me, especially people who think I'm a gendered female. I went from a place of sympathy to a place of empathy. I

could be sympathetic to how women are treated, and it really sucks that women are treated a certain way. But experiencing it is *sooooo* different.

Dani: I saw your Facebook post about being catcalled. . .

Ariel: I had an experience that was more recent than that. I was at a gas station, and I was taking my mom to a concert, and I had just gotten off of work. My car was full of all of my kids' stuff, and I was cleaning the garbage out of my car, and it didn't even occur to me that I'd get hit on. There was a guy in a car staring at me, and he got out and started following me around the car and started asking about my stockings . . . they were really cute with a pattern on them but they weren't fishnets or anything. And it was a new enough experience that I didn't think about why he was asking me about my tights while I was cleaning garbage out of my car. It was the least sexiest environment possible.

Dani: Yeah, the environment doesn't really matter, does it?

Ariel: Right. And as I was leaving he says, "I just want to let you know that I couldn't help and see you bend over." And I was like, "This conversation is done." And he says to me, "Hey, I'm just trying to tell you you're hot!" I didn't know how to handle the situation as a target. And he told me I should learn how to take compliments. I had heard this happens, but it was so different to experience it that way. It's really informative. And I'm someone who is still new enough in my transition that I want to be validated. In my head, yes, I want to be seen as an attractive female by a hetero man, but it is *not* validating. It is actually quite different. I felt sick, I wanted to go home and throw up. I was shaking and talked to my older son. I didn't know how to handle it.

Dani: Even if we do know how to handle it, we shouldn't be put in a situation where we have to be on guard. Like men are entitled to a "thank you" for harassing us.

Ariel: Right, it's that entitlement that I'm not used to seeing. About five months ago I had an experience at a beach in the middle of the day. I was collecting seashells for a project. It was a super femme moment, and I loved it, and it was great! But I just didn't think that being at the beach during the day posed a risk. This guy followed me around near a cliff and really forced himself on me. Some friends said I should have hit him, but you know what, that's not the point. Even if I defended myself and got away, every time I go to the beach I worry about that so I feel violated in that sense. And now when I go to the gas station I think I probably shouldn't clean my car out or bend over because some guy will check me out. I have to think about these things now. Everything you do, it changes how you act, and that's the part I didn't really key on when I wasn't seen this way, when I wasn't experiencing it firsthand. That same night after the gas station, I was talking to my mom about it. She grew up in the forties and fifties, and her reaction was like, "He went a little too far," but she just accepted it as normal behavior. It made me really angry and really sad.

Dani: What has your experience been with medical professionals?

Ariel: I kind of lucked out. And I know that Kaiser is the brunt of a lot of jokes, but someone somewhere in Kaiser really is pro-trans, and they are really on the forefront of trans health care. They have two trans clinics, one in San Francisco and one in Oakland. Once I reached them and talked to them, everything changed. I had pretty much come out a week before, I knew I wanted to start hormones as soon as possible. My fifteen-year marriage was imploding, and my whole world was going crazy. And the RN had me take a deep breath, had me calm down. They still have you see a therapist in case you need someone, and you see an endocrinologist. A week later, they walked me through the process. My endocrinologist saw me for an hour. And I started hormones that day. It was an amazing experience.

I left on this super high, though on the drive home I was really suicidal. On the one hand, I had met all of these people who were supportive, and I was starting my hormones and everything seemed on track, but at home, it was a battleground where I was constantly being told I was destroying the life we'd built, and there was this moment where I thought, "This is probably going to be the best it ever gets." It was the most suicidal I have ever been. I wasn't thinking I could be an effective parent, and I have a whole history with the Golden Gate Bridge, partly because I had a friend who killed themselves. They had come out in the nineties, and they were supposed to come to my house and never showed up, and I found out later they were having identity issues and thought they wouldn't be accepted. So every time I cross the Golden Gate I think about this friend who was in the closet. I had never walked across the bridge, and last year on my birthday in April I decided to walk across, and during that process I knew that I really needed to come out. So fast forward to that day in July, I was driving home and thought to myself, I could just stop and end on a high note. But I didn't. I'd like to say that I didn't because of my kids. I'd like to be that awesome person, but then I can get into this whole advocacy for depression. I'm very manic depressive. I'm not as safe when I'm manic.

Then it was just a process, so then I'd go down to San Francisco every two weeks for my estrogen shots. Thursdays became my thing. It was very therapeutic, my "me" time. As you know, as a parent and someone who works, we don't get a lot of "me" time.

Dani: Any negative side effects from hormones?

Ariel: I think I had so much going on initially, in the first six months, that it was hard to know what were hormones and what was the other stuff I was dealing with. The big difference I noticed was crying over happy stuff. Everyone said I'd be so much more emotional, and I thought that if something sad happened, I would cry, but that wasn't it. It was the happy stuff! I remember the first time it was a commercial and music kicked in, and I was so happy the dog was okay. And it was big, fat beautiful tears, and I loved it. It's inconvenient at times. So definitely, my emotions are way more on the surface. They are definitely there. There are days when I know I need to go home and cry; it's gonna happen if I want to or not. So I know I need to put on the songs that I like, get some red wine. . .

Dani: Cry night!

Ariel: Yes, definitely! I was a person who so didn't cry. I was so good at the role that I played. So bottled up. I am a very expressive person but my mannerisms have always been much more feminine. I tend to gush a lot and talk with my hands, but I couldn't do that as the person who I thought I was supposed to be. The more I played that male role, the more I was surrounded by people who liked that role. It reinforced it. I like to describe it as: I was a six-year-old girl who got cast in a play, but I had to play the boy part, and the play ended but the role didn't. My first real cognizant moment was when I was six. I found a cute pink cardigan, and I remember trying it on and loving it and knowing I'd get yelled at it I wore it. I grew up in farm country, and I loved getting dirty and playing outside, but I loved this other part too, but I knew that was not okay, and I felt really bad about it. And it has been since then I've had to bury it.

Over the years I learned to accent the things I did like. I've always been into movement. I wanted to do dance, but I did martial arts instead. And I love martial arts. I did it the most masculine way possible. I did kickboxing, fighting, I dislocated my shoulder, my knee, I broke my nose, broke my jaw. I fought for years. And I constantly worked to put on muscle, I was twenty pounds heavier then. I looked like a skinhead in my old driver's license.

Dani: How has it been dealing with the different messages you're getting about feminizing yourself through cosmetic surgery, feminine tattoos, etc.?

Ariel: I'll get more directly to that. . . . I have a really close friend who has been super supportive from the get-go and she's constantly validating me and says she thinks I'm even more beautiful as trans (she's pan), but at the same time she has—and not just her but people in my life who are supportive, but they like to tell me pretty much how to be as a woman: you're being too submissive, if you're being a woman you have to be stronger. I spent X amount of years being a role and being the best version of that role, and in every situation I had to figure out the best way to be, and that's really not who I am. If there's a potential physical situation, I can fight. I've had training! I don't forget that. But I am not that person. This is who I am and why is that a bad thing? I think there is, especially among the older vanguard of the feminist community, and rightly so, they are slightly more: "We have the right to be masculine," and I understand that because they were denied the right to be that way, but it doesn't mean there aren't femme people. You can be a cisgender male and be femme, you can be a cisgender female and be femme, you can be a trans this or that. I have a friend who is a trans man but likes to be very feminine and wears eyeliner, and he's like, "Why do I have to be a bodybuilder? I just identify as a man, but I still like to be emo and wear eyeliner."

For myself, I'm a pretty femme person. I love fairies and Disney princesses and mermaids! Give me shit about it, I don't care! Yes, this is my legal name, and it is from the *Little Mermaid* (laughs)! I watched the movie forty times as a little girl. While little boys wanted to date the little mermaid, I wanted to *be* the little mermaid. So when it came time to change my name I knew this was it, beyond a doubt, and people give me shit and say it's too feminine. I constantly get these messages. Just as we're starting to train society that identity and sexuality are different things, presentation can be different as well. You can have a masculine trans woman and a feminine trans man, and hopefully we can get rid of the whole binary concept altogether and recognize gender on a spectrum.

I had some people kind of accuse me, because I was going from one extreme to another, that I was reinforcing the binary gender. No, that's my path, and the reason I can go from one to another is because there is a spectrum to go on. And lots of people end up in the middle, and I'm a big advocate for using "they," all of those beautiful spectrums. Especially younger people in the trans community, they are really nonbinary, and I love them!

Along with trying to process that it's okay to be femme. So first I had to get that this is how I see it, and then there is how others see me. For me, I was forced to play this role, and when I came out, it was like taking a costume off, and now I could be me. I've always identified, and I'm just going to stop trying to be something. So a lot of people still see me as this guy trying to be female, and some would get mad if I tried to do anything stereotypical. It was till them trying to force me to be who I "should" be. My ex even asked me if I was going to be scared of spiders now. . .

Dani: Ha! So how do you navigate that and stay true to who you are despite the messaging you get from friends/family/society?

Ariel: Again, I didn't initially. I did deal with a lot of complications from my marriage, and in some ways that helped. Once I got over some of the suicidal thoughts, I had to deal with everything that came with the end of a fifteen-year marriage; that's a long time to be married. I had to deal with that and come to terms with co-parenting, and we had a band together and everything else. In dealing with all of that, it kind of allowed the transition part to happen in the background for the first six months. But at the same time, I didn't feel like I got to deal with a lot of things, like I should have focused on it a little more. It was a balance, but now I'm in a place where things are more stable. Now I'm trying to process all of the mixed messages about what I should or shouldn't be. That was part of what helped me to decide about feminizing my face. I decided I was going to do something that was affirming to me, and it is totally my choice, and I don't care what you think. Kaiser doesn't cover facial feminization as of yet. I decided I was just going to work on my nose. I had a very prominent nose, it was just like my father's. The dysphoria was only getting worse to the point where I hated looking in the mirror and I was getting sick. I thought I'd never look feminine enough with this very masculine feature. So I cashed out my retirement account, and I went for it. I had a big Roman statue nose, and now it's definitely more feminine and natural looking. I looked like I got hit by a bat for two months (laughs). My mother is Russian, and I look way more Russian now instead of the strong Scottish nose, and it was worth it. And the fact that I stood up for myself and look how I want to look, it's important

A lot of people support wanting to get bottom surgery, but "You want to change your face?!? That's not okay! You shouldn't do that!" Bottom surgery is potentially life threatening and more dangerous, but why are you okay with that and not my face? It made me realize that, A, people don't have to look downstairs if they don't want to, and, B, it kind of goes to this same idea of telling women what they should or shouldn't do. It's like guys telling women: "Don't wear makeup, I love you without makeup." You think you're being awesome, but you're still telling a woman what to do. If you want to do it, do it. I don't spend twenty minutes doing my eyeliner for some guy's approval. I'm doing it because I love that 1940s/50s Audrey Hepburn style, and I think it's gorgeous and classy.

Dani: What does self-care look like for you?

Ariel: It's something I've really just started to get into, and luckily this whole open gender fluid, artsy community is really into self-care. I have this friend who has this legitimate degree in herbalism, and she has these art potlucks, and I go over there, and we make lotions from scratch, and it's all super rich feminine energy, and it's very open to all genders and gender expressions. It's very in line with this softer, more feminine spirituality, and that's been really healing, having this group I can go and talk to, being free to express myself and my issues with being seen and treated as a woman in society, for good and bad, and learning how to negotiate and navigate that and having a support system. It makes me kind of sad for guys who feel like they need to live—even if they are cisgender and identify as male—I think there are a lot of times they might feel where they can't seek out that kind of support, and that is how society unfortunately treats men, as well.

With all of the hormones and surgeries going on, I'm much more sensitive to my diet than I was before. I get wicked bad hangovers, and it's because my body is processing the hormones.

Dani: And we're getting older!

Ariel: Exactly! It's that combination, and my body is legitimately going through a second puberty. And my estrogen is through the roof. I was like, "Give me more, give me more!" And then I got my labs back, and my doctor was like, "You gotta cut back, your liver will get destroyed." I was three times the upper limit of what a cisgender woman should have in her system. I thought, "How can that be bad?" (laughs) I was actually more even-tempered.

Getting a lot of labs and being cognizant of my sleep and what I eat is so important too. And because I'm going through so much transition not only having access to this wonderful support group but needing it and relying on it more too. I'm just so happy to have finally taken off that costume.

Origin

Wendy-O Matik

The binary gender dilemma is not an easy one
I stumble over inadequate words
and pronouns
and the intention behind their secret agendas.
Because I am biologically woman,
I am a walking assumption
the moment I step outside the safety of my door.
Because society defines me
by my cunt
by my tits
by my uterus
by the number of children I can
or cannot conceive,
I have felt the pressures of social conformity
narrowing my choices in life.
Because I feel comfortable mentally and emotionally
with the fluidity of gender
within myself,
I am less boxed in than most.
With fearless lovers of mine,
We are an amalgamation of woman and man
man and man
woman and woman
all at the same time
We toss out our gender along with our egos
and role play in the unknown

We forget our gender
We dismantle our preconceived notions of the sexes
We fuck our sexually limiting categories
We suck and kick and bite and cry
our way through to distortion
blurring the paradigm
to fit our fantasy.

Which brings me back to the
revolution of bodies and minds
the physics of our empowerment
virgin touches the whore
brown eats out black eats out red eats out white eats out yellow
cellular meets molecular
type A+ sucks type O
planetary dark matter bumps into galactic anti-matter
intuition tops cognition
hormones fucking hormones
fucking single celled amoebas
the origin of all living things.

In my fantasy
I cannot determine where my cock
becomes your cock
I cannot distinguish your fist from my pussy
From the primordial scream of our loving making
I am not concerned about our division of sex
our uncommon ground
our differences
I am sealing our fate in my ejaculation
because as a biological woman
I can
And because I am man enough to meet you half way
around the linguistic burden that we all share,
the borders of he-she-it
I lift up this final teardrop of our human essence
in reverence for the time to come

when you and I
cannot see or feel the separation
only the bloodline that runs in both our veins
as one.

Fucking Patriarchy through Radical Relationships

Wendy-O Matik

There is no remedy for love, but to love more.
—Henry David Thoreau

We lifted our shields in solidarity
for the coming revolution
and went to battle for love
knowing that centuries from now
we'd be minor footnotes in a book
documenting the return of the matriarch
real-to-life comic book heroes
setting sail on a new horizon
calling on the strength of all love warriors
before our time.
At last,
fulfilling our destiny.
(excerpt from the poem "Age of Swords" by Wendy-O Matik)

I'm a radical activist of the heart. I have always felt as if I have an enormous capacity to love everyone—the homeless guy down the street, the little old lady next door, someone I just had a five-hour mind-blowing conversation with, and then, of course, my friends, family, partners, and lovers. When I finally was able to admit to myself (without guilt) that I have a human right and obligation to myself to love as many people as I wanted or needed, then I became aware of how a monogamous relationship, outlined by the status quo, was never going to work for me. I would never be able to conform. Radical love, or the freedom to love who you want, how you want, and as many as you want, has become a way of life for me. Responsible open relationships seek to challenge patriarchy, the media, and our coerced social constructs of a relationship by imagining a nonhierarchical approach to love. As you redefine larger concepts like love, intimacy, sex, and relationships for yourself, you begin to disrupt the shackles of status quo that limit and restrict you and others from having healthier and more satisfying connections.

I am the author of *Redefining Our Relationships: Guidelines for Responsible Open Relationships*. The lived experience of a healthy, responsible, open relationship for thirteen years inspired me to write the book, as well as a lot of encouragement from friends. Despite the ending of that relationship, we spent a great deal of time negotiating what our relationship could be, or could have the potential to be, if we put our hearts and minds into it. We laid down a foundation of trust based on mutually agreed upon rules that helped us to grow and evolve as a couple. We have shared lovers, supported each other in having outside lovers, as well as supported our friends to forge relationships that better suited their lifestyles, particularly in the late eighties and early nineties when many of us had no real role models to follow.

The societal and cultural reality is that we are a far cry from sexual equality in this day and age. Men, straight or gay, have benefited from the luxury of sexual liberation without so much as their moral values being scrutinized by society. Women, whether straight or queer, have no such freedom. Labels such as slut or nympho continue to plague women who seek sexual autonomy. These stereotypes and misconceptions are perpetuated in the media, government, educational system, religious institutions, and even within the women's movement. We still have a long way to go before we can dismantle these derogatory perceptions and liberate ourselves from the social constraints that have been imposed upon us since birth. The first place to start is with yourself, confronting your own self-imposed guilt and your fears of stepping outside the standards of societal norm. It starts with freeing your mind, body, and heart to love openly despite judgment.

I'll be the last one to advocate one type of relationship over another—monogamy versus non-monogamy—because, in all honesty, I currently practice what Dan Savage coined "monogamish." As a single and fifty-one-year-old queer woman, I define this to mean that I mostly practice monogamy, because I'd like to make at least one relationship work, but I also still experience many romantic and loving connections with long-term trusted friends and lovers. What I am *more* interested in is planting the seeds of autonomy, when it comes to love and relationships. We have choices. We have options. There simply cannot be just one formula for everyone. Carve out your own lifestyle. Imagine your own ideal relationship. Radicalize your life and challenge yourself to have deep, meaningful relationships with anyone who you feel is important to you—including your parents, siblings, elders, friends, lovers, and neighbors. If you define "open" to include cuddling, kissing, and heartfelt communication, then work that into your life. If open means sexual liberation, then be honest with yourself and with your partner(s) and take the responsible steps to achieve this. Love is a revolution that starts in the privacy of your home and touches everyone you love and come in contact with.

I am advocating responsible relationships that are entrenched in the principles of honesty, communication, and consent. All relationships and friendships have spoken and unspoken guidelines and boundaries that are agreed upon. When you go outside the mutually agreed upon rules, then you betray yourself and your loved ones. That's cheating, and people get hurt. This is how jealousy gets flared and how couples start lying when they're not being honest about their true desires. This is the grey area of intimacy that I try to examine in my book. We all have natural tendencies to feel desire, to flirt, to fantasize—this is a healthy part of being human. It's when we deny these urges and suppress them that we run into trouble. In an ideal relationship of any kind, I would imagine that having an open and honest discussion about these fantasies would be a healthy place to start. In many ways, I wrote my book precisely for the people who don't want to scare away their partner with their desire to open up the relationship, as well as for those who want to make a commitment to avoiding stagnation, instilling honesty, giving voice to their true desires, dedicating themselves to creative relationship options, and supporting one another in their pursuit of the personal freedom to love many people.

Another way that loving with a radical and open heart dismantles patriarchy lies in a deeper examination of the three pillars of responsible open relationships: honesty, commitment, and consent. For example, these three critical principles are actually a direct attack on patriarchy when you consider what is occurring in the #MeToo movement. We see more obviously than ever how men's control of women's sexuality is often not honest or communicative or consensual. In other words, being responsible in all of your relationships and interactions with your fellow humans is an act against patriarchy, which is deeply irresponsible.

My book, in part, is an attempt to dispel the misconceptions and offer insight into an alternative view. It is my hope that my story reflects both the struggle inherent in living an alternative lifestyle, as well as the work that still needs to be done before there is greater societal acceptance. I write from one woman's experience and fight for autonomy. Part of my awareness and radicalization as a woman under institutionalized patriarchy is this struggle to break free of male concepts of a relationship, male domination of sexuality, male control over my freedom to live how I want, love who I want, and so on. I truly believe that we have a responsibility to challenge this patriarchal notion of a relationship and redefine something more empowering and more fulfilling for ourselves—this is part of what I discussed at my relationship workshops. But ultimately you have the right to love and live as you see fit, based on your ideals and values, while keeping respect and integrity at the core.

It's not easy to start being an activist in your own bedroom, in your own personal life and relationships. Even the most adventurous and most open-minded will struggle with their own internalized stereotypes, as well as feelings of shame and guilt. It's not a simple task to open a discussion up with your partner or lovers about how patriarchy affects you in bed, between the sheets. Most of us find it challenging to grapple with our own insecurities, jealousy, and possessiveness. Often we don't even have the safe space to discuss these topics openly. This was why I held monthly Radical Love & Relationship workshops for twelve years in order to create a supportive group environment and to build a community of visibility, validation, mutual understanding, and shared resources based on our common struggles. Open relationships take a lot of work, communication, self-disclosure, and transparency, and it is often easier to conform, rather than face all your fears and deal with the criticism and misunderstandings from others who may not support or understand. The bottom line is you have choices. If you don't honor these choices and the inherent responsibility that comes with them, then you'll never know the true potential of your heart.

Loving openly and freely in this day and age, whether you're straight or queer, is a political act. We are conditioned by outmoded social norms that limit our perceptions and shackle us to unhealthy cycles of dissatisfying relationships. Yet we live in a time where we can choose our own gender or redefine our own sexual identity. Isn't it safe to assume that we also have a right to decide what kind of relationship is more suitable to our lifestyle? Declare yourself a revolutionary of the heart. Find out how you can expand your potential to love, radicalize your lifestyle, and together we can threaten the social fabric of patriarchy!

The most vital right is the right to love and be loved.
—Emma Goldman

The place to improve the world is first in one's own heart and head and hands.
—Robert M. Pirsig

Resources from Wendy-O

Polyamory Books

Breaking the Barriers to Desire: New Approaches to Multiple Relationships by Kevin Lano and Claire Parry

Lesbian Polyfidelity by Celeste West

Living My Life: An Autobiography by Emma Goldman

Love in Abundance: A Counselor's Advice on Open Relationships by Kathy Labriola

Opening Up: A Guide to Creating and Sustaining Open Relationships by Tristan Taormino

Polyamory: The New Love without Limits by Dr. Deborah M. Anapol

Redefining Our Relationships: Guidelines for Responsible Open Relationships by Wendy-O Matik

Sex at Dawn: How We Mate, Why We Stray, and What It Means for Modern Relationships by Christopher Ryan and Cacilda Jetha

Skin: Talking About Sex, Class, and Literature by Dorothy Allison

The Ethical Slut: A Guide to Infinite Sexual Possibilities by Dossie Easton and Catherine A. Liszt

The Jealousy Workbook: Exercises and Insights for Managing Open Relationships by Kathy Labriola

The Lesbian Polyamory Reader by Marcia Munson and Judith P. Stelboum, eds.

Social Media Links

Check out local polyamory MeetUp groups in your area.

Check out polyamory groups on Facebook, such as:

https://www.facebook.com/groups/openrelationshipcommunitygroup/

https://www.facebook.com/groups/116269025065439/
Find poly-friendly relationship coaches and therapists, like:
www.juliannelovesme.com
www.kathylabriola.com/

What's Money Got to Do,
Got to Do with It?

Kara Vernor

I don't call him my lover, because: *gross*. My life is not a romance novel. He does not tear the clothes from my body as foreplay. The wind does not blow in his hair as he gently caresses my flowering sex. My guy doesn't actually have any hair, and there is no wind in our bedroom, just the occasional nosy cat brushing against our calves.

Calling him my boyfriend makes me feel like a teenager. He is not a boy, and I am not a girl. We've been together nearly ten years; we don't kiss at the movies or drive down country roads to have clandestine sex in the back of a truck (though I admit that still sounds fun). Perhaps the term would feel more natural if I lived in a city, but I live in provincial northern California where being unmarried, forty-four years old, and childless makes me a freakish outlier, and "boyfriend" only shines a light on this difference.

Significant other is probably the most accurate term for my guy, but it's dry and too broad. What is an other? Are my mom and brothers not significant others? My job? Ice cream?

Partner is politically correct but sexless—the polar opposite of lover. Plus, there are project partners and tennis partners and business partners. To me, the term most rings of a financial arrangement. Yet my "partner" and I have not signed any kind of contract together. We are not a union, according to the law.

Husband would clarify our relationship for others, but it has the stench of ownership, of coverture, and the sexist history of the institution that for so long stripped women of their personhood. Plus, it actually would turn us into financial partners, and that, at present, is the biggest issue of all.

I love weddings. I love witnessing two people standing up before their community and pledging their eternal love for each other, taking the huge leap of faith required to promise to stick with each other for the rest of their lives. No matter the divorce rate in the U.S., I love that people still believe in this promise and that many do keep it.

But a wedding does not have to become state-sanctioned marriage. We know this, right? The gay community certainly knows it. From time to time someone cautiously asks me when I'm going to get married or otherwise implies it's strange I'm not, and I want to say, "Are you asking me why I haven't tethered myself financially to my boyfriend?" Because that's what a legal marriage does—it establishes a financial contract. That is all it does. Certainly it can't make two people eternally monogamous or in love. Does such a contract help relationships? Is it hot?

A financial partnership within a romantic relationship often does make sense. If my relationship were different—if we had had kids together or were just starting out, or if we *had* to combine finances to arrange our lives as we wanted (like to get health insurance)—we might have gotten married. We still might if our circumstances change. But for now, when I think about the reasons *for*, they are all about contingency planning in the event of a disaster, reasons like:

- If he dies, I would likely avoid some legal battles with his family and ex-wife.
- If he's maybe going to die, I could make medical decisions when he can't.
- If he's sick and/or dying, I can visit him in the hospital.
- If one of us loses our job, we can get health insurance through the other's job.
- If he does die, I would be entitled to some government benefits.

Those certainly are valid reasons to marry, as health can evaporate in an instant, but I'm not convinced I can't get around some of these issues in other ways, like with a will, or marry quickly should they become relevant. The reasons against getting legally married feel more immediate and practical:

- His ex-wife could take him back to court and try to get more child support (which his son does not need—he is very supported).
- If we can no longer make it work, we would have to spend a lot of time and money dissolving our financial partnership. Statistically speaking, this is much more likely than his early death.

- My income might make it less likely for his son to get financial aid if he goes to college (though at this point it's likely he'll qualify).
- If either of us gets sued or suffers a catastrophic illness or other financial hardship, the other's finances and credit would be protected.

Weighing the odds, *not getting married* would be the smart bet, though while I believe it's important to consider the odds, the truth is there's a more significant reason I've avoided a state-sanctioned relationship. My boyfriend and I handle money differently, and I don't like the way he handles his.

I pay off my one credit card every month. I see it not as money I have, but as a convenience for purchasing something online or a backup in case of an emergency. I thankfully make enough money that I can see it this way. My boyfriend, who also makes enough to see credit cards this way, instead sees them as an extension of what is his. He wastes money paying fees on what he owes, and he keeps buying things he doesn't need while in debt: just the other day he bought a limited-edition book that is filled with drawings of nothing but penises and vaginas from a local illustrator for a hundred dollars. I don't sleep well at night when I'm in debt; if his money were my money, I wouldn't sleep at all.

I also sleep better knowing that if I want to—if I need to—I can make a clean getaway. My experiences growing up taught me to think like a single woman and not a wife. My mom divorced twice and remains single. My dad also divorced twice, his second marriage lasting just three months. I know firsthand that forever arrangements often are not, and I saw the toll that took on my mom, in particular. Add to that the behavior of men that's so often in the news, the domestic violence, sexual harassment, and sexual abuse they disproportionally perpetrate, and there are many reasons we ladies might want to be prepared to light that shit on fire and walk away. I started saving *fuck you* money early; I had a small pile of it long before I'd heard it called that (okay, it was more like a nearly imperceptible lump in my mattress, but the intention was there). In making important financial choices, I've always weighed whether they would bring me less or more freedom.

Am I cold in thinking this way? Does my pragmatism fly in the face of positivity and #GoodVibesOnly? of every romantic comedy I've ever seen? Our society upholds unconditional love despite the odds, validating only relationships that are *all in*. But I'd like to believe there's a version of love that doesn't mean silencing your common sense and risking your own well-being for someone else, that encourages an honest assessment of strengths and weaknesses and allows both people to buffer accordingly so that all aspects of the relationship are truly a choice, not a *have to*. That feels more genuine to me and more realistic given what we know about how often we find ourselves walking away.

For now, I'm not going anywhere. I love and cherish my boyfriend. I love his sense of humor, his kindness, the way he anchors me. Though sometimes stubbornly slow, I admire how he continues to learn and grow, how he wants to do the right thing. We have that indescribable mix of qualities that makes our individual brands of crazy much saner together, that inexplicable way we click. I would like to be with him forever. I would like to make that work.

And, of course, at some point, whether we marry or not, his financial situation will become inextricable from mine. What I can do in retirement, for example, will be dependent on what he can do, as well. The reckoning of our financial differences is coming regardless, but at least now our relationship is stronger, and we are more capable of handling it. We've had nearly ten years of navigating differences, and our fights have grown more productive along the way.

Money is almost always cited as one of the top reasons people divorce. Of course it is. That's almost like saying falling out of love is one of the top reasons people fall out of love. Living this way, unsanctioned and "in sin," means I may not have a term for my guy that conveniently conveys what we mean to each other, but overall I am better for it and so is our relationship.

Demystifying Sex Work

an interview with P.A.

Dani: My first big question: I feel like there are so many misconceptions about what sex work is and what falls under the category of sex work. So, from your point of view, what is sex work? And what is categorized as sex work?

P.A.: Sex work is basically any work that is selling some kind of sexual service or product. There are many different kinds of sex work. Escorting is what I do, it's a form of prostitution. So, all various forms of prostitution fall under the umbrella term of sex work. People who give sensual massages, like massage with a happy ending. That's certainly a form of sex work. But then there's also dancing at a strip club. That's sex work. Porn performers. That's a form of sex work. People who do [web]cam work, where the clients log onto a website and have interactions with people through the website and get a show. And it's all over the internet. So, camming. BDSM practitioners, I think most of them would probably consider themselves sex workers. Certainly there are some BDSM professionals who don't have sexual intercourse with their clients or may not even touch their client's genitals. It's really up to the provider. People who do sexological bodywork and surrogate partners, those kinds of professions. Surrogate partners work with licensed therapists to be with clients who have therapeutic issues around sexuality and intimacy. Sexological bodywork is a little bit more like massage, but there's also a lot of more therapy and coaching involved. I think most of those folks identify as sex workers, but some of them might not. It's a little bit of a gray area; with sexological bodywork, each provider chooses what kinds of activities they might want to do. So, I think some provide more of a sexual service than others. Another gray area is sugar babies, people who get paid for a date, and the date may or may not include any kind of sexual activity. I think some of those folks identify as sex workers, and some of them don't.

Dani: Okay, right.

P.A.: The term "sex work" was coined in the seventies. People started using it because we needed a term that encompassed all these different kinds of jobs that are selling sexual services in different ways. Or instead of selling sex, "selling sexuality" is a better way to say it. But some of those jobs, like prostitution, are illegal. And other jobs, like porn and stripping, are legal. There's a lot more stigma attached to some of those jobs than others. There's stigma attached to all of them, I would say. But, there's a lot more stigma attached to prostitution, for example. And so, people wanted to have a term that everyone could use. That they could say that they were a sex worker without outing themselves as an illegal worker. That's one of the reasons why we use that term.

Dani: I'm so glad you brought that up. It's really interesting to me too, because I've known lots of people that have been in those situations where they're a sugar baby, and it's so much more accepted than other types of sex work. But to me, you're exchanging companionship or some kind of sexual services for an apartment or a bunch of gifts and vacations. Maybe the currency looks a little bit different, but essentially it's the same thing. And just looking back through the years at people I've known in those situations, I think very, very few of them would've considered themselves sex workers. It's really interesting that that spectrum and the amount of stigma, and depending on what kind of services you are offering.

P.A.: Yeah. Definitely. If you think about the sugar baby situation, I would imagine that some people who are doing sugaring are selling more of the companionship. And other people are selling more sex. Everyone does it a little bit differently. And, of course, there are lots of women who are looking for a husband who is wealthy, who they can marry, and then they won't have to work. And so is that a form of sex work?

Dani: So, as far as your experience, do you have a main occupation? Is this something that you do full-time? Is this how you support yourself? How does it fit into your life as far as economically?

P.A.: Yeah, it is my only form of income. And I recently took a training to become a surrogate partner.

Dani: You're not Monday through Friday, 9:00–5:00.

P.A.: No, that would be exhausting. I only work enough to live comfortably and put a little bit away in savings, and that's it.

Dani: How did you get started?

P.A.: A friend of mine, in 2014. I was working at a little nonprofit and making sixteen dollars an hour and could barely support myself on that. And I was working more than forty hours a week. Working overtime a lot. And it was very stressful. I was looking for something new, because I was getting burned out. And I'd spent time voluntarily not working and living very minimally. And I was thinking about doing that again, because I was so burnt out. But I wanted to stay in the Bay. I need money, because I live in a capitalist system, and in Berkeley, California.

Dani: Yeah, in the most expensive part of the country.

P.A.: Yeah, exactly. And so, I was talking to people about job opportunities, and this friend of mine told me about how they had just started working at a new job, and they had also spent quite a while looking for work. And they had started working at a brothel in the Bay Area, an illegal brothel. There are legal brothels in Nevada. But that's the only place in the country where there's legal prostitution. This friend had started. . . "working at a house" is generally the way that people say it. It was run by a couple, a man and a woman. And they were doing very well financially. They were making a lot of money. And they were having a lot of fun. Basically, right off the bat I kind of knew that I would do well working there. I had never done any form of sex work before, which I think is a little unusual. I think a lot of people start with either dancing or massage or something like that. And I had done none, like no other forms of sex work. Unless you count the times when I was in college and I would have sex for access to parties and stuff like that. Because I totally did that. At the time, when I was in college and I was doing things like that, it just seemed like that was the thing that you did. And I was totally comfortable doing that. I had no moral qualms about it.

Dani: That's awesome.

P.A.: It really didn't seem that different from other ways that I had engaged in sexual activity. Except in this case, I was getting money. And I had to worry about being arrested. So, there was a big difference there. But I started at this same house where my friend was working. And my first client was amazing. He was very sweet. And very personable. And seemed to genuinely care about me, at least for the hour that we were spending together, you know. And it was so easy. He was even really attractive.

Dani: Oh, wow, you lucked out. That's great.

P.A.: I know, I think I did luck out. I mean, I don't care that much about what my clients look like. Because the fact that he was really nice was great. And I think, because of course I was nervous. It was my first time doing this thing. And I was nervous, but it was very easy, and I had a great time. And then my manager, the person who was running the house, handed me the wad of cash, and I couldn't believe my luck.

Dani: Like we were saying earlier, there are a lot of forms of sex work that are illegal. Is there any kind of union or organizing? Or a grassroots kind of group or something like that for support?

P.A.: That's a really good question. And honestly, I'm not sure of the best way to answer that. So, yes and no. There are a number of groups and organizations in the Bay Area that try to support sex workers in various ways. And there's the national group, SWOP, which is the Sex Workers Outreach Project. And they have chapters all around the country, if not the world. I don't know if they're international but certainly around the country. And there used to be a SWOP in the Bay Area, and I was a part of it. But it is no longer in existence, as far as I know.

There is the Saint James Infirmary in San Francisco, in the Tenderloin. And that is an amazing nonprofit organization that's been around for a while. And they do street outreach and educational programs and research, and they have health care stuff, like STD screening and that kind of thing. They have mental health services. They have licensed therapists, professional therapists, working there. So, that organization is rad, and I also used to be involved with a couple of their programs, but I'm no longer volunteering there. But, they do so much. And they're really helping the population that needs it the most, which is the population that works on the street, outside. And especially after the FOSTA-SESTA [Stop Enabling Sex Traffickers Act and Allow States and Victims to Fight Online Sex Trafficking Act] bill passed in April [2018].

And there's other groups popping up all the time. Particularly now since the FOSTA [Fight Online Sex Trafficking Act], there's a lot of groups of friends who are getting together wanting to start something. But, there isn't really anything else that's established, certainly not nearly as established as the Saint James Infirmary. And I would like to see more in-person groups. But, honestly, the internet provides a lot of community and support for a lot of sex workers, which is awesome. That's one wonderful thing about the internet. Personally, I'm more of a face-to-face kind of person. I like to have people who I'm seeing face-to-face. But, I have the privilege of being able to be out about my job for the most part; I don't have to worry so much about things like family finding out; I mean, I do worry about that. I don't have to worry about some other boss or some other job finding out and firing me, and I don't have to worry about exes finding out and hurting me or anything like that. I have this privilege in my life of being open about my work. And so I'm able to appreciate some of these in-person things. But for a lot of people that's not an option. It's not safe. So, the internet groups are really helpful for a lot of folks. And some of those, some of the internet community died, because of SESTA-FOSTA.

Dani: You brought up something that I wanted to ask you about too, about people finding out and how much secrecy is involved because of the stigma. And I'm wondering how much your friends, family, if you're in relationships . . . how much do people in your life know about what you do, and are you supported within your community?

P.A.: I'll start with my family. I've been escorting for about four years. I have not been in contact with my parents for about six or seven years. So I've been out of contact with them since before I was doing this. I would like to get back in contact with them someday, and I would like to be out to them, because I like be honest with people in my life, when I can. I'm a bad liar too. So that doesn't help. But, my mother, she's a survivor of sexual assault and incest. And she's very uncomfortable talking about sex. And I don't know how I would be able to bring up my work without terrifying her. Because she's terrified of sex generally; it's not even so much the job aspect of it. I think she would be terrified if she knew. It's a really delicate subject, and I'm going to cross that bridge when I get to it.

I am out to my partner's mother and her partner. I don't know them that well, but I've been with my partner for a few years now. And I feel like I want his family to be my family, and I don't want to lie. And his mom and her partner are pretty countercultural in a lot of ways. They're old hippies.

So we had a lot of conversations with them. And they had a lot of misconceptions about it. They worried that I was not safe. And that I was going to get an STD, which of course is always a possibility whenever you sleep with someone. They had a range of concerns. And we talked to them about all of them. And I think in the end they were still a little unsettled, but they're accepting of me.

Dani: That's so good. At least they're not conservative, Middle America Trump supporters or something.

P.A.: No. They're very much not like that.

In terms of my community, like my friends, I'm out to everybody. I feel like if I have a friend who is not okay with it, for whatever reason, I probably just wouldn't remain friends with them. I'm kind of picky about my friends, and I tend to have friends who are like me in a lot of ways. I've definitely had conversations with people where they are just worried about me. You know, they're just worried about my safety and that kind of thing. I tell them that some of their concerns are totally valid. Like, yes, I could get arrested. That is totally a possibility. Yes, I could get an STD, which is a possibility. For sure. There are risks. And I try to remind them that I was pretty slutty before I started this job, and I could've gotten an STD from any of my lovers. And in terms of physical harm, I used to work at my job at the nonprofit, though I'm not going to say what it was. I was putting my body in harm's way on a regular basis. And I had to go to the emergency room once because of something that happened at that job. I was definitely facing some level of danger at that job as well. And I ride a motorcycle. I could die on the freeway. And I know so many activists who put themselves in situations where they could get arrested for standing up for the things that they believe in; arrest is a total risk that they are willing to take. So, all of that is putting it in perspective. Yes, there are risks. I believe that there are risks with most, if not all, jobs. And I'm choosing to take those risks. And I feel like it's an educated choice. I think most of my friends get it.

Dani: One of the other things that I wanted to talk to you about is this idea that a lot of people kind of lump sex work in with sex trafficking. They see sex workers as victims. They see it as a really unsafe thing to be doing, especially for female sex workers. I'm wondering how you feel about that.

P.A.: So, it's just a flat-out myth that all sex workers are victims. Until recently, I was of the opinion, like many sex workers who work indoors, I think, and who choose the work, and who feel empowered by the work, I was of the opinion that there were voluntary sex workers. That was one group. And then there were trafficking victims. And that was a different group. And those two groups were very separate. And you shouldn't ever conflate the two. And that voluntary sex workers love their jobs. And trafficking victims are victims and are being harmed and are being exposed to violence regularly. I kind of had this idea that there are these two very separate groups of people, and I have recently learned that it's really not like that.

The way that I see it now is that it's complex. It's very complex. And there are people who identify as voluntary sex workers, like me, who if given the option to live in this world without working at all would take that option. I love my job. And I say that absolutely truthfully and honestly. But I also understand that I live in capitalism, where everyone has to have money in order to live comfortably. And I don't believe that is right. I personally believe that people should have food, water, health care, and housing, without having to work.

Dani: Right.

P.A.: Especially the kinds of jobs that people are forced into, when they're already low-income, and they don't have a lot of options. And of course, education also requires money. And opportunity and access. So, we live in this world where we're kind of all forced to choose some sort of work, or some people who can't work or don't work for whatever reason have a really tough life. And so, is it a choice? Yeah, kind of. Do I love it? Sure, I love some of my clients. Is it still kind of like I'm forced to do it? By the system, yes, sure. So, there's that level of it, right. There's the economic system level of it.

And then the other thing that makes those two groups not so separate, that I've learned, is that there are a lot of people who were forced into, who were trafficked, who were forced into selling sexual services, usually, I think, when they're teenagers, when they're younger. And they do it, and they get older, and they realize that this is way to make a living, and they continue to do it as an older adult, by choice. And, so, are they a trafficking victim or a consensual sex worker? They're both.

And then, of course, there's people who are forced into it, who don't want to do it, and who need services to get out, of course. I mean, everyone needs services. Of course there are some people who really do want to get out and who are under the control of someone else. That's how I've come to see it now. It's very complex.

I'm appreciating this interview, because I feel like I have the opportunity to go into this stuff with some depth.

Dani: Oh, good! This is so informative.

P.A.: Sometimes I have these chats with people that are really quick, and they ask me that question, but I only have thirty seconds to answer. And

I don't know how to answer that question. Because, you know, you've heard of the "Happy Hooker" stereotype?

Dani: Oh, yeah.

P.A.: On the one hand, I love that book. It's funny and fun and whatever. I do have a lot of fun at my job sometimes. And it's kind of wild, and I like being transgressive, and I think of it as kind of a kink for me. But also, I don't want people to get the idea that all sex workers feel that way, because they don't. Some people just see it as a job. And a lot of people feel like it's their only option. And, you know, so they do it. It's all right. But, they don't fall into the Happy Hooker stereotype. It really is a stereotype. It's much more complex than that.

Dani: I'm so glad that you spoke to the complexities of it too, because another thing, even just looking up online articles about sex work, criminalizing sex work, or sex workers rights, and there's nothing really out there. I feel like the information, because I'm not a sex worker, and I'm learning a lot just having this conversation with you and with other people I know that are sex workers, I feel like there's this really black and white where it's either all good and happy and money and joy, or it's like this devastating sex trafficking situation with this fifteen-year-old girl.

P.A.: Sure.

Dani: And, so, I just really, really appreciate your perspective that it can be a little bit of both. And there is a gray area. And it's not necessarily totally consistent throughout the experience of sex workers of different kinds too. I'm asking a lot of questions about stereotypes, mostly because of what I just said. Like the information that's available is not really that in-depth, especially if people are looking online, and there are all these misconceptions, right. So, following up with you saying that you actually really enjoy your work, and you really enjoy a lot of clients. . . There's this other perceived notion out there that if you are a sex worker and that's your occupation, then you're not going to necessarily enjoy sex outside of your job. I'm wondering how you feel about that?

P.A.: I'll start out by saying it's different for everyone. I suppose this goes for all the questions. But, this is so personal. It has definitely affected my sex life outside of my work. It's affected it in all kinds of ways. Some are good, and some are not good. I definitely have a lot less sex than I used to—outside of work. I have a need, a sexual need that has a lot to do with being sexually intimate with strangers and people I don't know very well. I get off on that. I used to hook up with people that I had just met, just for fun. And now I think that need is met through my work. It takes a certain amount of energy to do that, and I just don't have that energy.

Dani: Right. That makes so much sense.

P.A.: That being said, it's not as if all of the sex that I'm having with my clients is really good sex. My clients have this very common misconception that I get to have all of this amazing sex through my work, and they always say how envious they are.

Dani: That's so funny. So envious, and you're like, "Don't be."

P.A.: To be honest, the sex with my clients is pretty mediocre. Every once in a while it's good, for sure. And every once in a while it's pretty bad. And the fact is, when I'm working, I'm not there to get off myself. I'm there to provide a service for them. So, I'm not telling them what to do to please me. I'm not doing the things that I would normally do to have an orgasm. I'm just not, because that's not what I'm doing. I'm working for them. So, yeah, I do fulfill this kink need that I have to be intimate with strangers, but it's not like I'm having fabulous sex every time I sleep with a client. So there's that. I think because of my work, I am more demanding of my lovers outside of work. I sometimes get into this mode, especially like after a day where I've seen a few clients and I'm tired, and I've been in service mode for a while. . . I'm with my partner or lover, I just want them to do me.

Dani: Yeah. You're like, "I don't want to do the work right now. I'm tired. Somebody else do it for a change."

P.A.: Exactly. After doing that for a while, when I'm with my partner, I'm just like, all right, do it just this way. Don't do it any other way. Do it exactly the way I want it. I get more demanding and more picky. And I think if we were monogamous, then that could cause some amount of strain in our relationship. But we're not monogamous, and my partner has other lovers. And so I'm pretty confident that he has other people who he can get his needs met with, if I just need this one thing on one night or whatever. So being poly and being an escort really melds for me in a lot of ways.

Dani: Has being a person of color had any kind of impact on your life as a sex worker? Has it added any extra elements that you or situations that you have to navigate just because we live in a racist world?

P.A.: That's an interesting question. Yeah, so I'm half Asian and half white. I'm pretty white passing, and I identify as both white and a person of color, because I'm white passing. I don't know if I've quite figured this out just right, not for myself, but I've tried to use the Asian fetish to my advantage. I think sometimes it works, and I can get clients that's way. I definitely have a lot of clients who have an Asian fetish. They would not call it that. I think they know it's not PC to call it that, but that's what it is. And I know that that's what it is, because I find out through just knowing them that their wife is Asian, and all the other escorts that they see are all Asian. There's a long painful history, you know, around white men thinking that Asian women are subservient and all of that. I have tried to make money off of that. And I don't mind. I don't know why, but the funny thing is that I don't think I'm Asian enough for a lot of these guys, because I'm half white. I think that it's important to remember when discussing sex work of any kind that there's a lot of racism in the industry among clients, among workers, among managers. There's a lot of anti-black racism. It's very explicit.

Dani: On the part of clients or both workers and clients?

P.A.: The place where I see it is that, at least among escorts, black workers cannot charge as much generally. They can't make as much money. There aren't as many clients who are interested in seeing them. And I know that it's hard for dancers, as well. I have talked to a lot of people who have worked in clubs and I know that there are a lot of clubs that will only hire one black worker at a time. Like that kind of thing. And on the workers' end, there is a lot of anti-black racism. And anti, quote unquote, Arab racism. In the underground industry, there's not a whole lot of regulation, or it's self-regulated, right. So, racism that is always there, is very blatant. We generally don't see it as blatantly in other industries. I'm not experiencing those things firsthand. But, it's really real. And it's really detrimental. And I know that black and trans workers who are working outdoors are at the highest risk for violence—that's one of the reasons that I appreciate all of the work that Saint James does, because they're specifically working with folks who are working outdoors. I have a lot of privilege in the world and, thus, in my profession. So, I'm not experiencing that kind of racism that other people experience.

Dani: There's this thing in mainstream feminism that ignores transgender women's places in feminism and the importance of being allies to sex workers. So, from your perspective, two things: Why is it important that sex workers be supported by mainstream feminism? And how can people be better allies to sex workers?

P.A.: I think that since sex workers are women, many of them, not all of them, obviously. So many sex workers are women, that if someone is not supportive of sex workers, I would not consider that person a feminist. Feminists want women to have access to jobs. And equal pay. Ironically, sex work is like the one area of work where women make more money than men in our culture. Sex work is a way that women support themselves. Many sex workers are mothers. Many sex workers are caretakers of other people. So, to me, it's just a very obvious feminist issue. You asked whether I think sex work should be important to mainstream feminism. I mean, I don't know. If mainstream means that they're not supportive, then I don't care about mainstream. I think people who identify as feminists should support sex workers. And I think feminism should be trans inclusive. When it comes to trans issues, for me, is that I don't think anyone should be able to define anyone else's gender for them. So, if someone identifies a certain way, then that's what they are. End of story. And there are a lot of cis women who would disagree with that. And because I understand that trans women are women, the issues that they are facing are feminist issues, in my opinion.

Dani: And how can people be better allies to sex workers?

P.A.: On the interpersonal level, don't make jokes about prostitutes dying or being raped. Should be obvious. Yeah, those jokes are not funny. See sex workers as human beings who are just trying to support ourselves. Just like everyone else. And if a friend or family member comes out to you about being a sex worker, don't shame them for that. That's their choice. And depending on your relationship, it may or may not be appropriate to ask them questions about it. But I think, this goes with so many different things, particularly around sex and gender stuff. I think people sometimes feel like they have the right or are entitled to all of these answers around really personal issues. For other people. . . I'll come out to somebody as a sex worker, I'll say that I'm a sex worker, and they'll immediately ask, "Oh, how much do you make?" I mean, who else would you ever do that to? Personal information is personal. If the person wants to talk to you about it, then they can make that clear. Just allowing people to take the initiative around talking about personal information is important. And not making assumptions. Don't assume they're a Happy Hooker. And don't assume that they're a trafficking victim. They're just a person, living life, and they may have all kinds of different stories. And maybe sex work is one of those things. But, let them divulge information, and don't make assumptions. And that's just the interpersonal level. I mean, obviously I would love to see more positive representation or realistic representation of sex workers in the media. If your friend tells you that they saw a prostitute or saw an escort or got a massage or something, I would love for that to eventually just be a totally acceptable thing in our society. And people get so shamed for that. But, you know, if it weren't for our clients, we wouldn't have jobs.

Resources from P.A.
Podcasts
Sex with Strangers with Chris Sowa
"No More Safe Harbor," episode 119 of *Reply All* podcast

Websites
Sex Worker Outreach Project: http://www.new.swopusa.org/
St. James Infirmary: https://stjamesinfirmary.org/
The Honest Courtesan: https://maggiemcneill.wordpress.com/

Books
Paying for It: A Comic Strip Memoir about Being a John by Chester Brown
Playing the Whore: The Work of Sex Work by Melissa Gira Grant
Temporarily Yours: Intimacy, Authenticity, and the Commerce of Sex by Elizabeth Bernstein
Whores and Other Feminists by Jill Nagle

Auntie Starhawk's Sex Advice for Troubled Times

Starhawk

Resist the Patriarchy: Have Good Sex!

All the #MeToo posts and continual revelations of what women have always known and experienced about the ubiquity of sexual harassment and assault are tremendously important, empowering, and liberating, as they blow away the smokescreen that has obscured the truth of women's lives.

But in all the ferment that results, I hope we can remember that, while sexual assault is a Bad Thing, sex itself is a *Good Thing*!

The Bad is the assault part, the harassment, the rapes and quasi-rapes and coercion, the abuses of power—not sex. Sex is good! If we forget that, we sink deeper into the quicksands of life-denying, world-destroying patriarchy.

Life Force Is Sexy

By sex, I mean any way people come together in any combination that is mutual, consensual, pleasurable, and life-affirming. Sex is life force—whether that life becomes a new being or simply a reason for us older folks to enjoy living. In earth-based Pagan spirituality, sex is a way of experiencing the Goddess (or any form of the divine you prefer) within—the pulsating, vibrating, untamed passion of life itself.

That's really, really different from misusing sex to display power, to humiliate, embarrass, possess, or control another.

We live in a pleasure-denigrating culture, steeped in old religious thoughtforms and current economic conditioning that removes value from our embodied experiences of passion, ecstasy, and connection in order to control and exploit us. Rape culture underlies patriarchy, and it's the opposite of a life-embracing, loving, and sex-loving culture.

In our world, sex is also an arena of tremendous vulnerability and wounding. So, how is a sensitive person to proceed? How can we ever connect with potential partners in pleasure in a world that sometimes feels like a minefield of opportunities to inadvertently offend or injure someone? What should I do if I'm genuinely attracted to someone and want to pursue the possibilities?

Take Your Old Auntie Starhawk's Advice

1. Examine the power relationships

Are you this person's boss, teacher, elder relation, spiritual leader, caregiver, casting agent, doctor, potential funder, or something like that? Is there some power differential between you, beyond the variances of privilege that are always with us? If so, I'm sorry, forget it. If the attraction is a true one, it can wait until you extricate yourself from the power relationship, until the course is over or one of you moves to a different job. Until then, there's no way to have a truly consensual relationship—no matter how many attending physicians sleep with their interns on *Grey's Anatomy*!

2. Examine the situation

Are you both/all awake, conscious, and capable of making clear decisions? As in, not drugged, inebriated, in the midst of a mental health crisis, etc. If the answer is no, stop and wait.

3. Use your words

A lot of sexual attraction proceeds from body language and subtle signals. I was raised in the fifties, when women were taught not to be the aggressors but to signal our willingness in subtle ways. And our unwillingness, for that matter—not to slap Uncle Joe's hand when it strayed to our thigh but to quietly move away and not spoil the party. That worked great for abusers, not so great for most of us. Plus men were never taught how to read those signals. Some intuitively got it right—others read everything short of a sock to the jaw as a sign of attraction.

Happily, in these enlightened days, we are all free to ask directly, and that's probably a good policy no matter how honed your intuition. Saying something like: "I'm feeling very attracted to you—are you interested?" is not harassment, provided no other power differentials are in operation, and provided the object of your desire is truly free to say "no." Talking doesn't have to be a legal negotiation—it can be romantic and sexy, as in this (I hope tantalizing) excerpt from my latest novel *City of Refuge*, where a priestess of the Temple of Love initiates a former soldier into the mysteries of sacred sexuality:

> She smiled back, her eyes teasing again. "Then let's play a game. I'll ask you for something, and then you can ask me. Either one of us can say 'no' at any time, or 'yes.' But I want you to describe in detail everything you want to do to me, and everything you want me to do to you. It will heighten the pleasure. Do you agree?"
>
> "Give it a try."
>
> "Then ask me for something," she breathed into his ear. "And say 'I.' Always say 'I.'"
>
> "Can I kiss you again?" he whispered softly.
>
> "Yes."
>
> Kissing. They had never bothered with such preliminaries in the rec room. But he liked it. His lips touched hers, his daring tongue sought the cave of her mouth, a foretaste of that deeper cave.
>
> After a long moment, she pulled back and in a husky voice asked him, "Will you caress my nipple with your fingers, through my gown?"
>
> They played a duet of request and fulfillment.
>
> "Kiss you one more time? With your eyes open?"
>
> "And now unbutton my gown, if you will, and do the same on my bare flesh . . . please. . ."
>
> "And can I touch your ass?"
>
> "And would you now stroke the fringes of the flower. . ."
>
> The game went on for hours. The sun went down, and Lilith drew him inside, into a candlelit chamber with a big, soft bed in the middle and mirrors on the walls. River found that the talking and describing slowed their lovemaking to a maddening pace. But then he relaxed into it, and began to enjoy it. He experienced everything twice, once in the describing, once in the doing.
>
> Until finally she asked him, "May I prepare your shaft to enter the chamber?"

"Oh yes!"

She slipped a condom over him, stroking him as she did, and murmuring what sounded like a prayer: "I place this here as a sign of our deepest love and respect for the great powers that generate life. I place this to honor the act we are about to do with reverence and care for one another, for our health and safety. All acts of love and pleasure are my rituals!"

She drew him into her. Their eyes locked.

"Now, no more talking," she said. "No more need to ask. I am yours. You are mine."

4. Use protection

Condoms or other barrier protection if STDs are an issue, birth control if a pregnancy is possible and unwanted. Incorporate them into sex play if they seem too clinical—you're an imaginative being and I'm sure you can figure out how.

5. Bad sex happens

Even when it's all consensual, sometimes the fireworks just fizzle. You don't share the same tastes or get into the same rhythm. Sometimes, especially in long relationships, you may respond more out of accommodation than overwhelming passion: "My partner is eager, I'm frankly more into reading a book and going to sleep, but I enjoy pleasing them, and I know I'll get into it once we start." Life is full of ambiguities. Leave room for them. Relationships are fraught with imperfections and disappointments, but we're humans, and working through those things is how we embrace the wonderful depths and richness of other humans. For undying, unflagging devotion—get a dog!

6. The most important thing

Treat your partners with consideration and respect. That's really what it all comes down to, isn't it? That goes for how you talk about the incident afterwards, as well as what you do and say before and during. You don't have to pledge undying love or get married. Sex can be many things—the glue that holds together a lifelong commitment or a fleeting interlude of ecstasy or everything in between. But you do have to honor and respect your partners, speak well of them, keep the boundaries that allow for true intimacy, and speak the truths that make for real connection.

Follow these simple guidelines and maybe we can create a culture that encourages pleasure, joy, and true romance between empowered, lusty, passionate, life-loving beings adoring and pleasing one another in a world where all of life can thrive.

Love as Political Resistance: Lessons from Audre Lorde and Octavia Butler

adrienne maree brown

Audre Lorde taught us that caring for ourselves is "not self-indulgence, it is an act of political resistance," and although we know how to meme and tweet those words, living into them is harder. We have a deeper socialization to overcome, one that tells us that most of us don't matter—our health, our votes, our work, our safety, our families, our lives don't matter—not as much as those of white men. We need to learn how to practice love, such that care—for ourselves and others—is understood as political resistance and cultivating resilience.

We don't learn to love in a linear path, from self to family to friends to spouse, as we might have been taught. We learn to love by loving. We practice with each other, on ourselves, in all kinds of relationships.

And right now we need to be in rigorous practice, because we can no longer afford to love people the way we've been loving them.

Who have we been loving?

> —the people who cross our physical or virtual paths, spark the flame of our interest, earn our devotion and respect and protection.

> —our own family, because of blood.

> —people we are committed to but don't like anymore.

How have we been loving?

> —defining love by obligation.

> —celebrating love on externally marked holidays.

> —keeping the realities of love behind closed doors.

> —framing love up as a fairy tale on social media.

> —as a product we give each other.

> —as a limited resource that gets swallowed and used up, tied in plastic when we're done, and piled up out of sight.

> —prioritizing romantic love over self, comrade, and friend love.

This kind of love is not sufficient, even if it is the greatest love(s) of our lives. The kind of love that we will be forced to celebrate or escape on Valentine's Day is too small.

We're all going to die if we keep loving this way, die from isolation, loneliness, depression, abandoning each other to oppression, from lack of touch, from forgetting we are precious. We can no longer love as a secret or a presentation, as something we prioritize, hoard for the people we know. Prioritizing ourselves in love is political strategy, is survival.

From religious spaces to school to television shows to courts of law, we are socialized to seek and perpetuate private, even corporate, love. Your love is for one person, forever. You celebrate it with dying flowers and diamonds. The largest celebration of your life is committing to that person. Your family and friends celebrate you with dishes and a juicer. You need an income to love. If something doesn't work out with your love, you pay a lot of money to divide your lives, generally not telling people much unless it's a soap opera dramatic ending. This way of approaching love strangles all the good out of it.

What we need right now is a radical, global love that grows from deep within us to encompass all life.

No big deal.

One of my favorite reframes on romantic love is "relationship anarchy" from Andie Nordgren:

> Love is abundant, and every relationship is unique
> Love and respect instead of entitlement
> Find your core set of relationship values
> Heterosexism is rampant and out there, but don't let fear lead you
> Build for the lovely unexpected
> Fake it til' you make it
> Trust is better
> Change through communication
> Customize your commitments

To help make this a true day of love, here is brief radical love manifesto:

Radical Honesty

We begin learning to lie in intimate relationships at a very early age. Lie about the food your mother made, to avoid punishment, as you swallow your tears, about loving this Valentine's Day gift, about the love you want and how you feel. Most of this is taught as hetero-patriarchy 101: men love one way, women another, and we have to lie to impress and catch each other. Women are still taught too often to be submissive, diminutive, obedient, and later, nagging and caregiving—not peers, not emotionally complex powerhouses, not loving other women and trans bodies. These mistruths in gender norms are self-perpetuating, affirmed by magazines and movies, girded up at family dinner tables.

We also learn that love is a limited resource, and the love we want and need is too much, that we are too much. We learn to shrink, to lie about the whole love we need, settling with not-quite-good-enough in order to not be alone.

We have to engage in an intentional practice of honesty to counter this socialization. We need radical honesty—learning to speak from our root systems about how we feel and what we want. Speak our needs and listen to others' needs. To say—I need to hear that you miss me. When you're high all the time it's hard for me to feel your presence. I lied. The way you talked to that man made me feel unseen. Your jealousy makes me feel like an object and not a partner. The result of this kind of speech is that our lives begin to align with our longings, and our lives become a building block for authentic community and, ultimately, a society that is built around true need, real people, not fake news and bullshit norms.

Healing

Trauma is the common experience of most humans on this planet. Love too often perpetuates trauma, repeating the patterns of intimacy and pain so many of us experienced growing up in racist and/or hetero-patriarchal environments. Shame might be the only thing more prevalent, which leads to trauma being hidden, silenced, or relegated to a certain body of people. If we can't carry our trauma and act normal, if we have a breakdown or lose our jobs/homes/children, there is something wrong with us. What we need is a culture where the common experience of trauma leads to a normalization of healing. Being able to say—I have good reasons to be scared of the dark, of raised voices, of being swallowed up by love, of being alone. And being able to offer each other: I know a healer for you. I'll hold your hand in the dark. Let's begin a meditation practice. Perhaps talk therapy is not enough. We should celebrate love in our community as a measure of healing. The expectation should be—I know we are all in need of healing—so how are we doing our healing work?

Learn How You Change

Most of us resist changes we didn't spark. We feel victimized, and so we try to hold tight to whatever we figure out as a way to survive. We spend too much time watching change happen with our jaws dropped, writing what the fuck over and over. It is time to learn Octavia Butler's lessons—both that "the only lasting truth is change," and that we can, and must, "shape change." So we need to observe how we respond to change: Does it excite us so much that we struggle with stability? Or do we ignore changes until it's too late? Or fight changes that are bigger than us? It takes time and assistance to feel into and find the most strategic adaptation.

Build Communities of Care

Shift from individual transactions for self-care to collective transformation. Be in community with healers in our lives. Healers, we must make sure our gifts are available and accessible to those growing and changing our communities. Be in family with each other—offer the love and care we can, receive the love and care we need. Share your car or meals with a healer in exchange for reiki sessions. Facilitate a healing group in exchange for massages. Clean a healer's home as a barter for a ritual to move through grief. Pay healing forward—buy sessions for friends. Let our lives be a practice ground where we're learning to generate the abundance of love and care we, as a species, are longing for.

On Valentine's Day, commit to developing an unflappable devotion to yourself as part of an abundant, loving whole. Make a commitment to five people to be more honest with each other, heal together, change together, and become a community of care that can grow to hold us all.

Burnout, Sacred Leadership, and Finding Balance

an interview with Gerri Ravyn Stanfield

Dani: What is your role at Acupuncturists Without Borders?

Ravyn: I'm the executive director. I've worked for nonprofits all my life, and it's been an incredible experience to move into nonprofit management in a bolder way.

Dani: I know this is a relatively new role for you, but have you been involved with the organization for a long time?

Ravyn: Yes. I went to Nepal on a service trip with AWB, because I was really trying to figure out what, if anything, I could contribute to the problem of sex slavery. We partnered with some different NGOs and nonprofits in Nepal to train health care practitioners and acupuncturists and set up regular clinics in places where women and girls are recovering from trafficking. That could be sex trafficking, but also organ trafficking is pretty problematic there.

We do a lot of training. I would say that's the main function of our organization. We do a particular kind of mobile clinic using a five-point protocol that's really good for trauma and post-traumatic stress and addiction. We teach health care providers how to set up mobile clinics. We got started after Hurricane Katrina, so we've used it extensively in disaster situations, but then began to move into connecting with folks who asked us to come and train them and starting to make some really amazing relationships with different healers all over the world, traditional healers, and also folks that are practicing different kinds of medicine. We do world healing exchange trips where we go and learn a little bit. In Nepal, we got to work with a traditional herbalist and a shaman. We got to meet and work with community organizers and acupuncturists, because Nepal has an acupuncture license. Those acupuncturists are phenomenal. After the 2015 Nepal earthquake, they were out doing these local clinics, and they'd just been through the earthquake themselves, and they were out within days and probably treated about eighty thousand people.

Dani: That was such a terrible earthquake. Aside from your work with Acupuncturists Without Borders, how would you describe yourself? Do you use the term witch or priestess, as far as your spiritual activism goes?

Ravyn: There's a long, long tradition of people reclaiming words that have been used against them as insults, so I'm happy to identify as woman, queer, witch. More or less to honor the blood that's been spilled [from] my people throughout time, right. Simply doing what I have the privilege to do every day. I think about that. I can speak my mind. I can run an organization. I can teach. I can write. I can work for social change. I generally don't live in fear that I'll be killed for it, but these times are changing.

Dani: Fuck, I know. I was just going to say that.

Ravyn: I feel like I owe that debt to the people that came before me and fought for my freedom. I think for that reason, I also strongly identify with being a healer and an alchemist. I didn't know this when I started doing my research to write *Revolution of the Spirit*, that the root of the word "heal" is an Old English word, and it's "hal," H-A-L, and it means "to make whole." I come back to it in almost everything I do, because that sometimes feels like something I could reach. Maybe I can't fix everything that's broken or this world that seems utterly broken, but I can work to make it whole.

Dani: You're a writer as well. Can you tell me a little bit about what you write and how that fits in or how you even make time for it?

Ravyn: I have written since I could pick up a pencil, and I move around. I'm very genre-fluid. I write fiction and nonfiction and poetry. I've published one creative nonfiction book that's about the places where art and medicine and spirituality meet. I'm really encouraging healers to restore or invent spirituality and medicine again. I feel like I use writing as therapy. I've used writing as a way to stay hopeful. I learned from Lidia Yuknavich that grief and depression and rage could be generative spaces.

I think even just linking writing to everything else, sometimes I feel like the answer is to write into the rupture, the answer for me, the answers for how do we deal with what we witness in the world. It's just that using those spaces as generative has really gotten me through some of the most painful times in my life. I guess I think about whatever I'm writing, there's a way that storytelling makes you put the event, whatever it is—sometimes a horrible event—in the center of the story and not at the end. Then write your way out of it and think about how you want it to end.

Dani: This big, huge question that I have for you is: What does it mean to you, with all of these different identities you have, and all of this creative work, healing work, spiritual work, what does it mean to you to move through the world as a woman doing this work? Especially right now?

Ravyn: I mean, it's so huge. It's so huge. I think that I don't know how to separate my womanhood from my personhood so that I think it's pretty phenomenal that I can often forget the ways that, if I'm just feeling into what it is to be a person, I can sometimes forget for a moment that what it means to be a woman and how women, different backgrounds and colors and forms and shapes and all of the ways that women manifest in the world, are not valued immediately, and that we have to fight to be seen and heard. I think that it's so interesting to think about moving in the world as a woman.

I think it falls to women much of the time to do a lot of the transformative work that's required in culture. I don't want to speak for all women, but I think that a lot of folks that I'm working with and talking to and listening to are trying to do the work of building relationship or rebuilding relationship, so whether that's with families or relationship to land base or relationship to an ethnic or cultural background that they've been separated from, there's so much, I think, needed right now about restoring relationships. For some of us, it's about making repairs, acknowledging what harm has been done. I think that often falls to women, that work of relationship. I don't think that's the way it has to be, or even the way it should be, but it's certainly the way that socialization and maybe even some neuroscience sets it up for us.

Dani: Right, where it's almost just expected of us even though a lot of these repairs that need to be made, maybe, going out on a limb, some of those fractures in our lives, in our history, were not necessarily caused by other women. It's interesting that it's like, "Okay, we're suffering the trauma, and we're suddenly finding ourselves in this place of needing to also do this extra work." It's like overcome it and fix it. Right?

Ravyn: Yup. Agreed. Agreed. I was really struck by your question you asked me before of how activism and healing work has affected me physically. I think that level of exhaustion that you just mentioned feels like a common denominator in the lives of most of the women I know. Obviously, for a multiplicity of reasons, and yet that urgency burnout cycle that I think comes along with activism and healing work and needing to fix it, not being satisfied with the way that things are, and having a difficult time to figure out when to stop and rest, or even if that's an option to you, because I think for a lot of women it's not an easier, obvious option.

Dani: That's such a big one, because just talking to different women for this project and being around a lot of women in my life, just the burnout and the stress and the health issues from being in these caretaker roles, whether it's through parenting or healing work or activism, especially as we get older, I feel like, "I just don't have the energy." But then I feel this responsibility. You know?

Ravyn: Yeah. Some of these questions, Dani, are so amazing, because they really do ask me to dig a bit. I was thinking about self-care, and I love how you came right out and said, "Some people feel like it's negative or it's selfish." I guess, when I think about self-care, when I talk about it, and I'm, again, thinking about to peers or to acupuncture patients or to friends or fellow organizers, I'm talking about self-care that does recognize that privilege is available to some and maybe not to all. Self-care still holds the responsibility of changing the culture, but boy. . . When I say self-care, I'm thinking about the ability to love yourself, no matter what's happened to your body or your life and just this radical notion of parenting yourself as well as you can with the resources available to you, regardless of how you were parented.

Dani: Right, right. How do we do that? Because I know that just for me, growing up, the way that I was raised, where I'm one of ten children, and we grew up very, very poor, and I never saw my mom take care of herself. I never saw any women in my family do anything nice for themselves. There was a lot of abuse and neglect and all of those things. Even now, it's like decades of therapy and all of this stuff, I always still, it's not huge, but I can feel it. There's like a little nugget, a little kernel of guilt when I take the time to care for my body, go to therapy. I don't know if any of us have the answers, but how do we do that, especially now when we're bombarded with negative information every fucking hour today? It's so hostile. I'm feeling increasingly unsafe. How do we learn to fucking slow down long enough to replenish and take care of ourselves in this world? It's so hard. Help me, Ravyn!

Ravyn: I wish I had a clear pathway and a clear guide. I will say that this thing that you named, the bombardment and the not being able to slow down, does sometimes feel like a place where we can begin. The neuroscience that I've been learning these days—I'm a big brain geek—is that the default mode network is the part of the brain that gives us our self-talk. Just going back to this thing that you named about family, and I certainly have a similar experience, very self-sacrificing women who didn't care for themselves, and then certainly would look down on me for things like not having children. What am I doing then with my life? This default mode network is so interesting, because, like I said, it manifests our self-talk, so it's whatever the soundtrack is playing in our heads when people aren't around. The research that I've read shows that most people have such a brutal default mode network playing that they can't be alone with their own thoughts. It's like you're beating yourself up constantly, for everything. Who wants to listen to that? Who wants to unplug and slow down and listen to your brutal self-talk? Just interrupt it, this horrible soundtrack. Things like, could be video games, could be alcohol, could be substances. Sometimes it's sleep, but also things that we might think of as more positive, like meditation or mindfulness or acupuncture or being able to be with another loving person and activate some neurons and get a different story. I think that when we say, "How are we going to make time for self-care? How are we going to interrupt these patterns?" It's like we have to start to develop this self-compassion. It seems so silly and new age. I almost don't even like the sound of myself saying it, but it's like this developing the witness to your own experience, your own pain, and your own emotion, and being able to be with yourself and to say things like, "It makes sense that you feel this way." I worked with an incredible therapist actually when I had very little money, and she saw me for very little money. Literally all she would do is give me compassion.

Dani: Aw, that's so great.

Ravyn: But it was so hard. I just was like, "What do you mean?" She's like, "It just sounds like you are working so hard and you're so exhausted." I was just falling apart. Just to be met with your own truth by a voice who isn't saying, "You suck. Do it better, harder, more, faster." There are some meditations or practices that I feel like have been really helpful.

In some ways, the love of my life was my grandmother. No matter what was going on in my family, my everyday family, being able to see her. . . She didn't even live near me. But our contract together was love.

I think I learned later that we didn't even agree politically, but I didn't know that. We didn't have time to argue. We just were loving each other. Sometimes I will do a practice where I actually try to see myself through her eyes, especially when I'm being the worst to myself, and just imagine what it's like to look at me through these eyes of love.

Dani: It's so interesting too, because it's so easy to be compassionate and supporting and loving to our friends and people that we care about. I catch myself when I start beating myself up. I would never, ever fucking say this to my friends or my kids. Why am I doing this? Then I'll be like, "Oh, well, because they deserve better than me." Or whatever shitty thing it is.

Ravyn: It's so easy. I absolutely agree, but this to me is what revolutionary health care looks like. It's this way that we turn all the hatred and the dismissal and the fear of this and the fear that's been instilled in us, turn it on its head and try to figure out what a radical thing it would be to love and forgive yourself, while not escaping from the world and not being able to do things to make change and building relationships across cultures and all kinds of lives that exist. I think women sometimes get taught how to love someone, and if there's any way that we have been loved by someone, and, really, they say it only takes one adult. It doesn't even have to be a family member. One adult that loves and believes in you can make a huge difference in your psychology, just to have that one experience. Just lifting that imprint a little bit and turning it on ourselves, I mean, I just think health care has got to be part of the revolution, or we're just all going to be stuck in our trauma default network brain telling us that we're nothing and don't deserve to exist and don't deserve to take care of ourselves. It's like, who can change the world with that soundtrack?

Dani: Exactly. I think about what's going on in the world right now, and I'm like, "Of course, the most revolutionary thing we can do right now is take care of ourselves and each other," but we're also completely stunned right now.

Ravyn: I think some of the kinds of radical connections that we're being asked to make right now are exciting. I think they're painful. I think we're having to listen to each other and potentially stories of generational pain and trauma. I think we're having to be really curious about where people are coming from and not assuming that we know anything about their story. Do you know adrienne maree brown's *Emergent Strategy*, the book? She says this thing in *Emergent*. . . I mean, she says a lot of brilliant things, but this question why is so important to community organizing, wondering, being curious about people and where they're coming from, asking why people behave the way they do. I think I always try to speak with the idea that we are there to stop harm and make repair. If we don't understand, that's what I hear so much from people these days, like about all of this stuff: Why? How could this be possible? How could people do this? On some level, it's immoral. It's awful. They must be monsters. Then I think about the brain on trauma and what happens to the brain after generations of trauma and how these stories continue to play out again and again. Some of this, I think, is still this possession trauma. People being able to move and act as a collective because of the many different forms of colonization that has made that a reality.

Dani: So many layers to it.

Ravyn: So many layers, so many layers. When someone is doing something abusive or horrible, much of the time, in their brain and in their neuroscience, they are completely checked out. That is a big way that people can carry out major abuses and commit moral injury. Check out, detach. The shitty thing is someone is detached and hurting you, you also connect to that state of detachment, because you start to imitate people. Again, everybody's brain goes into trauma, and nobody's nervous system is calm. It's just the snake eating its tail, like there's no end to it unless we can really interrupt cycles of unhealed trauma.

Dani: Yeah. We have a lot of work to do in this world, oh, my god, and this country too. We have all this trauma that we're not even really super aware of, that certainly hasn't been healed if we're not aware of it, and then we go and act out and oppress other people wherever we go. It's just this never-ending madness. It's madness.

Ravyn: I think we are asked to transform in these places where we've lost maybe the most precious things or maybe these places where everything we once believed has collapsed or fallen apart and we have to reshape and shift. Maybe even in the wreckage, try to find art and wisdom. I think, maybe that part for me doesn't have to be exhausting. I don't actually think that's all about seeking and doing. I think sometimes that is about just slowing down and letting myself feel it and weeping and writing into. . . I think about ruptures a lot.

Dani: Rupture is a good word.

Ravyn: Yeah, like writing into these cracks and ruptures. Wounds are really interesting physically. Depending on how deep they are, but usually if something really is wounded or gouged, there's that protective network of fibers, the scab that forms over the top of it. But it actually heals from the bottom up.

Dani: You don't really think about that because you're only seeing it from the outside.

Ravyn: There are these things about wounds, like now I'm thinking more about the metaphor of it, but it's like. . . I think we have to sit with the wounds, like actually feel them, talk about them, certainly our personal wounds, but absolutely these cultural wounds that are expressed but not discussed. Then, I don't know, I'm a big fan of trying a lot of different medicine and seeing what works.

Dani: From where I'm sitting, I see you as someone that's been able to really weave all of these different, very important aspects of being a fucking human in this world: activist, spiritual and physical healer, etc. I know you mentioned earlier that you don't necessarily see your healing work from your social justice work as very separate. I know this is a big part of Reclaiming too; How do you do it? What kind of advice would you have for someone? What's the importance of merging those different pieces? I just know my background being a "radical" activist for a long time, and in that social justice activist direct action world, everyone was a fucking atheist. And they were self-righteously atheist.

Ravyn: Yes, yes. Like, "God is bullshit, and if you believe in that, you're an idiot."

Dani: Right. Then, on the other side, like taking herb classes and being in meditation or spiritual groups, doing my healing, more Sonoma County woo stuff. On the other side, it was like, "Oh, well if we just all love and meditate." It was very interesting for me when I finally was like, "Fuck these extremists. I can be both at once." It was kind of hard for me, because I didn't really feel like I found a place until I found Reclaiming in the mid-late nineties and was like, "Oh. Yeah, I am okay having both of these."

Ravyn: What a dichotomy. I mean, you express it so well, that it is such a dichotomy, I think.

Dani: Yeah. "No gods, no masters!"

Ravyn: I feel like it can't be said enough how amazing Octavia Butler is, the sci-fi writer. Her ideas that all community organizing is science fiction, because we're making worlds. We're creating something that doesn't yet exist. I feel like this kind of storytelling, that's the only thing that ever made sense to me. I think that's the way I connect in art, in social justice, in spirituality. It's like going into the story itself. I guess I feel like sometimes it's the story of my actions trying to be congruent with my values, or we're trying to ask our culture to become a vision that we're dreaming. That just seems to unify for me, like telling the story of the world that we want. Then making art out of rubbish. I think I can't say enough, taking responsibility for the ways that we've caused harm and asking to hear other stories that aren't the same as our story. I don't know. That feels like my religion. I don't know if that really answers your question.

Dani: It's great. I'm into it.

Ravyn: It's the place where I can connect and even just go, "Okay. What is the story of anarchy?" The story of anarchy, maybe, and one version could be this idea that the potential inside each human being is realized and we no longer need charismatic white male leaders with money to tell us how it's going to be. Then, just like, "Okay. Fine. That's pretty magical, y'all."

Dani: Ha!

Ravyn: I'm not saying it's impossible, because I think it's completely possible, but that is a very magical story right there.

Dani: It totally is. It's a beautiful thing too.

Ravyn: I don't minimize fairy tales. Myths are true stories, like stories that are so deeply in the human psyche that we can't lose them, even though some myths have existed for thousands of years in different forms. Then spirituality is often the story of how we came to be or what we do when things dissolve or how we process destruction and death. Then one of the definitions of art I love is: making relationship between two things that aren't necessarily alike. I certainly am an imperfect human like all the rest, and when something doesn't feel good, I often move towards stories, collective stories where people are trying to do that, especially when the values are around human beauty and survival and relationship with our planet in ways that we can move into a more egalitarian and liberated world.

Dani: I know that you've done a lot of work with Acupuncturists Without Borders, but I didn't realize that the population you were serving when you were in Nepal were mostly women and children recovering from being trafficked. How do you manage to just not give up? How do you still find joy, still build relationships, and not give up, just say, "Fuck it," and go work for corporate America, when there's so much suffering? It just seems insurmountable to me sometimes.

Ravyn: I will say I think joy is a tall order sometimes. I think there's this idea that we can live in a joyful state all the time, and if we're not doing that, then something's wrong with us. I will say, "No, no. I think it's actually right to weep for what you witness in the world." Let it touch you. Let it wash over you. And, again, coming back to self-care and relationships with other people and being able to tell stories and take breaks, all of that feels deeply important, I think, with witnessing suffering. I really like what Joanna Macy says about hopefulness being something . . . you have to practice feeling it. There's no evidence or reason to feel it. It's not looking good. I think about that, and I'm like, "Okay, hope is my martial art. I have to come to it and practice it." Even if I don't feel hopeful at all, what are my options? I can certainly take myself out, or I can live as if I did feel hopeful and see what happens. Sometimes I think asking people to find their way to joy is sometimes too big.

Dani: It's a little bit of pressure.

Ravyn: It's too much pressure, yes. I can almost always get to a feeling of being grateful, and that could be pretty simply sometimes I'm just grateful for the things I haven't yet lost because life is really a big losing game. In the end, we kind of lose it all. I also can think about this story I love: after the siege in Leningrad, again, the city's decimated. Basically, nothing left, and the musicians took what was left of the orchestra, and they made their way down to the town square, and they played music for hours. I'm not saying you have to do that.

Dani: This is "Ravyn's postapocalyptic checklist: find all the instruments, create an orchestra in the rubble."

Ravyn: There's something about that level of destruction. Again, just thinking that we had an unprecedented year of disasters last year all over the world, really, as you were just talking about the fires. There's just shit that we see people do, like neighbors who haven't talked. They live by each other for twenty years and never have spoken. Then after a flood or an earthquake, they're sharing resources, and they suddenly become this collective, and they're worried about all their members and lending each other stuff. People who have boats are out for fourteen days just trying to make sure everybody's out. There's something that does get awakened, this kind of gold of humanity, maybe, after the worst has happened. We definitely see it after disasters. Like I said, it's tricky when people are traumatized, but that transformation I think is the best possible outcome.

Right now, many of us, not all, but many people on the planet, get to have this illusion that we don't need each other. We get to live in these bubbles where we supposedly just get to choose who we're around and who our Facebook friends are . . . and not talk to anybody. While I value privacy and choice, I also think that this lie that we're independent is maybe one of the things to go in these big transitional times. I feel like the planet is like, "Hurry up!"

Dani: Get your shit together, people!

Ravyn: Get your shit together!

Dani: I'd also love to talk about sacred leadership and what that means to you.

Ravyn: I think leadership is so tricky. It's like we've got this model, it's the one rich white guy who tells us how it is and people support them, or they overthrow them, and that's all we know. Even though we have these governmental bodies, everything's so corrupt, and it's all about money. I just think people are also growing very tired of that, and so I think, as the modern world, as our world, as it gets faster and less personal and more and more brutal, I think that I like to work with leaders, people who want to make a difference and people who want to challenge these trends of corruption and isolation and disassociation and overwork, and who want to learn to work collectively.

I think that there's also this way that we're being asked to challenge all these systematic injustices. I think that people are wanting that training as well; how to work collectively, how to gain confidence, but also how to challenge racism, sexism, and transphobia and homophobia as it comes up, that how each of us or those of us that feel called to that kind of work to help create space where any voice could be heard.

I think that a lot of what I've found is that I think people who have a tendency towards wanting to practice healing are actually some of our best leaders. And they're not often the people who are drawn to leadership. In fact, I never wanted to be in leadership. I wanted to have fun. I feel like my entire life, because I was a responsible human being who was very helpful, I was constantly given leadership and responsibility; it feels like it was kind of handed to me sometimes by teachers and other folks. Again, I think when it's just an individual doing that, that's where the burnout and exhaustion happens. But what I think of as sacred leadership is this learning to work collectively in an embodied way, and do a lot of listening and a lot of creating space and helping to synergize ideas and coming right back to that, "What do we do to make the world whole?" Some of that takes confidence building, and I think that is probably the thing that I would say to these people that I'm like, "Oh, you would do such a great job in leadership," and people are like, "No way, I'm too shy" or "No way, I'm not a good public speaker." I think that so much of the abilities that we assign to leaders can be learned. I think the qualities of sacred leaders or the kind of leadership that we're speaking right now are the things that tend to be inherent in people that want to heal. I would say people who want to heal instead of perform, perhaps.

Dani: Thank you for saying that. I've been noticing, especially in the "healing communities," different problematic things, like a lot of male healers in our community where we live, and I am generalizing here, are like, "Oh, I'm an activist. I'm a healer." But it's this very performative, kind of self-serving, predatorial kind of thing. Actually, specifically a couple of men that I know. They're like, "Oh, I'm a leader, and I'm doing this great thing, and I'm this healer." But then they use it as this playing card to really . . . treat women like garbage, basically. There's that, and I just noticed that more and more, and I'm trying to be intuitive about it and not so investigative, but there's that performance piece, and then there's that heart led leadership piece, so I'm just glad that you've said that. It's something that's been on my mind and a topic of a lot of conversations, especially in my activist community, too where everyone's like, "Oh, there's this new guy in town who's an activist that has no history of doing social justice work." Great for you, white guy, that's stepping it up, but what are your intentions? Where the fuck have you been? Welcome, but also: I got my eyes on you. You better watch your back.

Ravyn: Yeah, good. I think just coming back to that question of why, it's like why do you treat women this way? Not this particular woman and the sad story that I'm sure you have and a great excuse and reason, but why? Where does that come from, dude? Where did you learn that? What is telling you that is a reasonable thing to do? Why do you think people don't see it?

Dani: Man, that's so frustrating.

Ravyn: I loved you saying, "I have my eye on you," because I think in some ways that's the power of community. Again, I'm still operating under this idea that no one is really disposable, so at some point, all these people are going to have to get educated and come along for the ride.

Dani: I see a lot of people wanting accountability, and then other people going, "Oh, you're after revenge." It's like, no. There's a difference. There's a big difference between those things. Sometimes it's a gray area for me.

Ravyn: We've got to deal with that as anybody who has European ancestry, anybody who has privilege, anyone that is responsible, and anyone who is a United States citizen. We've got a lot of accountability to take. I think we got to get stronger about it within ourselves and being both strong and gentle with each other around it.

What Is a Home?

Sanam Mahloudji

Last Friday afternoon, my Iranian grandmother was anesthetized in a white operating room, in a hospital in America, where a doctor removed the uterus that had housed my mother sixty-two years ago. At about the same time, our new president announced the United States would no longer be a home for millions of people like my grandmother, because of an attribute they were born with: country of origin as genetic defect.

The next day, my grandmother drank tea, reclining on her American hospital bed, as disturbing news reports and social media posts lit up my phone. Refugees and travelers from banned countries were being stopped at airports, turned away. America is the only country my family has called home since 1979, when we fled Iran. And now America had included my beautiful motherland, home of poets and jagged mountains, among the nations banned. All Saturday, I cried. I grieved. Iran then said it would take "reciprocal measures," though it wouldn't exclude those with valid Iranian visas, and I no longer had a grip on the meaning of "home."

My face felt hot, my body weak.

But in my despair, I remembered something important: I know America as intimately as I know my mother and grandmother, their bodies my other homes. I studied in its schools, I read its books, and years ago, I'd practiced law in its courts. On Sunday, I left my three-year-old twin daughters at home with my husband, their father. I rode with a friend to Los Angeles International Airport, where thousands of people held up signs that said, in various ways, "No," that America is its people. America is me, and it is us.

Among all the activists, I also saw a man in a suit with a sign that read "Lawyer." I cried. I hadn't gone to the airport with an agenda; I just knew that I couldn't stand what our new president had done. I'd left the law to write fiction after my father's death nearly a decade ago and hadn't practiced since. But while the crowd chanted, "No bans. No walls. Sanctuary for all," I kept an eye on the lawyer, because at that moment, he was the embodiment of what I believed in: equality, freedom, and fairness.

I thought of my grandmother in the hospital, how she became an American years ago under a different president, one I mostly disagreed with but with whom, in retrospect, I shared some core beliefs. My grandmother, like myself, was a citizen now, and I refused to let our family or other families like ours be tossed aside without a fight. I wasn't ready to claim the law just yet, but at the end of that day, back at our apartment, I wrote to organizers online with offers of help, telling them: *I speak Farsi. I'm a lawyer.*

I worried. The truth is I speak Farsi only well enough to talk to my grandmother about her day. The truth is my father died never recovering from being in exile. When he died, I vowed that I wouldn't do the same, that I would recover by exploring who I really was: a writer, an artist. And even before I dropped the law, I hated being called a lawyer. I would even cringe.

But on Monday morning, I made a choice. After getting my daughters to preschool, I drove to LAX again without knowing if I would be needed, afraid that my Farsi and legal skills were imperfect. I listened to Iranians on NPR talking about heartache and havoc.

The morning was hot and sunny. I was wearing my new activist uniform: heavy-duty boots, waterproof jacket. I had an apple and full bottle of water in my bag. When I walked into the terminal, I immediately found the tables that had been set up for those offering legal help. Behind them, attorneys in discussion or typing on laptops. Almost all of them were women in their own versions of activist uniforms. On the tables themselves, there were sign-up sheets for volunteers, forms to fill out while speaking to people detained or their family members. Afraid that my Farsi would be inadequate, I told one of the lawyers that I only spoke Farsi with my grandmother. She smiled and said that was great.

I borrowed a marker and wrote a message on a manila folder. It said in English, "Volunteer lawyer. Do you need help? I speak Farsi." Feeling bold, I headed out to another terminal holding up this sign. Along the way, I was joined by other women lawyers, and we rushed around from one terminal to another. We put our bodies where the glass doors opened, available in case someone was questioned or detained. "I feel a little exposed holding this sign," I said. The others nodded.

We headed back to the tables, which I was starting to think of as lawyer headquarters. There, an Iranian woman was crying; in Farsi, she said her sister had been detained. She and her sister had been in Tehran, because their mother had a heart attack. But at first, I couldn't quite figure out which tense she was using. Did her mother already have a heart attack—or was the woman worried the new president's policy would give her mother a heart attack, in the way a heart is said to break from longing?

Both made sense to me.

Later, I stood with my sign near the area where those held by customs could exit by walking up a wide ramp. There, I spoke to a few young women from Iran who'd safely made it out and recommended that travelers come through Abu Dhabi. Officials there were fair.

Suddenly, a lawyer approached, joined by an Iranian woman who'd just arrived. The lawyer asked if I could speak Farsi to her. Her cousin had a green card in good standing but was detained anyway. We spoke in Farsi; the lawyer nodded and walked away. After she left, the woman offered to switch to English—she was American too, after all.

"Of course," I said; then, emboldened, "but I can speak either." She responded in perfect English. So in English I asked her for her name and her cousin's name. She said, "Oh, do you want me to write it?" With a name like Sanam Mahloudji, I've said the same thing nearly my entire life. Though America is my home, it has trouble writing and reading me—and people like me.

"No problem," I said. "I can write it, just tell me."

"Oh, right," she nodded. "You know." She told me their beautiful Iranian names, and I spelled them out with ease. She smiled, and I smiled too, because my America is a land of immigrants. In that moment, she was an Iranian American client, and I was an Iranian American lawyer. Neither of us needed to explain ourselves.

Don't we all deserve that? I won't let this new president take that possibility away, even if sometimes it feels like an impossible dream.

I plan on going back to LAX this week, though now that a federal judge in Seattle has temporarily blocked portions of the travel ban, I'm not sure what to expect.

But I know America. I studied in its schools. I practiced in its courts. I know its laws and its values. I feel a kinship with the ACLU attorneys who, though vastly outnumbered, must face the thousands of attorneys our new president will have at his disposal. I have faith in the U.S. Constitution; I know that it's greater than any one person, any one president. America is still my home—the home of my grandmother and my daughters, a home that will keep restoring itself and growing more just. But only if we stand up for ourselves—and for each other.

Discovering the Radical Possibility of Love

Melissa Chadburn

This is a story of how I got accustomed to life without a home. Without the anchor of a biological echo. Without my compass.

I was young—only fifteen—and I had entered a place of strange rules. The group home was temporary, only two weeks to a month. What was allowed versus what was not allowed at Stepping Stones was so random and absurd it was like navigating public transportation in Los Angeles. Cussing was okay. Sleeping during the day was not okay. If you were sixteen or older, you were allowed to smoke—but no one who worked at Stepping Stones was allowed to give you a cigarette. Instead, you could pick one up that was dropped on the floor or left in an ashtray and smoke that.

Before this, I had never heard of two women of color living with each other as life partners.

It was in this small group home in Santa Monica, up past "lights out" under a small blanket by flashlight, that I read Alice Walker's *The Temple of My Familiar* for the first time. The novel portrays three main relationships, deftly weaving between characters and time to tell a story about womanhood, colonialism, racism, spirituality, and the trauma we carry with us in our blood.

But it was the relationship between Celie and Shug that most caught my attention: before this, I had never heard of two women of color living with each other as life partners. Celie and Shug's relationship had been alluded to in the prequel, *The Color Purple*, but *The Temple of My Familiar* went deeper, picking up where the couple's story left off, in their later years.

Throughout the narrative, these women touch one another's lives, directly and indirectly. Celie's only experience with sexual pleasure is with Shug. Eventually, as their relationship develops, she goes off to live with her. What they have is more than lust, more than physical attraction: Celie and Shug both care for each other.

Even if she was a fictional character, Celie was my reason to reach.

Reading about a love that was safe and happy was all the more wild to me from under a used, stained sheet in the twin-sized bed I slept on. (Notice I say the bed, not my bed.) To think that I had a sister somewhere who had survived being separated by half the world from the people she loved; who had survived an abusive husband; who had survived illiteracy, economic violence, racism, and captivity; and then was able to find love in another woman. Even if she was a fictional character, Celie was my reason to reach.

In the small world I grew up in, there was only fast food and public transportation and cockroaches and rabbit ears extended with hangers on top of the television. In the small world I grew up in, there were frozen dinners and reusing the aluminum sectional containers that held the frozen dinners. There was no staying and keeping people or them keeping you in that world. There was lots of moving—every six months or less, another.

It was not lost on me that this was a time when I was coming out of destruction.

My other choice was back in a one-bedroom apartment in our lower-middle-class neighborhood, Palms. The apartment where my mother locked me in her closet or forced me to clean all night. Our apartment where I constantly got told what to do but tried my best to look badass. It was not lost on me that this was a time when I was coming out of destruction.

Then, once in the group home, there was yet another thing: touch. No one was allowed to touch me. It was for my safety. It was in my best interest. But there was nothing I wanted more than to feel a nice, strong, firm touch. Not bashful. Not flinching.

We broke this rule in our own ways. In the afternoons when they were bored, some of the girls played with me, played with my hair, my face. Outlining my lips with a dark brown pencil and then filling them in with a deep shade of red—the color of blood. They paid attention to me some afternoons the same way that my mother's boyfriends had paid attention to me. I would take some other girl's eyeliner, burn the tips of it, and roll the warm pencil over my lids. It made me look tired and uninterested. My innocence was gone. I was becoming an angry, wild thing.

The book is founded on a time before men began to claim proprietorial rights over women and children.

The Temple of My Familiar is founded on a prehistoric utopia, a time when men and women lived apart, coming together only for the purposes of procreation. A time before power seeking. A time in which apes and lions shared our world in peaceful companionship. A time before men began to claim proprietorial rights over women and children. In the book, this aggression not only poisons the lives of warring humanity but also the intimacy that had previously existed between people and animals.

At the time, I was dealing with proprietorial rights too: in the group home, I had become chattel. The chattel of L.A. County. *The Temple of My Familiar* made me think about how it felt to be human before capitalism wove its corrupted web around our lives. Before the system. Before earning points for being clean and not cussing. Before I learned all of Stepping Stones' strange rules and their names. This is called being good. This is called being invisible. This is called wanting to be touched. This is called touching other boys and girls. This is called getting caught. This is called getting written up.

I remember watching a group of boys run away from a window and wanting desperately to chase after them. But I quickly learned that there were rules and names for this too. That would be called runaway. That would be called juvenile delinquent. That would be called juvenile hall. That would be called no more high school. That would be called no more college. That would be called going to jail. That would be called hopeless.

There was love out there for me to take any way I wanted. In a house. With a woman.

Before the book, I stayed up nights playing all my faults over and over again in my mind, all the possible ways I may have broken one relationship or another. The people I lost, the people I left. I was turning into a ball of regret, and then *The Temple of My Familiar* gave me the freedom to dream. Beyond this place of one thousand rules. Beyond a case number ascribed to me. There was love out there for me to take any way I wanted. In a house. With a woman. Not a fetish. Not a statement. Not a struggle. But an everyday thing.

Like the author, Alice Walker, wrote in her poem "Silver Writes": "It is true—/I've always loved/the daring/ones." Years after leaving Stepping

Stones, that same radical pulse lives in my every day—and, eventually, I found who I'd been looking for.

I know today that there really is nothing more revolutionary than growing old with someone, and fighting, and getting sober together, and running together, and having pets, and cleaning the house together, and making a mess of everything together, and still being there the next day. Like when she spoons me, she clasps my butt with her left hand and reaches around and clasps my left tit with her right hand and I feel buckled into happiness. And when she doesn't, I'm wishing she was; and then about two minutes into it sometimes I'm wishing I could move. Because I get hot. And if I move it's okay because now I'm loved enough to know—she won't leave me. She is my king, my queen, my lion, my familiar.

Desert Rain

Avery Erickson

The first desert rain of the season starts to fall, light as a feather at first. Then, a torrent. Rain hitting the truck like trumpets sounding, honoring my willingness to rise to the challenge and take the risk of moving alone to become a full-time, live-in co-parent to two. Overnight. With someone I am not in a romantic relationship with.

I've since been told that this rain is a welcome, a good omen.

I roll across the Arizona-California border, alone, trailer and motorcycle in tow behind my silver, sun-scorched, 275 thousand–mile Tacoma—"Ziggy" (Stardust). This poly, trans-femme queerdo from San Francisco, leaving my home that midwifed and birthed me for ten years. Stepping into the unknown, moved by the magic of synchronicity.

To a red state.

Well, crimson, really.

Crimson like open carry laws and rifles at coffee shops. Like ex-Sheriff Joe Arpaio, rampant racial profiling, and ICE detention centers.

The first thing I see as I enter Arizona is a spray-painted sign that declares, "Trump and Pence for 8."

We're not in Kansas anymore, Toto, I think-quip to myself. I'm moving toward something, but in this moment I am alone. I feel a gripping tightness in my gut survival place.

I may be physically alone in this moment, but recalling that we all met—my co-parent and spirit kids—because of magic and fate helps ease the sense of hypervigilance and isolation. Because the story played out in my lived experience, in real life, in real time, I sometimes forget how surreal it truly is.

And it's a story that needs to be told, in times like these, for people like us.

It's a story of mystery, of higher love, of trust in life and willingness to take risk. It's about community, family, self-forgetting, while becoming one's most authentic self. Becoming bigger than one thought they could be in this life.

•

Meow Wolf—neon human-sized fish tank diorama, a drummable polythene mastodon ribcage, laser harps. Think: art installation meets fantasy play space for kids and adults alike. Very Santa Fe. I'm traveling alone in New Mexico to clear my head after extricating myself from a tumultuous and emotionally abusive relationship. A relationship that mimicked the deeper layers of trauma that I experienced as a young person. A relationship that broke me open so I could see the next layer of healing, so I could be forged anew and available to the next stage of my life.

I stroll through faux smoke, dodging kids and families rushing around from one room and one level to another. I stop to admire, and play a little bit, the plastic life-sized mastodon with icy, neon red ribs as percussion.

Abruptly I hear a small voice behind me, "Hey, we know you!" A smaller voice still, chimes in alongside the first, "Yeah, we know you!"

I turn around and see two young girls, eight and ten at the time, whom I had met days before at an intentional community in the Sangre de Cristo Mountains outside of Taos, in northern New Mexico. Define irony. Land of Enchantment indeed. What's in a name?

I had met them briefly at community mealtime, the eldest one being the most outgoing. I was instantly impressed with the fierceness of her presence, her passion for knowledge about animals, her apparent lack of fear of other people. The younger one, more reserved, shy. More of an artsy self-described doer than a talker. Their biological parent, M, I met only for a moment. Then, being on a family road trip, they went on their way back to Arizona days before I left that community to continue on my own.

They would later tell me that not only had they originally intended to already be back in Phoenix to prepare for school starting again, but they had been at Meow Wolf for eight hours that day already, had left, then returned for no apparent reason.

In other words, there were multiple reasons that they shouldn't even have been in the State of New Mexico, much less at the same location at the exact same time as me.

I've lived long enough to recognize synchronicity in strangeness, in the seemingly improbable and impossible. Clearly, I was supposed to spend time with these people, but for what reason I did not know. I simply know to recognize and follow guidance, life seeing fit to only show me the next one step, if that.

The girls take me by the hand, "We want to show you stuff!"

"Okay!"

All journeys, all change, all healing, start with "okay," with *yes*. And, *I don't know*.

The four of us spend hours together. I have the best time.

Nearing closing time, I find myself not wanting our time together to end. I invite them out for dinner at the dime-a-dozen New Mexican restaurant that shares a parking lot with our meeting place.

As we sit at a small table, close, cohesive, and I have a strange and unfamiliar feeling in my body. *What is this feeling?* I am feeling what I now understand to be belonging, safety, presence, family.

But I don't even know these people, says Brain. *But I do*, says Heart.

It is the same feeling I experience when we eat our first meal, picnic style, in the house we lease to try co-living after I move to Phoenix.

Grace and awe coming full circle. I tear up, as per usual. The older one looks at me, rolls her eyes saying, "Again??"

•

Six months after colliding with them in Santa Fe, I arrive in Phoenix by land for the first time. All previous visits were short stints by plane, one even overnight to surprise the eldest for her first ever music recital. I roll into their apartment complex, jittery from days of road and months of excitement-joy-fear. More feelings than hyphens or commas can express.

I've changed my entire life and bet it all on love, connection, and family.

I park my truck and trailer on the street, out of sight. I want to surprise them even though the kids have apparently been counting down the hours until my arrival. It is my first time feeling this welcome and wanted in life.

As I move states, seemingly away from a space that one would assume is more safe for someone like me, in reality I am moving toward having a loving, functional family for the first time in my life—the ultimate opportunity for service, and to be healed, as well. Healing self through giving what I didn't get. The irony is that it is physically in a place categorically more hostile to me as a living, breathing being, and to our nontraditional, queer family.

I call my co-parent, M, on the phone.

"Hi."

"Hello!"

"How are you?"

"Where are you??"

"Knock, knock, I'm outside. . ."

I watch from the other side of the apartment complex, hidden, as M and the girls rush outside full-bore, searching for me. I savor the sight just for a moment, but let it go on for a little while longer, since the girls love pulling pranks, and one can't not play back.

And so it begins—our unicorn family, a living breathing weeping laughing example of union in spirit, of resistance, of change, expansion, and possibility. Of choice. Family of choice. And, at the same time, choiceless in the way that love makes demands. It demands that we walk our path, and in return it throws open all the doors, clears the path.

Burns a life down sometimes, to make the path.

Parenting with M, another trans person, proves to be an opportunity to become more my authentic self, to embody the divine feminine, the Mother, that which births not just the nourishing feminine but the active and directive masculine. The ability to creatively be whatever is needed, within the realm of my own authenticity, in service to the ideal of unconditional love for others.

I am able to be a mother-like parent, without being biologically capable of bearing children. Life instead births them for me, enabling me to embody this sacred archetype and calling.

•

Weeks after arriving, we experiment with different approaches to my being in their lives in ordinary life. Two days on as a parent, one day off, at their apartment for four days, on my own and apart for three. No set agenda, no preconceived notions. Just allowing the format of our family to organically unfold through constant check-ins and communication among all four of us. As we try different permutations, we find that me being deeply involved, indeed a live-in parent, is what feels best for everyone.

It is world-changing to have earned the trust of children and their biological parent. To experience the privilege to guide them in life.

In the words of Our Lady of Perpetual Grace, Tracy Chapman, "Iiiiiiiiiiiiii had a feeling that I belonged. . ."

We discuss and negotiate co-living. We use consensus-based decision-making with the kids wherever possible, seeking to teach them about being participative and empowered members of a community. Illustrating through action—we pray—a truly feminist and nonhierarchical approach to living.

The school year is about to end, but I want to be as involved as I can in the girls' education and parent community. To take the dive. There's one final parent event of the school year in a week's time.

•

I arrive alone to the youngest's elementary school Parents' Night Out. I meet and greet the suburban, middle-class, seemingly heterosexual, cisgender, mostly white parental units. Me—deep voice, strong jaw, tits, short shorts, and a blazing heart of love and commitment.

Commitment to walking wherever I must walk, to educate wherever I must educate, for the sake of myself, my kids, our family, and what our family represents. For the sake of other queer and trans families that exist, have existed, and will exist in the future. We must be visible, must stand in our truths, and say I am here, we are here, we are good, we are healthy, we are the future, and we are full of love, possibility, and empowerment.

Exist. Stand. Walk. Talk. Speak. Educate. Connect. Resist. Deconstruct. Construct. Build.

The other parents are very kind and inviting, and I tell them my story. The story. Our story.

"So, wait. You're not married to their other parent? They're not your partner?"

"We call ourselves Partners in Parenting, and Partners in Growth. But, no, romantic partnership is not our primary commitment to each other."

"And they're not your kids?"

"They're not from my body, if that's what you mean. But they're my spirit kids. They feel like my kids. The kids I *get* to love, support, and parent."

I watch their faces contort in confusion; I can see the relay signal not totally landing.

This does not compute, their micro-expressions scream. Their microaggressions.

I watch with amusement at the strain they think they're hiding on their faces, as they go from box to mental box, trying to stick me in. Box me in. Define me.

Cage me.

"We have a fairly nontraditional family structure," I say, reining in their circuitous attempts to make sense of it all.

"Ah, I see. . .," each person I speak with that night says in their own way.

I drink my club soda and head home.

•

A summer later, I'm at our same daughter's Fall Back to School Night, my first as a parent.

I arrive first, and as I stand waiting for M and the kids an obstinate sense of otherness gnaws at the base of my ribcage toward my heart. I greet the woman standing next to me to soothe my tension. We do the suburban small talk—you know, what grade is your kid in, blah, blah, blah.

Then she adds, "Are you waiting for your husband too?"

I smirk inside, appreciating the multileveled hilarity of her question-presumption.

"Um, sort of. . .," I respond. *Not really.*

We stumble through pseudo-conversation for another minute until the fam shows up and we proceed to the classroom.

Earlier that week I was picking the youngest up from her first day of fourth grade, her last year at this school. I walked onto campus among the soccer moms and dads in flip-flops and tanks, a little lost, a little out of place, and looking for her in my—again—short shorts, tank top, boobs, and a recently shaved face.

My desert-suburban, nonbinary femme uniform.

As I walk into the entrance of the elementary school (which suddenly seems to be made of eggshells), I recall the news articles I've read about parents fearing trans children, not to mention trans parents. I think of the parents in Achille, Oklahoma, openly advocating for castrating a twelve-year old trans girl on her first day of school for using the girl's bathroom, with Facebook comments like, "If he wants to be a female make him a female. A good sharp knife will do the job really quick."

That district had to temporarily shut down the school to protect her.

This was August 8, 2018.

This tension simmers below the surface of my consciousness as I traverse campus, looking for our nine-year-old. To celebrate her first day of her last year of elementary school, like any family.

The weight and pain of anticipating conflict, danger, ostracization. The same fear that moved me to do competitive martial arts for seven years long before transitioning, just to feel safe walking in the world. All of these feelings and fears, for walking on an elementary school campus for a kid I love.

Visibly queer and suspect. Visibly trans and suspect. Misgendered as male and suspect.

With these feelings, fears, and social realities in my body, in our bodies, M and I sit in our fourth grader's classroom, soaking up what information we can in what headspace remains while contending with these stresses.

In the name of her education, in the name of love and family.

•

There is no unique, special ending.

All there is is the magic and awe of having found love and family. For those of us who did not have familial love that could be trusted, this is earth-shattering.

All there is is the reality that so many people of oppressed groups face in the United States. People of color, refugees and migrants, language minorities. All there are are stories of love and survival in a system that seeks to prevent that. A system that hates femininity, that hates women. That hates non-white people. That hates queer, trans, and intersex people. That hates poor people.

And yet, we march on, in daily life and beyond, metaphorically and sometimes literally, to claim our existence, humanity, dignity, and safety. Our power. Life.

As the late Reverend Leonard Cohen remarked, "Remember when I moved in You/And the holy dove was moving too/And every breath we drew was Hallelujah. . ."

And perhaps at those times, may we be graced with the cooling salve of desert rain.

Transmigration

Milla Prince

In my people's ancient cosmology, the dead visit the living in the form of little birds: humble Sparrows, bright red Bullfinches, Waxwings, yellow-bellied Titmice. Crowding around the bird feeder, they are travelers from the Other World, gobbling up their rightful offerings. When we feed them, we feed our ancestors, our small gods, our immediate, departed relatives. Maybe this is why I have a soft spot for birds. Small birds, yes, the Flickers of the unearthly neon-orange wings, Winter Wrens as small as your thumb and as loud as anything that populate the woods; but also Ravens, Crows, and, most importantly, Seagulls. Albatrosses may have a special place in lore, but I think the "common" Seagull is the most under-appreciated bird in our collective imagination. Raven may have created the land I now live on *and* whispered into the ear of the Norse High God, but Seagulls can feast on fresh clams and french fries on the same day, fly, swim, and walk the earth, travel hundreds of miles to inland towns like my landlocked hometown, and nest on tiny tidal islets out in the wild straits of the Pacific. Seagulls, in my mind are a liminal bird, forever traveling between realms, stealing hot dogs right out of your hand, then vanishing into the mist with an eerie screech to travel into the under-world, the past, or maybe the future.

On the tidal shores of Clayoquot Sound, on the parking lot of a Walmart in Grants Pass, on the deck of one of Washington State's many ferries, I keep a keen eye on a Seagull emerging from the mist. They are my signs, my ghostly visitors. I watch them crack open clams, bicker, and soar on storm winds. I try to catch their yellow-rimmed night water eyes. Sometimes the darkness looks back at me, head cocked and curious. "Are you my father?" I ask, trying to sound casual. Usually, they fly away, feigning ignorance.

What I actually know about my father fits into a cluster of words longer than a sentence and shorter than a paragraph. It fits into a large, plain envelope. I know his name and his approximate age. The name is so common in the Arabic-speaking world, that it almost seems like an obstacle, or an alias. It is not Google-searchable, but over the years I've searched it often anyway, turning up a sixteen-year-old in an Israeli military prison, an advisor to a dictator, assassinated in Syria in the early 2000s, and, once, a journalist on the Gaza Strip. My breath catches as I scroll through the image search, trying to match software engineers and proud grandfathers to his picture. I know that he was Palestinian, whatever that means. It is a country without borders, under occupation, its residents unable to gain any citizenship, not free to leave, or stay. I know that he was a refugee. I know a few other details, like stars in the bottom of a well, ephemeral and too precious to share. In the single photograph of him and my mother together, he is wearing large sunglasses, obscuring much of his face. In the photo, it is always the spring of 1978. They are student radicals, brought together by the international solidarity movement. The image is a close-up, their two faces barely fitting into the frame. They are smiling.

I know his handwriting, which like mine, varies wildly from letter to letter. He sent these dispatches to my mom when she was pregnant with me. Most of them are postcards and can't really be called a correspondence, as it seems she rarely replied. I keep them in an envelope in my desk. These postcards, mundane, lovesick, and in our digital age, hopelessly dated, are the final physical transmissions between me and my father, though at the time neither of us had any idea the other existed. One, from Beirut in the fall of 1978, reads: "I don't died yet. Are you happy? I hope so."

The last letter is dated in the end of November 1978. I was born the next January.

My mother never told him she was pregnant with me. She didn't want to complicate things, and it only occurred to her years later that things tend to get complicated anyway. That a child might like to have a father, a father might have the right to know of their own child. By then, he was nowhere to be found, with his common name, his confusing nationality, his migrant whereabouts. The letters my mom's friend Ali sent to his last known address, inscribed in his elegant Arabic script, came back covered in stamps and scribbles that amounted to "no forwarding address."

Like all lost parents, my father played an outsize part in the story of my life. His absence was more like a presence, a void that my imagination rushed in to fill. My father was a story I told myself when I wanted to escape the feeling that I had come into the world as a complication, an anomaly.

He was always the hero of all of my childhood fantasies about belonging, about a wider world where there were other people like me, or at least more like me. My longing for a father was just as much a longing for a place people couldn't tell anything about me just by looking at me. It was the longing for someone who would know how to cut my hair so that I didn't look like a cocker spaniel. A longing for the old ladies on the train to stop asking my mother stupid questions. Growing up on what seemed like the far edge of the known world, in a small town in Eastern Finland, I was constantly reminded of the fact of my father's absence by strangers and family members alike. "Who's girl *are* you?" the Romani ladies would ask at the grocery store, and even though I was only six years old, I knew exactly what they meant. I looked different, only half like most people. I was dark, with a thick brow and thicker hair, and my skin had a green, underwater tint to it in the winter and grew brown in the brief subarctic summer. Even the Romani ladies didn't think I was one of theirs, but maybe half.

One of the hardest things about a missing parent is the surplus of emotion they leave behind. There is this longing for love that you can never have, but equally all this love you yourself have that has nowhere to go. Our culture is so obsessed with romantic love as the ultimate form of affection between people that we neglect to pay heed to the power of all the other kinds of love that exist. The love between a parent and a child is primordial, loud, born out of the mysteries of cell division. Unable to give that love to anyone, to my mother, my grandmother, who both had their own specific love and resentment in my heart, that love was left to fester; it became longing and grief and rage and other more amorphous, nameless things.

What we don't know about lost parents can fill whole books from the simplest to the most complicated: what their voice sounded like, or how their hair settled after a swim, to whether they believed in an afterlife, or if they ever dreamed of us? Do we have siblings? What are the names of our grandparents? The map is filled with blank areas whose inhabitants are invisible to me. "Here," says the edge of the known world, "there be dragons."

For the longest time, I thought that my only inheritance from the lost side of my family tree was good teeth, a lot of body hair, and some form of survivor's guilt. I knew that my father came from a war-torn, occupied land, and it didn't take a lot of imagination, mixed with nightly news from the Middle East, to imprint me with an idea of the possibility of a very different life, one less safe and quiet than the one I had ended up with.

Determining my genetic inheritance was mostly the process of elimination: if you don't have your mother's nose, your grandmother's smile, or your grandpa's hair, then those must be the traits belonging to some other genus hiding within you. I was a nervous child, clumsy, dreamy the way some kids are. From the moment I could sit up, I always had my nose in a book, long before I actually learned to read. The reality of the world, the loud noises, other children, physical activities made me uncomfortable. I spoke under my breath to chairs and stones, to flowers and Sparrows. Stories seemed more real to me than houses. Was that something from my father's side? Or just the personality I was born with? Without a point of comparison, nature and nurture become easily convoluted.

Finland is an insular culture, on the far reaches of the Earth, and in my childhood very much a homogenous society, one with easily defined boundaries and experiences universal to most people in that culture. Any experience outside of that was terra incognita, a land unknown and unfathomable. My genetics made me a person of the edges. Never fully there but with nowhere else to go. My father made me a liminal person, someone without a fixed sense of identity or place. He was a refugee, and I became an immigrant. He didn't have a homeland, and I left mine when I was nineteen and have lived most of my adult life somewhere else. My country and my culture didn't really know what to do with people like me; there was no place for us to fit in. Yet, and in the end, I found it easier to be a stranger in a strange land than among the only people I'd ever really known.

The Finnish word for a person of mixed heritage back then was "half-blood." The culture didn't really have a concept for the idea that you could be Finnish *and* something else. You could only ever be half. And anyway, how could I claim to be Finnish and Palestinian, when I didn't have any Palestinian culture, I had never been to Palestine, didn't speak Arabic, and didn't even fully understand what being Palestinian meant? I couldn't.

But I also couldn't claim to be full Finnish in spite of being born and raised there, because it was obvious that there was an unknown quantity to my being. When people see you only as half of something, they only see the half of you they don't recognize. A part of you is always obscured.

At some point, I stopped believing that I would ever actually find him. For years, conditioned on fairy tales and Hollywood, I held onto the fantasy that someday we would find and recognize each other, the kind of serendipity that only exists in movies but somehow feels real enough to be possible. But sometime in my twenties, I was finally able to let go of the necessity of direct, concrete answers to all the questions I had about him and accept that any new information would probably come from self-knowledge and examination and the broader context of the culture and place he came from. I realized that there were pieces of him embedded in the unlikeliest of places.

When I was seven, I went on my first trip without my mother. Some family friends of ours organized a group tour of Tunisia, and when my mom was unable to go, she decided to let me go on my own. It was the kind of thing that single parents often do, a blind trust in the good sense of their prematurely mature children, in the helping hands of the village that should have always been there.

I loved Tunisia. It felt to me like a skin I could slip into that fit me perfectly. The air, the food, the way people looked at me, all seemed utterly different and familiar at the same time. Everything that had a texture about it felt tangible to me: the buildings, the pastries, the clothes, even the air; which smelled like sesame seeds and honeycomb and sandalwood. At dusk, the cities came alive in a way that was the opposite of a Scandinavian town: all the lights flickered on, the noises became louder and louder, the doors flew open, and people emerged through them, moving with purpose in the night.

One day, we were walking in some historic site, a walled in courtyard with beautiful tiles and a pomegranate tree. One of the women handed me a pomegranate, cut into neat quarters. Putting a handful of the gemlike, juicy seeds in my mouth, I had an almost immediate physical reaction to them. I burst out laughing, loudly and delightedly, so much so that I startled myself. Years later, on the advice of a friend, I bought a Palestinian cookbook and started cooking it from the beginning, chronologically, like a novel of dishes. The first section is all about spices, and I decided to create one of the mixes, Baharat, in my mortar and pestle.

Grinding the spices slowly, as they began to blend together, I experienced the exact same reaction: the joy in the shock of recognition.

My body, it seems, remembers things I can't recall in this life. Stored somewhere in some as of yet unnamed cellular memory are small pieces of ancestral remembrance that respond to food, pieces of culture, language, and smells, like ships in the dark sea respond to a beacon; they signal back in recognition. My love of spicy foods and strong coffee, things both anathema to the culture I was raised in, are suddenly given meaning and context. Pomegranate seeds and cardamom pods may not be much of an inheritance, but they're precious to me. None of my family like to cook, but I have always loved food and kitchens, and so, as I cook my way through the food of my Palestinian ancestors, I picture myself as a part of lineage of people who enjoyed preparing meals; who ground their spices just like I do, but probably made much better falafel. When I offer it to them, I ask for blessings, but also forgiveness, because it still falls apart each time. I imagine generations of aunties shaking their heads at my earnest efforts. The birds that come and eat it off the little platter on the stoop don't seem to care as much.

I had always assumed that over time, the story of my father would start to make sense to me, that the pieces of information would eventually coalesce together and form whatever I was looking for: my father or myself. That if I kept trying, I would one day be able to tell this story in a way that made sense. I would imagine telling it to my children, maybe over a dish of breakfast hummus, how I might be able to present them with enough of their lost grandfather, so that they wouldn't feel as bereft of their heritage as I had. Maybe I would trace their features with my finger, naming each part and putting it on the map of our family: "There is your father's nose, your grandmother's mouth, set determinately, there are my cheekbones, and your great grandmother's cowlick (I have it too!), and here, here is your grandfather's smile, his dimples, see right here, in this picture? Do you see it?"

When we were around thirty-five, my husband and I had a serious conversation about having children, or rather *not* having them. Becoming adults in the Anthropocene, a world poised on the tipping point of some kind of collapse or another under the sheer weight of humanity, we kept failing to figure out what we would tell our hypothetical children about the kind of future we'd be able to provide them with. In a world being unmade, it seemed less and less important for us to pass on our genes, which were unknown and flawed at best, just to contribute converting everything on Earth into the biomass of humanity.

Some people may think of choosing to not have children as an ending: of your family line, of your ancestor's heritage, a terminus for the number of family members you will have. For me, that decision brought up even more questions about how to reconcile my father into my family, now determined in its size and constellation. If you never have children, who will you be an ancestor to? Regardless of our choices, passing our genes down any human lineage is hard and unlikely work. Many people's lines carry on for just a few generations before they are extinguished. But having human children is not the only way to be part of a lineage on this Earth.

I can't help but wonder not only if my father had any other children but also what he might have told those children, about the world, about our shared future. And if he didn't have other children, ones he actually knew about and raised, did he persist in being a good ancestor anyway, tending something; a garden, a circle of friends, or a revolution? From what little I know about him, he was someone who grew up in a refugee camp and still believed in a better world and hoped, fought, and worked for it. No matter what kind of man he actually was or became, that is an inheritance I can receive from him.

I am no longer concerned with the actual man, because I know I can never find him, not on the internet, not through serendipity or genetic testing or my mother's flimsy memories. After all those years of being lost, I now think of him as being everywhere. He is no longer an absence but a presence. He lives inside my blood cells, red and white, traveling through my aorta daily, carrying oxygen and epigenetic baggage. Sometimes I catch the ghost of his face under my own features. I see my father in the last remaining old-growth forests of this land that is neither of our homeland, that is other people's unceded land. I can visit him in the roses in my garden, the native ones, as well as the cultivars. The roses carry a whole family of lore and meaning, they're where both of my lineages meet: the Palestinian side, with their thousand-year practice of rosewater and candied roses, and the Finns, with their Solstice Roses and rose hip preserves made in the fall to keep them healthy trough the long winters. In the morning papers I read about Salmon trying in vain to travel up a dammed river, and I think of my father. News reports of refugee children, imprisoned journalists, people working to gain back their traditional lands come to me as echoes of my father's life. The love I feel for him no longer sits directionless and static in my heart.

Every day, from one moment to the next, I try to put that love into action, to disperse it as far and wide as I can. I hope to become a small mother, one of many parents, a partial ancestor to many beings. To work the best I can in tending, planting, nourishing, and protecting them in my short lifetime.

Naturalists and biologists always tell us not to anthropomorphize anything that isn't human, but I think we need to anthropomorphize *everything*. Not to center perceived humanness, but rather to see the "people-ness" of all beings. To not distinguish between animate and inanimate but to seek kinship. In an animistic worldview you can have a stone for a cousin, a mouse for a sister, and, maybe, a bird for a father. The transmigration of the soul is not a linear process that occurs after a tidy death as a tidy rebirth into a new form. In my experience, it is an active and ongoing work of seeing all the world alive.

On the beach, I find his name is etched by worms inside a roll of birch bark in script illegible in any human language. "Are you happy?" I ask a passing Gull, fish guts dangling from his mouth. "I hope so."

Acknowledgments

This collection obviously would not be what it is without all of the contributors and the stories they share here. Thank you for your work and your belief in this project; you all deserve gold medals. I am so grateful to call many of you my friends and to live in this world with you all.

Big love to the folks at PM Press for jumping on—and encouraging—this project from Day 1, especially Ramsey Kanaan and Steven Stothard, who answered my endless questions. Thank you, also, to Michael Ryan for the eagle eye with copyedits.

A huge shout out to (and mini–worship session of) Mikayla Butchart for her brilliant art and cover design!

Thank you to Demetria Provatas and the Woodland Keep Residency on Lopez Island, Washington, where the early work on this anthology (in zine form) first began.

I would not have been able to meet my deadline during such a personally and globally tumultuous time without my closest longtime friends and supporters of my work, especially Meredith Johnson: thank you for the endless walks to visit "my" barn owls at the Laguna de Santa Rosa, pep talks, rant sessions, and tacos. And big love to my small circle—and wider community—of witches, herbalists, activists, writers, healers, and general badasses. I appreciate and adore you so much.

And to the wonderful feminist male allies I've been lucky to have in my life: you all make it safer for "angry feminists" like me to exist in the world, and I love you.

And finally, to my fabulous, tolerant, and patient children, Simon Winter and Ava Harvest, who this book is for, I love you.

Contributors

adrienne maree brown is the author of *Emergent Strategy: Shaping Change, Changing Worlds* (AK Press, 2017) and the coeditor of *Octavia's Brood: Science Fiction from Social Justice Movements* (AK Press, 2015). She is a writer, social justice facilitator, pleasure activist, healer, and doula living in Detroit. Her essay, "Love as Political Resistance" was previously published at bitchmedia.com.

Dani Burlison (she/her) is the author of *Some Places Worth Leaving* (Tolsun Books, 2019), *Dendrophilia and Other Social Taboos: True Stories* (Petals & Bones Press, 2013), a collection of essays that first appeared in her *McSweeney's Internet Tendency* column of the same name and the *Lady Parts* zines. She has been a staff writer at a Bay Area alt-weekly, a book reviewer for *Los Angeles Review*, and a regular contributor at *Chicago Tribune*, *KQED Arts*, *The Rumpus*, and *Made Local Magazine*. Her writing can also be found at *Ms. Magazine*, *Yes! Magazine*, *Earth Island Journal*, *WIRED*, *Utne*, *Ploughshares*, *Hip Mama Magazine*, *Rad Dad*, *Spirituality & Health Magazine*, *Portland Review*, *Shareable*, *Tahoma Literary Review*, *Prick of the Spindle*, and more. Her writing also appears in several anthologies. She lives, teaches, and writes in Santa Rosa, California (Southern Pomo Territory).

Mikayla Butchart is an award-winning illustrator, artist, and designer. Originally from Northern California, she received her master's degree in illustration from the School of Visual Art in New York and now resides in Portland, Oregon, www.mikaylabutchart.com.

Melissa Chadburn has written for *NYTBR*, *Buzzfeed*, *Poets & Writers*, *American Public Media's Marketplace*, and dozens of other places. She is a contributing editor for *The Economic Hardship Reporting Project*. She is editor-at-large for *DAME Magazine*. Her essay, "The Throwaways," received notable mention in Best American Essays and Best American Nonrequired Reading. Her debut novel, *A Tiny Upward Shove*, is forthcoming with Farrar, Straus, & Giroux. Her essay, "Discovering the Radical Possibility of Love" was first published at shondaland.com.

Airial Clark is the founder of *The Sex-Positive Parent*. She has a master's degree in Sexuality Studies from San Francisco State and is also the parent of two tweenage sons. Airial graduated from University of California Berkeley in 2007 with a BA in English Literature and Anthropology. She is a contributing writer for *Good Vibrations Magazine, The Sex Positive Photo Project of the SF Bay Area*, and *Shades Magazine*. She also has writing in *Rad Families: A Celebration* (PM Press, 2016).

Leilani Clark is a food and culture writer based in Northern California. She is the editor of *Made Local Magazine*, a print magazine all about food and agriculture in Sonoma County, and a regular contributor at *Civil Eats, KQED*, and *The Press Democrat*. A former staff writer at *The North Bay Bohemian*, Leilani's writing has been featured at *Mother Jones*, the *Guardian, Sonoma Magazine, Time Magazine.com, Food & Wine.com*, and *Edible Marin & Wine Country*. She was a 2014 California Endowment Health Reporting Fellow, and her feature story about a federal crackdown on Northern California medical marijuana dispensaries won a California Newspaper Publishers Association award in 2013. She graduated with a BA in English Literature from University of California San Diego and an MFA in Writing and Consciousness from the California Institute of Integral Studies in San Francisco.

Deya is an undocumented student from Mexico completing a double major in Sociology and Legal Studies at University of California Santa Cruz.

Vatan Doost is a pseudonym used for protection by this amazing Iranian-born American writer. In Farsi, Vatan Doost means someone who loves their culture, people, and country; a patriot of sorts, if you will.

Avery Erickson (they/them, she/her) is a transfeminine, nonbinary person, holistic health practitioner, and writer/artist. Their work as a

Chinese medicine doctor, acupuncturist, and herbalist focuses on trauma recovery and spiritual (re)integration, specifically early childhood and sexual trauma and its somatic manifestations. They are in the process of codeveloping a queer and trans, earth-honoring sustainable community outside of Taos, New Mexico.

Ariel Erskine (she/her, they/them) is a filmmaker and illustrator and the drummer for the folk-punk band Gender Trash. Living in Petaluma, California, with her three children, Ariel is a proud pan, trans-woman seeking to bring attention to the rights of the LGBTQIA community and other social and civil liberties issues through her art and community activism.

Margaret Elysia Garcia is the author of *Sad Girls & Other Stories* and *Mary of the Chance Encounters*, a reporter, contributing editor for *Hip Mama Magazine*, and recently wrote for *Dame Magazine* and *Ravishly*. She's the cofounder of Pachuca Productions—a Latina microtheater company—and has produced two productions through her company, and three of her plays were produced through Wretched Productions film company and dramaworks theater companies. She is currently working on a nonfiction book called *Throwing the Curve*, on alternative modeling and burlesque dancing as a means to sustained body positivity.

Silvia Federici is a feminist writer, teacher, and militant. In 1972, she was cofounder of the International Feminist Collective that launched the Wages for Housework campaign internationally. Her books include *Witches, Witch-Hunting and Women* (PM Press, 2018), *Caliban and the Witch: Women, the Body and Primitive Accumulation* (Autonomedia, 2004), and *Revolution at Point Zero* (PM Press, 2012). She is a professor emerita at Hofstra University, where she was a social science professor. She worked as a teacher in Nigeria for many years and was also the cofounder of the Committee for Academic Freedom for Africa.

Ariel Gore is the founding editor of *Hip Mama* and the author of ten books of fiction and nonfiction, including the critically acclaimed novel *We Were Witches* (The Feminist Press, 2017). She has won an American Alternative Press Award, the LAMBDA, the Rainbow Book Award, and an Arizona-New Mexico Book Award. Her writing has appeared in hundreds of publications, including *The Rumpus, Psychology Today*, and the *San Francisco Chronicle*.

Michelle Cruz Gonzales is the author of *The Spitboy Rule: Tales of a Xicana in a Female Punk Band* (PM Press, 2016). In the 1990s, Gonzales, now an English professor, played drums in and wrote lyrics for the groundbreaking female punk band Spitboy. Gonzales has contributed to *Hip Mama Magazine*, published in anthologies, literary journals, and more recently *Latino Rebels*. She is featured in the 2017 documentary *Turn It Around: Story of East Bay Punk*.

Phoenix LeFae is an eclectic magical practitioner, author, Tarot reader, rootworker, and professional Priestess, who has been walking the path of the Witch for many years. Her writing has appeared in the following anthologies: *Pagan Leadership Anthology, HooDoo Shrines and Altars*, and *Brigit: Sun of Womanhood*. She writes for *Reclaiming Quarterly* and blogs at *The Witches Next Door*. Phoenix has had the pleasure of teaching and leading ritual globally. Her book about working with gods, ancestors, and the fae will be published soon by Llewellyn Worldwide. Her essay "I'm a Hysterical Woman" was previously published at patheos.com.

Sanam Mahloudji is a writer living in London. Her fiction has appeared in *McSweeney's Quarterly, Passages North*, and *Crab Creek Review*. She was nominated for a 2018 PEN/Robert J. Dau Short Story Prize for Emerging Writers. The essay anthologized here was adapted from a piece that first appeared in *GOOD*.

Wendy-O Matik is a freelance writer, poet, radical freethinker, and holistic nutritionist. Since the release of her book *Redefining Relationships* (Defiant Times Press, 2002) she has taught over a hundred Radical Love & Relationship Workshops globally, excavating important social trends and reshaping the future of alternative relationship models for the twenty-first century. As an activist for social change, Wendy is pushing the boundaries on firmly rooted notions in mainstream society on relationships, love, gender, sexual equality, and sexual politics. She spends most of her time on a farm where the animals outnumber the people.

Melissa Madera is originally from Washington Heights, New York. Melissa (aka the abortion diarist) is a first generation Dominican-American and the Jill of all trades at *The Abortion Diary*. Melissa travels the world with her podcast and is a story sharer and dedicated story listener, recovering academic, multimedia historian, full-spectrum doula, and a bilingual reproductive justice educator and advocate. She has also been a high school teacher, adjunct college professor, and gynecological teaching associate, and has trained in Restorative Therapeutic Yoga (as well as an Anusara Yoga two hundred–hour YTT), Thai Yoga Bodywork, and Reiki I.

Nayomi Munaweera was born in Sri Lanka. She grew up in Nigeria and immigrated to Los Angeles with her family in the early eighties. She is the award-winning author of the novels, *Island of a Thousand Mirrors* (St. Martin's Press, 2014) and *What Lies Between Us* (St. Martin's Press, 2016). She has been named one of "Twelve Women of Color Writers You Need to Know" by *Bustle Magazine* and "One of the Asian American Women Writers Who are Going to Change the World" by *Electric Literature*. Her short fiction and nonfiction are also widely published. Munaweera is also widely anthologized. Her essay "Thoughts on Mother's Day" was previously published at *Huffington Post*.

Christine No is a Korean American writer and filmmaker. She is a Sundance Alum, VONA Fellow, two-time Pushcart Prize Nominee, and Best of the Net Nominee. You can find her work in *The Rumpus, sPARKLE+bLINK, Columbia Journal, Story Online, Apogee, Atlas and Alice*, and various anthologies. Christine is the assistant features editor at *The Rumpus* and a contributing writer at *Panorama: The Journal of Intelligent Travel*. She also sits on the board of Quiet Lightning, a Bay Area nonprofit literary organization. She looks good on paper, but she spills a lot. Like a baby. She lives in Oakland with a pit bull named Brandy. Say hi here: christineno.com. Her essay "Chama" was previously published at *The Rumpus*.

P.A. is a sex worker in the San Francisco Bay Area. She is thirty-four years old, queer, and cis. Her father is Japanese from Hawaii, and her mother is first-generation Polish-Jewish. P.A. grew up outside Seattle, moved to Los Angeles for college, and has remained in California ever since. She has been escorting for four years, initially for a house and now independently. Sex work is her only form of income. She strongly believes that sex work is the healthiest, most fun, and most interesting way for her to survive in our capitalist society. She is soon to be moving in with her amazing partner; she currently lives with her beloved tiny terrier Asha.

Laurie Penny is an award-winning journalist, essayist, public speaker, writer, activist, internet nanocelebrity, and author of six books, including *Unspeakable Things* (Bloomsbury, 2014), *Everything Belongs to the Future* (Tor, 2016), and *Bitch Doctrine* (Bloomsbury, 2017). Laurie writes essays, columns, features, and gonzo journalism about politics, social justice, pop culture, feminism, technology, and mental health. When she gets time, she also writes creepy political science fiction. Her essay "How to be a Genderqueer Feminist" was first published at Buzzfeed.com.

Milla Prince grew up in the endless boreal forests of Eastern Finland, about two hundred miles from the Arctic Circle and a hundred miles from the Russian border. Her work as a writer and folk herbalist is grounded in her people's ancestral folk medicine and her culture's surviving land-based practices. Among her many passions are connecting people with their own ancestral folk lineage with plants and writing about the intersections of old ways, ancient practices, and the modern world. Through her work, she shares plant medicine, ancestral herbalism, community resilience, reciprocity, animism, and folk magic for the wild and wooly times we live in. Milla is an immigrant to what we currently call the USA and lives on a small island on unceded Coast Salish Territory. You can often find her in the kitchen cooking salt out of seawater and reading sci-fi novels. She has two cats. Sometimes, she is two cats.

Bethany Ridenour (they/them) is a teacher and student of ancestral skills. For as long as they can remember they've turned to the trees and animals in the forest for council. Bethany believes strongly in the healing powers of nature, believing that strengthening our connection with the natural world can improve our interpersonal relationships and emotional well-being. Bethany has found that working the hands with elements of nature brings some of the deepest healing and feels like it is their path to help bridge the gap between humans and nature, bringing to light how that relationship can help heal trauma. Bethany has worked with many different natural elements, with a strong emphasis on different ways of processing skins (e.g., making and using brain-tan, bark-tan, rawhide, and furs), earth pigments, and is a professional broom maker at Bristleandstick.com.

Lorelle Saxena is an acupuncturist and mother. Her writing revolves around the shared human experience and finding the beautiful and extraordinary in everyday life. Her proudest accomplishment is being a nice person most of the time.

Anna Silastre is a writer and teacher from Sonoma County, California. She's written and performed for the North Bay Cabaret, Get Lit, and a couple slams in the Bay. She once wrote the sales pitches for a salami company, and at one point rode her bike around Santa Barbara writing articles about sea creatures and boy scouts. She currently writes lessons and progress report comments for the most amazing eighth graders in Newark, New Jersey. She plans to start a doctorate in Education at Teachers College, Columbia, next fall. Anna Silastre is not this person's real name, but in the interest of protecting herself and those she loves, she is using this name instead of her own.

Gerri Ravyn Stanfield is the author of *Revolution of the Spirit: Awaken the Healer* (Holy Risk Press, 2018), a guide to liberate the healing superpowers within us. She has been published in *Nailed Magazine*, *Voice Catcher*, *Rebelle Society*, *Elephant Journal*, *Wake Up World*, and *Tattooed Buddha*. She is the executive director of Acupuncturists Without Borders and creates modern ritual and theater art, combining music and poetry to make contemporary offerings of the human imagination.

Starhawk is an author, activist, permaculture designer and teacher, and a prominent voice in modern earth-based spirituality and ecofeminism. She is the author or coauthor of thirteen books, including *The Spiral Dance: A Rebirth of the Ancient Religion of the Great Goddess* (Harper & Row, 1979), the ecotopian novel *The Fifth Sacred Thing* (Bantam Books, 1993), and its sequel *City of Refuge* (Califa Press, 2016). Her most recent nonfiction book is *The Empowerment Manual: A Guide for Collaborative Groups* (New Society Publishers, 2011), on group dynamics, power, conflict, and communications. Her essay, "Auntie Starhawk's Sex Advice for Troubled Times" was previously published on her blog at starhawk.org.

Patty Stonefish comes from a strong line of matriarchs—Lakota, Russian, and Polish. She is the founder and joint lock ninja behind Arming Sisters. Born in North Dakota and raised throughout the countryside, Stonefish has over a decade of martial arts and women's self-defense experience. She has utilized these journeys to change the way women's self-defense is applied. Aside from martial arts, her mind has been shaped through extensive world travel, completion of her BA in Veterinary Science, yoga teacher training, and activism across Indian Country. She believes in unicorns, breaking down barriers, healing, culture, and, above all, humanity.

Kara Vernor has had fiction pieces published in the *Los Angeles Review, Green Mountains Review, Fanzine, No Tokens*, and elsewhere, and her fiction chapbook *Because I Wanted to Write You a Pop Song* is available from Split Lip Press. She is the recipient of an Elizabeth George Foundation scholarship, and her stories have been included in Wigleaf's Top 50 Very Short Fictions, the Best Small Fictions finalists, and Outpost 19's Golden State 2017 anthology.

Kandis Williams, born 1985 in Baltimore, is based in Los Angeles and Berlin. Primarily working with collages and drawings, her engagements branch out to encompass mediums such as text and contemporary dance, to examine sociocultural constructs of race, place, history, and the self. Williams received her BFA in 2008 from the Cooper Union School of Art, New York. Her work has been exhibited at Night Gallery, SADE, the Underground Museum, and Human Resources in Los Angeles, the Studio Museum in Harlem, New York, and the Breeder in Athens, Greece.

Michel Wing (they/them) is the author of a poetry collection *Body on the Wall* and a coeditor of *Cry of the Nightbird: Writers against Domestic Violence*, a benefit project for YWCA Sonoma County, and their work with domestic violence prevention. Michel's poetry and creative nonfiction have appeared in *Sinister Wisdom, The Gay & Lesbian Review, Melancholy Hyperbole, Rain & Thunder*, and several anthologies, most recently *Digging Our Poetic Roots: Poems from Sonoma County* (WorldTemple Press, 2015). In October 2012, two of their poems were shown in Sacramento in an exhibit at the California Museum, Creating Freedom: Art & Poetry of Domestic Violence Survivors, with the poem "Dreamwork" taking first place honors. Michel lives in Las Cruces, New Mexico.

Lidia Yuknavitch is the author of National Bestselling novels *The Book of Joan* (Canongate Books, 2018) and *The Small Backs of Children* (HarperCollins,

2015), winner of the 2016 Oregon Book Award's Ken Kesey Award for Fiction, as well as the Reader's Choice Award, the novel *Dora: A Headcase* (Hawthorne Books, 2012), and a critical book on war and narrative, *Allegories of Violence* (Routledge, 2001). Her widely acclaimed memoir *The Chronology of Water* (Hawthorne Books, 2011) was a finalist for a PEN Center USA award for creative nonfiction and winner of a PNBA Award and the Oregon Book Award Reader's Choice. A book based on her recent TED Talk, *The Misfit's Manifesto*, was released in October 2017. Her essay, "Explicit Violence" was previously published at *The Rumpus*.

ABOUT PM PRESS

PM Press was founded at the end of 2007 by a small
collection of folks with decades of publishing, media, and
organizing experience. PM Press co-conspirators have
published and distributed hundreds of books, pamphlets,
CDs, and DVDs. Members of PM have founded enduring
book fairs, spearheaded victorious tenant organizing campaigns, and worked
closely with bookstores, academic conferences, and even rock bands to deliver
political and challenging ideas to all walks of life. We're old enough to know what
we're doing and young enough to know what's at stake.

We seek to create radical and stimulating fiction and nonfiction books, pamphlets,
T-shirts, visual and audio materials to entertain, educate, and inspire you. We
aim to distribute these through every available channel with every available
technology—whether that means you are seeing anarchist classics at our bookfair
stalls, reading our latest vegan cookbook at the café, downloading geeky fiction
e-books, or digging new music and timely videos from our website.

PM Press is always on the lookout for talented and skilled volunteers, artists,
activists, and writers to work with. If you have a great idea for a project or can
contribute in some way, please get in touch.

PM Press
PO Box 23912
Oakland, CA 94623
www.pmpress.org

PM Press in Europe
europe@pmpress.org
www.pmpress.org.uk

FRIENDS OF PM PRESS

These are indisputably momentous times—the financial system is melting down globally and the Empire is stumbling. Now more than ever there is a vital need for radical ideas.

In the years since its founding—and on a mere shoestring—PM Press has risen to the formidable challenge of publishing and distributing knowledge and entertainment for the struggles ahead. With over 300 releases to date, we have published an impressive and stimulating array of literature, art, music, politics, and culture. Using every available medium, we've succeeded in connecting those hungry for ideas and information to those putting them into practice.

Friends of PM allows you to directly help impact, amplify, and revitalize the discourse and actions of radical writers, filmmakers, and artists. It provides us with a stable foundation from which we can build upon our early successes and provides a much-needed subsidy for the materials that can't necessarily pay their own way. You can help make that happen—and receive every new title automatically delivered to your door once a month—by joining as a Friend of PM Press. And, we'll throw in a free T-shirt when you sign up.

Here are your options:

- **$30 a month** Get all books and pamphlets plus 50% discount on all webstore purchases

- **$40 a month** Get all PM Press releases (including CDs and DVDs) plus 50% discount on all webstore purchases

- **$100 a month** Superstar—Everything plus PM merchandise, free downloads, and 50% discount on all webstore purchases

For those who can't afford $30 or more a month, we have **Sustainer Rates** at $15, $10 and $5. Sustainers get a free PM Press T-shirt and a 50% discount on all purchases from our website.

Your Visa or Mastercard will be billed once a month, until you tell us to stop. Or until our efforts succeed in bringing the revolution around. Or the financial meltdown of Capital makes plastic redundant. Whichever comes first.

Witches, Witch-Hunting, and Women

Silvia Federici

ISBN: 978-1-62963-568-2
$14.00   120 pages

We are witnessing a new surge of interpersonal and institutional violence against women, including new witch hunts. This surge of violence has occurred alongside an expansion of capitalist social relations. In this new work that revisits some of the main themes of *Caliban and the Witch*, Silvia Federici examines the root causes of these developments and outlines the consequences for the women affected and their communities. She argues that, no less than the witch hunts in sixteenth- and seventeenth-century Europe and the "New World," this new war on women is a structural element of the new forms of capitalist accumulation. These processes are founded on the destruction of people's most basic means of reproduction. Like at the dawn of capitalism, what we discover behind today's violence against women are processes of enclosure, land dispossession, and the remolding of women's reproductive activities and subjectivity.

As well as an investigation into the causes of this new violence, the book is also a feminist call to arms. Federici's work provides new ways of understanding the methods in which women are resisting victimization and offers a powerful reminder that reconstructing the memory of the past is crucial for the struggles of the present.

"*It is good to think with Silvia Federici, whose clarity of analysis and passionate vision come through in essays that chronicle enclosure and dispossession, witch-hunting and other assaults against women, in the present, no less than the past. It is even better to act armed with her insights.*"
—Eileen Boris, Hull Professor of Feminist Studies, University of California, Santa Barbara

"*Silvia Federici's new book offers a brilliant analysis and forceful denunciation of the violence directed towards women and their communities. Her focus moves between women criminalized as witches both at the dawn of capitalism and in contemporary globalization. Federici has updated the material from her well-known book* Caliban and the Witch *and brings a spotlight to the current resistance and alternatives being pursued by women and their communities through struggle.*"
—Massimo De Angelis, professor of political economy, University of East London

Re-enchanting the World: Feminism and the Politics of the Commons

Silvia Federici with a Foreword by
Peter Linebaugh

ISBN: 978-1-62963-569-9
$19.95   240 pages

Silvia Federici is one of the most important
contemporary theorists of capitalism and feminist
movements. In this collection of her work spanning over twenty years, she provides
a detailed history and critique of the politics of the commons from a feminist
perspective. In her clear and combative voice, Federici provides readers with an
analysis of some of the key issues and debates in contemporary thinking on this
subject.

Drawing on rich historical research, she maps the connections between the
previous forms of enclosure that occurred with the birth of capitalism and the
destruction of the commons and the "new enclosures" at the heart of the present
phase of global capitalist accumulation. Considering the commons from a feminist
perspective, this collection centers on women and reproductive work as crucial
to both our economic survival and the construction of a world free from the
hierarchies and divisions capital has planted in the body of the world proletariat.
Federici is clear that the commons should not be understood as happy islands
in a sea of exploitative relations but rather autonomous spaces from which to
challenge the existing capitalist organization of life and labor.

*"Silvia Federici's theoretical capacity to articulate the plurality that fuels the
contemporary movement of women in struggle provides a true toolbox for building
bridges between different features and different people."*
—Massimo De Angelis, professor of political economy, University of East London

*"Silvia Federici's work embodies an energy that urges us to rejuvenate struggles against
all types of exploitation and, precisely for that reason, her work produces a common: a
common sense of the dissidence that creates a community in struggle."*
—Maria Mies, coauthor of *Ecofeminism*

The Spitboy Rule: Tales of a Xicana in a Female Punk Band

Michelle Cruz Gonzales with a Foreword by Martín Sorrondeguy and Preface by Mimi Thi Nguyen

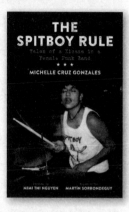

ISBN: 978-1-62963-140-0
$15.95   160 pages

Michelle Cruz Gonzales played drums and wrote lyrics in the influential 1990s female hardcore band Spitboy, and now she's written a book—a punk rock herstory. Though not a riot grrl band, Spitboy blazed trails for women musicians in the San Francisco Bay Area and beyond, but it wasn't easy. Misogyny, sexism, abusive fans, class and color blindness, and all-out racism were foes, especially for Gonzales, a Xicana and the only person of color in the band.

Unlike touring rock bands before them, the unapologetically feminist Spitboy preferred Scrabble games between shows rather than sex and drugs, and they were not the angry manhaters that many expected them to be. Serious about women's issues and being the band that they themselves wanted to hear, a band that rocked as hard as men but sounded like women, Spitboy released several records and toured internationally. The memoir details these travels while chronicling Spitboy's successes and failures, and for Gonzales, discovering her own identity along the way.

Fully illustrated with rare photos and flyers from the punk rock underground, this fast-paced, first-person recollection is populated by scenesters and musical allies from the time including Econochrist, Paxston Quiggly, Neurosis, Los Crudos, Aaron Cometbus, Pete the Roadie, Green Day, Fugazi, and Kamala and the Karnivores.

"The Spitboy Rule *is a compelling and insightful journey into the world of '90s punk as seen through the eyes of a Xicana drummer who goes by the nickname Todd. Todd stirs the pot by insisting that she plays hardcore punk, not Riot Grrrl music, and inviting males to share the dance floor with women in a respectful way. This drummer never misses a beat. Read it!"*
—Alice Bag, singer for the Bags, author of *Violence Girl: East L.A. Rage to Hollywood Stage, a Chicana Punk Story*

Revolutionary Mothering: Love on the Front Lines

Edited by Alexis Pauline Gumbs, China Martens, and Mai'a Williams with a Preface by Loretta J. Ross

ISBN: 978-1-62963-110-3
$17.95   272 pages

Inspired by the legacy of radical and queer black feminists of the 1970s and '80s, *Revolutionary Mothering* places marginalized mothers of color at the center of a world of necessary transformation. The challenges we face as movements working for racial, economic, reproductive, gender, and food justice, as well as anti-violence, anti-imperialist, and queer liberation are the same challenges that many mothers face every day. Oppressed mothers create a generous space for life in the face of life-threatening limits, activate a powerful vision of the future while navigating tangible concerns in the present, move beyond individual narratives of choice toward collective solutions, live for more than ourselves, and remain accountable to a future that we cannot always see. *Revolutionary Mothering* is a movement-shifting anthology committed to birthing new worlds, full of faith and hope for what we can raise up together.

Contributors include June Jordan, Malkia A. Cyril, Esteli Juarez, Cynthia Dewi Oka, Fabiola Sandoval, Sumayyah Talibah, Victoria Law, Tara Villalba, Lola Mondragón, Christy NaMee Eriksen, Norma Angelica Marrun, Vivian Chin, Rachel Broadwater, Autumn Brown, Layne Russell, Noemi Martinez, Katie Kaput, alba onofrio, Gabriela Sandoval, Cheryl Boyce Taylor, Ariel Gore, Claire Barrera, Lisa Factora-Borchers, Fabielle Georges, H. Bindy K. Kang, Terri Nilliasca, Irene Lara, Panquetzani, Mamas of Color Rising, tk karakashian tunchez, Arielle Julia Brown, Lindsey Campbell, Micaela Cadena, and Karen Su.

"This collection is a treat for anyone that sees class and that needs to learn more about the experiences of women of color (and who doesn't?!). There is no dogma here, just fresh ideas and women of color taking on capitalism, anti-racist, anti-sexist theory-building that is rooted in the most primal of human connections, the making of two people from the body of one: mothering."
—Barbara Jensen, author of *Reading Classes: On Culture and Classism in America*

"For women of color, mothering—the art of mothering—has been framed by the most virulent systems, historically: enslavement, colonialism, capitalism, imperialism. We have had few opportunities to define mothering not only as an aspect of individual lives and choices, but as the processes of love and as a way of structuring community. Revolutionary Mothering arrives as a needed balm."
—Alexis De Veaux, author of *Warrior Poet: A Biography of Audre Lorde*

Sisters of the Revolution: A Feminist Speculative Fiction Anthology

Edited by Ann VanderMeer and
Jeff VanderMeer

ISBN: 978-1-62963-035-9
$15.95   352 pages

Sisters of the Revolution gathers a highly curated
selection of feminist speculative fiction (science fiction,
fantasy, horror, and more) chosen by one of the most respected editorial teams
in speculative literature today, the award-winning Ann and Jeff VanderMeer.
Including stories from the 1970s to the present day, the collection seeks to
expand the conversation about feminism while engaging the reader in a wealth of
imaginative ideas.

From the literary heft of Angela Carter to the searing power of Octavia
Butler, *Sisters of the Revolution* gathers daring examples of speculative fiction's
engagement with feminism. Dark, satirical stories such as Eileen Gunn's "Stable
Strategies for Middle Management" and the disturbing horror of James Tiptree Jr.'s
"The Screwfly Solution" reveal the charged intensity at work in the field. Including
new, emerging voices like Nnedi Okorafor and featuring international contributions
from Angelica Gorodischer and many more, *Sisters of the Revolution* seeks to
expand the ideas of both contemporary fiction and feminism to new fronts. Moving
from the fantastic to the futuristic, the subtle to the surreal, these stories will
provoke thoughts and emotions about feminism like no other book available today.

Contributors include: Angela Carter, Angelica Gorodischer, Anne Richter, Carol
Emshwiller, Eileen Gunn, Eleanor Arnason, Hiromi Goto, James Tiptree Jr., Joanna
Russ, Karin Tidbeck, Kelley Eskridge, Kelly Barnhill, Kit Reed, L. Timmel Duchamp,
Leena Krohn, Leonora Carrington, Nnedi Okorafor, Octavia Butler, Pamela Sargent,
Rose Lemberg, Susan Palwick, Tanith Lee, Ursula K. Le Guin, and Vandana Singh.

"The VanderMeers are a literary power couple."
—Boing Boing

*"A very laudable trait of the editors is their egalitarianism, their refusal to distinguish
between lowbrow and highbrow, using quality and impact as their only yardsticks."*
—Barnes and Noble